Benjamin Y. Conklin

A Complete Graded Course in English Grammar and Composition

Benjamin Y. Conklin

A Complete Graded Course in English Grammar and Composition

ISBN/EAN: 9783337779146

Printed in Europe, USA, Canada, Australia, Japan

Cover: Foto ©Thomas Meinert / pixelio.de

More available books at **www.hansebooks.com**

A COMPLETE GRADED COURSE

IN

ENGLISH GRAMMAR AND COMPOSITION

BY

BENJ. Y. CONKLIN,

PRINCIPAL OF GRAMMAR SCHOOL NO. 3, BROOKLYN, N. Y.

NEW YORK, BOSTON, AND CHICAGO
D. APPLETON AND COMPANY
1889

PREFACE.

This book is designed to be a practical working manual for the assistance of the teacher as well as the pupil. The author has sought to present the subject in an easy, natural, and progressive way, and, as far as possible, to avoid repetition; yet, by a judicious selection of graded sentences and carefully arranged questions for review, to keep before the mind of the learner what he has already learned.

Indeed, in their gradation, the sentences themselves are a concrete presentation of the whole subject. The questions at the end of the lessons are so framed as to require the pupil, after studying the text carefully, to formulate his own answers. This fact will often make it necessary for the teacher to examine a lesson with the class before assigning it to be learned.

The theory of the book is the gradual development of the sentence; the method, inductive. Beginning with the simplest form of the sentence, as "Birds fly," only one new element is added in any single lesson; so that a thorough mastery of each lesson ought to result.

The author has endeavored to avoid an excess of language-work on the one hand, and too much formal parsing and analysis on the other. Analysis and synthesis are carried along together, in due proportion and relation. By this method of treatment, the pupil acquires not only a knowledge of the structure of the sentence, but also the power to *use* language.

From the beginning to page 60, the gradual development of the sentence, and the *nature* and *office* of the different parts of speech, are the leading features. Not till pupils become familiar with the relations that the words in a sentence bear to each other, are they prepared to learn the proper forms that words should assume to suit those relations; the learning of these forms should therefore be deferred until this point has been reached.

The book is sufficiently elementary in the beginning to be put into the hands of pupils in the lowest grammar grades, and sufficiently advanced to cover all that is required of the highest grammar classes, thus compassing the entire range of the usual *two-book* course. It is intended to be taught in the order in which it is arranged; but those who may prefer to teach the attribute complement, or the conjugation of the verb, before its introduction in the regular course, will find little inconvenience in doing so.

Instead of examples of false syntax for correction, exercises are given for filling out sentences by supplying the correct forms of words in blank spaces, which, perhaps, is a better way of accomplishing the same object. But for the convenience of such teachers as deem the correction of false syntax profitable, carefully selected examples are given in the appendix.

The aim of the book is to make the study of English grammar more interesting, and thus to render the progress of the pupil in it more rapid, and his mastery of it more complete.

As to the merits of the book, and the wisdom of the plan, the author leaves his co-workers to judge for themselves.

B. Y. CONKLIN.

BROOKLYN, N. Y., *November, 1888.*

CONTENTS.

	PAGE
Introduction: Objects—Ideas; Noun; Verb; Sentence	1–11
Grammar—its Divisions	12
Parts of Speech; Table; Definition	13
Simple Subject and Predicate	14–15
Adjectives—Descriptive and Limiting; Modified Subject	16–19
Analysis and Composition	20–23
Articles; Synthesis; Composition	24–27
Adverbs—Modified Predicate; Analysis; Composition	28–32
Conjunctions—Simple and Compound Sentences	33–34
Analysis and Synthesis; Composition	35–37
Transitive Verbs—Object Complement; Analysis	38–43
Synthesis; Models for Written Analysis	44–45
Diagramming	46
Nouns—Common and Proper; Composition; Letter-writing	47–53
Pronouns—General Use	54
Contracted Compound Sentences; Analysis; Synthesis	54–59
Nouns and Pronouns—Inflection	60–91
Quotations—Direct and Indirect	92
Oral Parsing Models	93–94
Double Possessive Forms; Relative Pronouns	95–97
Verbs—Tense and Number; Synthesis	98–102
Verbs—Agreement with Subject; Composition	103–108
Natural and Rhetorical Order of Words	109–110
Analytical Parsing	111
Interrogative Adjectives and Adverbs	112
Review by Sentences; Synthesis	113–115
Prepositions—Adverbial Objective; Analysis; Synthesis	116–138
Words Misused; Analysis; Intermediate Expressions	139–142
Abbreviated Compounds; Series of Words; Punctuation	143–147
Uses of Articles; Arrangement of Adjectives; Punctuation	148–152
Verbs—Regular and Irregular	153–156
Apposition; Analysis; Possessive Case; Synthesis	157–162

CONTENTS.

	PAGE
How to use Sit, Set, Lie, and Lay	163
Attribute Complement; Copula; Analysis; Parsing	164–171
Verbs—Active and Passive Voice	172–174
Independent Element—Nouns; Interjections	175–178
Adjectives—Inflection; Use; Position	179–189
Adverbs—Classes; Use; Formation	190–193
Varying Parts of Speech	194
Infinitives	195–202
Participles	203–210
Conjunctive Adverbs—Complex Sentences; Analysis	211–213
Relative Pronouns—Complex Sentences; Analysis	214–225
Interrogative and Responsive Pronouns	226–227
Abbreviated Clauses; Nominative Absolute; Synthesis	228–230
Conjunctions—Co-ordinate, Subordinate, Correlative	231–232
Complex Sentences—Kinds; Analysis; Classification	232–236
Compound Sentences—Classification	237–238
Elliptical Sentences—Analysis	239–240
Bad Construction Improved	241–242
Punctuation—Semicolon and Colon	243–244
Verbs—Modes; Conjugation	245–258
Analysis of Poetical Selections; Poetic License	259–260
Verbs—List; Irregular and Defective	261–263
" —Infinitives; Uses	264
" —Shall and Will; Uses	265–266
Rules—Capital Letters	267
" —Syntax	268
Composition—Subjects	269–270
APPENDIX—Diagramming	271–278
Rhetorical Figures	285–286
Versification	287
Recasting Sentences	288
Other Characters used in Writing	289–290
Index	291–296

HINTS TO TEACHERS.

IF children could always *hear* correct language, they would learn to *use* it correctly. But many are accustomed to hear language full of glaring errors, and thus a habit of incorrect expression is formed both in speaking and in writing. To correct this habit is the work of the teacher.

In teaching grammar, it should never be forgotten that the real object is to teach pupils *how* to speak and to write the English language correctly, and how to read it intelligently. Analysis and parsing are only means to this end.

Teachers should require pupils to write all their composition exercises neatly, and to re-write them—making all the corrections themselves—after the errors have been indicated by proper marks made by the teacher. Discretion must be used, however, in giving proper aid, at first, in making corrections.

Teachers should not confine themselves entirely to the questions in the text-book, and they should avoid a stereotyped form of questioning.

The questions in this book generally come after the text, and on this account pupils may not always be able to formulate concise answers to them; therefore, before each lesson is assigned, it should be carefully read with the class, and judicious aid should be given in formulating answers.

A great advantage is gained by recapitulating important points in each lesson at its close. The teacher should be specially careful to see that pupils thoroughly *appropriate* the thoughts contained in the text before requiring them to commit any part of a lesson to memory.

In assigning subjects for compositions, teachers should be very careful *not* to select topics that are beyond the ability of pupils to comprehend, nor those that will require *too much* searching in books of reference. The *object* should be *to get from pupils a correct expression of the thoughts that they already have,* or that they may *readily* acquire by observation and reading, rather than to have them try to produce labored essays on abstract themes.

ENGLISH GRAMMAR AND COMPOSITION.

INTRODUCTORY LESSONS.

I.—OBJECTS—IDEAS.

Questions.—1. What things do you find in a garden? 2. What do you see in the park? 3. What do you hear at a concert? 4. Mention five things you have seen in the street. 5. Mention five things you see in this room.

1. Things are called **objects**. We learn about such things, or objects, in various ways:

We learn about some things by seeing them; as, a *man*, a *tree*.
We learn about some things by hearing them; as, *music*, *noise*.
We learn about some things by feeling them; as, *velvet*, *iron*.
We learn about some things by tasting them; as, an *orange*, *vinegar*.
We learn about some things by smelling them; as, a *rose*, *cologne*.

Questions.—We learn about some of these objects in *more* than *one* way. In how many ways do we learn about an *orange*? about *velvet*? about a *clock*?

2. The *sense of seeing*, the *sense of hearing*, the *sense of feeling*, the *sense of tasting*, and the *sense of smelling*, are called *the five senses*.

Direction.—Name the five senses.

3. There are *some* things, however, that we do not perceive * through these five senses; as, *anger, joy, wisdom, memory*.

Anger is *something*; *something* means *some thing*; therefore, *anger* is an *object*. *Memory, joy*, and *wisdom*, are objects also.

---

* Teachers should explain words that are not familiar to the pupil.

4. We learn about such things as *memory, joy, sorrow,* etc., by *thinking* about them.

Direction.—Mention other things about which we learn by thinking.

Questions.—How do we learn about *houses? gold? silk? pain? life? flowers? apples? sugar? pride? folly? truth? pity? iron? kindness? falsehood? milk?* Mention the five senses.

II.—NAMES.

5. When I say *knife,* or write *knife,* the *word* that I speak or write is not the object itself; it is only the *name* of the object.

Questions.—What are the words *pencil, desk, boy, book?* Is the boy sitting beside you a *name,* or an *object?* If I call him a *boy,* or *James,* what are the words *boy* and *James?*

6. Every thing that we can perceive by the senses, or that we can think about, has or may have a name.

Questions.—1. Is your desk a *name* or an *object?* 2. Is your *hat* a name? 3. Is the word *pencil* a name? 4. Is the word *hat* a name? 5. What is your slate? 6. What is your knife? 7. Has every object a name?

Direction.—Write three names of trees, in a column on your slate.
Write three names of persons in the same way.
Write three names of different natural divisions of the earth's surface. Also three names of each of the following things: Cities; rivers; things made of paper; of leather; of iron; of glass; of wood; things found in a store; things that we learn about by seeing; by hearing; by feeling; by tasting; by smelling; by thinking.

Questions for Review.—1. How do we learn about objects? 2. How many senses have we? Name them. 3. Is the pen you write with a name or an object? 4. What is the *word* pen? 5. What is an object? 6. What do we learn about an orange by the sense of seeing? 7. What do we learn about it by the sense of feeling? 8. What do we learn about music by the sense of hearing? 9. How do we learn about hardness? 10. Can we see goodness, or only the result of goodness? 11. How do we learn about light? 12. How do we learn about heat? 13. Can we see pride, or only the result of pride?

III.—NOUNS.

7. Words that are names of objects, we may call *name-words*. In grammar they are called nouns, because the word **noun** means **name**.

8. Definition.—A **noun** is a *word* used as a **name**.

9. Objects may be separated into classes; as, *persons, animals, places,* and *things.*

A noun may be the name of a person; as, *boy, son, George, father.*
A noun may be the name of an animal; as, *dog, fox, horse, elephant.*
A noun may be the name of a place; as, *city, London, park, town.*
A noun may be the name of a thing; as, *cap, tree, foot, glass, truth.*

10. A noun is the name of any person, animal, place, or thing.

Direction.—Write three names that are names of persons; three each of animals, places, things found in the kitchen, things found in the earth, and things used by carpenters.

Questions.—Is your *hat* a *noun* or an *object*? What is the word *hat*? Is the word *horse* a noun? Is the word *orange* an *object* or the *name* of an object? Is your *brother* a noun?

11. Definition.—A noun that names only a **single object** is called a **singular noun,** or a noun in the **singular number**; as, *boy, girl, hat, chair.*

12. Definition.—A noun that names *more* than *one object* of the same kind is called a **plural noun,** or a noun in the **plural number**; as, *boys, girls, hats, chairs.*

Questions for Review.—1. What is a noun? 2. Why is the word *house* a noun? 3. A noun may be the name of an object belonging to how many different classes? 4. Name the four different classes of objects mentioned in this lesson. 5. How many senses do we possess? 6. Name them. 7. By how many of the senses may we learn about a city? an apple? memory? thunder? lightning? fire? milk? velvet? 8. Is your book a noun or an object? 9. What is the difference between a noun and an object? 10. What is a singular noun? 11. What is a plural noun? 12. To which class of nouns does City Hall belong? 13. To which of the four classes does grasshopper belong? 14. To what class does cousin belong?

IV.—SENTENCES.

* **Questions.**—The names of a number of objects have been written and mentioned. Do any of these objects *act*, or *do* anything? Do *horses*? Do *people*? Do *birds*?

Direction.—Think about these three objects—birds, frogs, dogs—and tell what they do.

Exercise.—John, state your thought about what birds do. "Birds sing."

James, was that your thought about birds? "No, sir. Birds fly."

William, state your thought about what frogs do. "Frogs jump."

Charles, state your thought about what dogs do. "Dogs bark."

Each boy has stated or expressed his thought; in other words, each has made a statement; each has asserted a fact.

How did you state or express your thoughts? "We expressed our thoughts in words."

Is there any other way of expressing our thoughts? "We can express thoughts by motions or signs."

How do we generally express our thoughts?

13. The statement, "Birds sing," is called a sentence; so are the statements, "Frogs jump," and "Dogs bark."

14. Sentences are either spoken or written.

15. Definition.—A **sentence** is a combination of words so arranged as to make complete sense.

Questions.—1. In how many ways may we express our thoughts? 2. What name is given to the statement, "Wolves howl"? Why? 3. What is a sentence? 4. Make *two* sentences stating how horses travel; *one*, stating what kind of noise monkeys make; *one*, stating what kind of noise pigs make.

V.—VERBS.

1. The dog barks.

Explanation.—In this sentence, *dog* is the name of the object that does something, and the word *barks* shows what the dog *does*.

    1. The bird sings.
    2. The duck swims.
    3. The horse runs.

Questions.—1. What does the word *sings* show in sentence 1? 2. What does the word *swims* show in sentence 2? 3. What does the word *runs* show in sentence 3?

Direction.—Select, in the eight following sentences, the name of that which does something, and also the word which tells what it does.

MODEL.

"The soldier fights" is a sentence, because it is an arrangement of words making complete sense. *Soldier* is the name of the person that *does* something; and *fights* tells what the soldier does.

1. The soldier fights.
2. The horse trots.
3. Grass grows.
4. The snake crawls.
5. Fire burns.
6. The bird flies.
7. The rat gnaws.
8. The diamond sparkles.

Explanation.—In the sentence, "The soldier fights," the word *fights* expresses an *action*. Words that are used *to express action* may be called *action-words*; in grammar they are called **verbs**.

16. In each of these eight sentences a statement or *assertion* is made, and the *verb* is the word that makes the assertion.

17. Definition.—The *word* used *to assert* something of some person or thing is called a **verb**.

18. Every sentence must contain a verb. A verb is sometimes composed of more than one word; as, "Dogs *will bark*."

Direction.—Select the verb in each of these eight sentences, tell why it is a verb, and also what person or thing the assertion is made about.

VI.—COMPOSITION LESSON.

Direction.—Form sentences by writing a verb in the blank space after each noun, so that it will make sense, beginning each sentence with a capital letter, and ending it with a period:

1. Ducks ——
2. Wolves ——
3. Girls ——
4. Men ——
5. Flowers ——
6. Trees ——
7. Fire ——
8. Rivers ——
9. Bears ——
10. Apples ——
11. Boys ——
12. Birds ——

19. Rule.—Every sentence must *begin* with a capital letter.

Direction.—Form sentences by writing a noun in the blank space before each verb, being careful to attend to capitals and punctuation:

1. —— ride.
2. —— grow.
3. —— sail.
4. —— plow.
5. —— drink.
6. —— fight.
7. —— run.
8. —— study.
9. —— melts.
10. —— smile.
11. —— creep.
12. —— steal.

Direction.—After writing these sentences correctly, select the nouns and verbs, and tell why they are nouns or verbs.

MODEL.

"Ladies ride" is a sentence, because it is a combination of words making complete sense. "Ladies" is a noun, because it is a name. "Ride" is a verb, because it expresses action.

Note.—Sentences should express what is true or reasonable.

1. Birds teach.
2. Snakes bark.
3. Growl crickets.
4. Ladies croak.
5. Horses sing.
6. Crawl frogs.
7. Dogs chirp.
8. Men fly.
9. Fishes trot.

Questions.—Do these words as they are here arranged make complete sense? Are they proper sentences? Why not?

Direction.—Select such nouns and verbs as will, when combined, make complete sense.

Review Questions.—1. What is a sentence? 2. With what must the first word of a sentence begin? 3. What is a noun? 4. Is the noun *wolves* singular or plural? 5. What is a verb? 6. What is the singular of each noun in these nine sentences? 7. What must every sentence contain? 8. How must each sentence begin and end?

VII.—DECLARATIVE SENTENCE.

Remark.—This lesson, and the three that immediately follow, are given here to aid pupils in reading, in writing short compositions, and also to prepare the way for the analysis of sentences. The sentences given, however, should not be used for analysis, as they are unsuitable for this purpose for beginners.

20. A sentence may be a *statement*, a *question*, a *command*, or an *exclamation*.

1. Henry jumped.
2. Mary laughed.

INTRODUCTORY LESSONS.

Explanation.—Sentence 1, "Henry jumped," is a statement; it states or declares a fact, and is therefore a declarative sentence. So is sentence 2.

21. Definition.—A **declarative sentence** declares or *asserts* a *fact*.

22. Some sentences do not declare facts, as will be seen by observing the following:

1. Henry jumped. A statement or assertion—declarative sentence.
2. Did Henry jump? A question—interrogative sentence.
3. Do not jump, Henry. A command or entreaty—imperative sentence.
4. O, how Henry jumped! An exclamation—exclamatory sentence.

Names of persons, like *Henry*, *John*, *Mary*, are called proper nouns, and must always begin with a capital letter. Other nouns, like *boy*, *girl*, *man*, *desk*, are common nouns, and must *not* begin with a capital letter unless they begin a sentence.

Questions.—1. Why must *did* and *do*, in 1 and 2, begin with a capital letter? 2. Why must 1 end with a period? 3. What kind of a sentence is 2? 3? 4? 4. What four things may a sentence be made to express?

23. Rule.—Every declarative sentence must end with a period.

Direction.—Form declarative sentences by writing a verb in each of the blank spaces below, observing the rule for punctuation:

1. Parrots ——
2. Weeds ——
3. Robins ——
4. Snow ——
5. Mice ——
6. Boys ——
7. Spiders ——
8. Rivers ——
9. Snails ——

Direction.—Fill out the following sentences by using proper nouns in 1, 3, and 5, and common nouns in the others:

1. The dog bit ——.
2. —— eat hay.
3. The hunter shot a ——.
4. The dog swam across the ——.
5. The man called ——.
6. The girls went to ——.

VIII.—INTERROGATIVE SENTENCE.

1. Did Henry jump?

Questions.—When I say, "Did Henry jump?" do I state a fact? Do I ask a question?

24. A sentence used to ask a question is called an interrogative sentence, because *to interrogate* means *to ask*.

25. Definition.—An **interrogative sentence** is one that *asks a question*.

Direction.—Write the following sentences, tell what kind each is, and why, and place the proper punctuation mark after each:

26. Rule.—Every interrogative sentence must end with an interrogation point.

1. John found a ball
2. Where is my book
3. Mary went to school
4. Did James buy a top
5. When did you come back
6. The farmer sows his seed

Direction.—Change the following sentences into interrogative sentences, and place the proper punctuation mark after each:

1. They retired early.
2. Mary is happy.
3. William can write neatly.
4. Boys like fun.
5. Girls like nice dresses.
6. John found a knife.

Questions.—1. What kind of sentences are these as they are here printed? Why? 2. What is a declarative sentence? 3. An interrogative sentence? 4. What punctuation mark must follow a declarative sentence? 5. How must a sentence begin? 6. How must an interrogative sentence end?

IX.—IMPERATIVE SENTENCE.

1. Henry, stop that noise.
2. Do not jump.
3. Give me some bread.

Questions.—Does sentence 1 make a statement? Does it ask a question? Does 2? Does 3?

Explanation.—Sentence 1 makes a command. Sentence 2 makes an earnest request. Sentence 3 expresses a strong wish.

Such sentences as these three are called imperative sentences, because the word *imperative* means *commanding*.

27. Definition.—An **imperative sentence** is one that makes a *command*, or an *earnest request*.

Direction.—Write the following sentences, and tell what kind each is, and why, and place the proper punctuation mark after each:

28. Rule.—Every imperative sentence should end with a period.

    1. John, bring me that book
    2. William bought this book yesterday
    3. Do not let the book fall
    4. Where did Henry buy the book
    5. Mary, do not soil the book
    6. Bring the book to me
    7. Will you lay this book on the table
    8. How often must I speak to you

X.—EXCLAMATORY SENTENCE.

When our feelings are excited either by anger, fear, joy, or sorrow, we express ourselves with strong feelings, or emotion; that is, we cry out, or exclaim.

Direction.—Write the following sentences, and tell which express strong feeling:

    1. This lake is beautiful.
    2. O, what a beautiful lake this is!
    3. It thunders.
    4. Did you hear it?
    5. How dreadfully it thunders!

Questions.—Does sentence 1 express emotion? Does 2? Does 3? Does 4? Does 5?

29. Definition.—An **exclamatory sentence** is one that expresses *strong feeling* or *emotion*.

Direction.—Write the following sentences; determine the class to which each belongs; place the proper punctuation mark after each, and give reasons:

30. Rule.—Every exclamatory sentence should end with an exclamation point (!).

    1. Did William laugh
    2. How fast it rains
    3. O, how that child cries
    4. Bring the child to me
    5. How the wind blows
    6. See that beautiful bird
    7. Bring me the bell
    8. Joseph ate an apple
    9. Do not spill the ink
    10. What a beautiful garden you have

Review Questions.—What are the four classes of sentences into which language is divided?* 1. What is a declarative sentence? 2. With what should a declarative sentence end? 3. What is an interrogative sentence? 4. With what should an interrogative sentence end? 5. What is an imperative sentence? 6. With what should an imperative sentence end? 7. What is an exclamatory sentence? 8. With what should an exclamatory sentence end? 9. What is a sentence? 10. What is a noun? 11. What is a verb?

XI.—COMPOSITION LESSON.

31. Arrangement.—*Margin*, of about an inch and a half at the top of the page.

Heading, in the middle of the page (from left to right).

Heading, must begin with a capital letter, end with a period.

Principal words in the *subject* must *begin* with a *capital* letter.

Margin, of about three quarters of an inch on the left of the page.

Paragraph line, half an inch to the right of the marginal line.

32. Punctuation.—Words spoken or written by another person, when introduced into one's own composition, must be inclosed in quotation marks (" ").

A *hyphen* (-) must join the last syllable of an unfinished word, at the end of the line, to the rest of the word.

A *new paragraph* may be made when there is a change from any particular part of the subject, about which we are writing, to something different.

33. Rule.—The first word of a full quotation must begin with a capital letter.

Directions.—Copy the following composition, observing carefully the *arrangement, capitals,* and *punctuation*:

---

* Pupils should frequently be required to distinguish these four classes of sentences in their reading-lessons.

THE PERFUME OF FLOWERS.*

Some flowers have no odor whatever. By odor we mean any smell, whether agreeable or offensive. The elegant japonicas of various colors, and the beautiful cactus, in all its varieties, have little or no odor.

There are some flowers that give out an odor that is not fragrant. A fragrant flower is one that emits an agreeable smell. The dahlia emits an odor that is not fragrant. *Perfume* is only another name for fragrance.

Every fragrant flower is a perfume-factory. Sometimes a large number of these factories of one kind grow together, and then the air is filled with the perfume that they make.

The fragrance from the flowers of the grape-vine is very delicious. It is of this that Solomon speaks when he says, "The vines with the tender grape give a goodly smell." † And yet the flowers are so small and so near the color of the stem and leaves that you would not notice them unless you looked particularly for them.

Direction.—For a subsequent lesson, write this on the blackboard in solid form, leaving out periods and quotation marks, and require pupils to replace them properly, and to break the composition into paragraphs. Or, the paragraph may be dictated to the class.

Questions.—1. How many margins should there be on a page of written composition? 2. How wide must they be? 3. Where must each paragraph begin? 4. Why does "Solomon" begin with a capital letter? 5. What punctuation marks inclose what Solomon said? Why? 6. Of what do these marks consist? 7. Are the commas *inverted* at the right or the left of the words inclosed? 8. For what is the hyphen used in this lesson.

---

* "The Perfume of Flowers" is the *heading*.

† When only a part of a sentence is quoted, the first word should not begin with a capital letter; as, Mary used the words, "a fragrant flower," in the wrong sense.

ENGLISH GRAMMAR.

XII.—THE PARTS OF SPEECH.

34. Definition.—**English Grammar** teaches how *to speak*, *to write*, and *to read* the English language correctly.

The object of language is the intercommunication of thought. We have already learned that our thoughts are expressed in sentences, and that sentences are composed of words. Grammar may therefore be said to treat of sentences and of the words that compose them.

35. Orthography treats of letters and their combination into syllables and words [spelling].

36. That part of grammar which treats of words *separately*, is called **etymology**.

37. That part of grammar which treats of words *combined in sentences*, is called **syntax**.

38. Syntax * treats of the arrangement of words in sentences according to established usage; in other words, syntax treats of the *relation* which words bear to one another in a sentence.

Questions.—1. What is *English grammar*? 2. What is *orthography*? 3. What is *etymology*? 4. What is *syntax*?

There are many thousands of words in the English language; yet they may be assorted into eight different groups or classes, each class having a name of its own.

39. Many of the words of our language are *names*, and belong to the class called *nouns*. A large number of words express action, and are classed as *verbs*. The following arrangement will show the division of words into the eight classes:

---

* This may be omitted, if it is desired, till needed in the regular order of progress.

PARTS OF SPEECH.

Nouns.	Pronouns.	Adjectives.	Verbs.	Adverbs.	Conjunctions.	Prepositions.	Interjections.
Joseph			jump				
horse			swim				
street			run				
man			sing				
tree			cry				
table			walk				

If these columns were long enough, all the *names* in the language could be put in the *noun column,* all the *verbs* in the *verb column,* all the *adjectives* in the *column for adjectives,* etc., thus separating the words of the language into eight classes. The *noun* and *verb* columns are here filled because these two parts of speech have been used in the preceding lessons.

40. Each of these eight classes of words—*nouns, pronouns,* etc.—is called a **part of speech.**

Questions.—1. What part of speech is *horse, table, man, Joseph, walk, swim, run, tree, sing, jump, street, cry*? 2. How many parts of speech are there?

Remark.—The names of the eight parts of speech are not now to be memorized. They are here introduced to show pupils what they will have to learn. These names can be fixed in the pupil's mind, however, by requiring him to reproduce the diagram every time a new part of speech is taken up, and to fill the proper column with words of the new part of speech, taken from the sentences used, and by asking each time how many of the eight he has learned, and how many yet remain to be learned.

41. Definition.—A **part of speech** is one of the classes of words into which the language is separated.

In order to determine to which of these eight classes the different words in our language belong, we must discover the *use* of each in a sentence; or, in other words, what they *do* in a sentence.

Questions.—1. What is a noun? 2. What is a verb? 3. What is a sentence? 4. What is meant by a part of speech? 5. How many parts of speech are there? 6. Of how many parts of speech do you know something? 7. How may we determine to which part of speech a word belongs?

XIII.—SUBJECT AND PREDICATE.

1. Horses trot.
2. Wasps sting.

Questions.—1. When I say, "Horses trot," about what do I speak? 2. What do I say about horses?

42. There are *two parts* in every sentence: first, that about which the assertion is made; and, second, *what is said* or *asserted* of it.

Direction.—Write the following sentences, and mention the name of the person or thing about which the assertion is made in each; also state what is asserted in each. Care should be taken with punctuation and capitals:

1. Men talk.
2. Monkeys chatter.
3. Crickets chirp.
4. People think.
5. Parrots imitate.
6. Wasps sting.

43. Definition.—The **subject** of a sentence is that part about which something is asserted.

44. Definition.—The **predicate** of a sentence is that part which makes the assertion.

Direction.—Name the *subject* and the *predicate* in each of the six preceding sentences.

Note.—In the sentence, "Children sing," the word *children* is a *noun*, and it is also the *subject* in the sentence; **noun** is its **part of speech name**, and **subject** is its **sentence name**. *Sing* is a verb, and it is also the predicate in the sentence; **verb** is its **part of speech name**, and **predicate** is its **sentence name**.

45. Definition.—A **verb** is a *word* used *to assert* something of its subject. [18.]

Note.—The verb is the predicate when it is used alone to make an assertion about the subject. In the sentence, "John spoke hastily," the whole predicate is *spoke hastily*; but the verb *spoke* is the most important word used in making the assertion.

Remark.—*To assert* is *to affirm* or to declare that a thing *is*, or *is not* so. But *assertions* are considered by grammarians to include *commands* and *questions*.

Questions.—1. What is the subject of a sentence? 2. What is the predicate of a sentence? 3. What is an assertion? 4. What, besides statements, do assertions include? 5. Is "Will you go?" a statement? 6. Is "Bring the book to me" a statement? 7. In "Wasps sting," what are the *part of speech* names? 8. What are the sentence names? 9. How many names has a noun in a sentence? 10. How many names has a verb in a sentence? 11. What are they? 12. How many parts to every sentence? 13. What is a verb?

XIV.—SIMPLE SUBJECT AND SIMPLE PREDICATE.

1. Men walk.
2. Children cry.

Direction.—In selecting the subject and predicate, look *first* for the predicate. Then ask a question by using *who* or *what* before the verb, thus: *Who* walk? Answer, "Men. Therefore, *men* is the subject." In this way find the subject in each of the following sentences:

1. Robins sing.
2. Hens cackle.
3. Lions roar.
4. Lilies bloom.

5. Cherries ripen.
6. Men work.
7. Calves bellow.
8. Babies cry.

46. The *subject* of a sentence sometimes names the *actor*; the *verb expresses the action*; as, "Men *eat*." "Men *write*." "Men think" [mind action]. "Girls study" [mind action]. "Boys play."

47. The sentences used in this lesson are of the *simplest kind*, for in each there is only a *single word* [noun] for the *subject*, and a *single word* [verb] for the *predicate*. Such a subject is called a **simple subject,** and such a predicate is called a **simple predicate.**

Direction.—Supply a simple subject for each of the following verbs:

1. —— twinkle.
2. —— growl.
3. —— squeal.
4. —— flows.

5. —— study.
6. —— smile.
7. —— gnaw.
8. —— steal.

ADJECTIVES.

Direction.—Supply a simple predicate for each of the following subjects:

1. Farmers ———.	7. Stars ———.
2. Snakes ———.	8. Lions ———.
3. Bees ———.	9. Wolves ———.
4. Fishes ———.	10. Cows ———.
5. Flowers ———.	11. Rats ———.
6. Rain ———.	12. Birds ———.

Review Questions.—1. What is a singular noun? Plural noun? 2. What does English grammar teach? 3. Of what may English grammar be said to treat? 4. What is etymology? 5. What is syntax? 6. Into how many classes are all the words in the language grouped? 7. What general name is given to these groups? 8. Of how many of these parts of speech have we learned something? 9. What two important parts in every sentence? 10. What is the subject of a sentence? 11. What is the predicate of a sentence? 12. How may you find the subject? 13. What is an assertion? 14. What do assertions include?

XV.—ADJECTIVES.—MODIFIED SUBJECT.

1. Boys study.	4. People sleep.
2. Birds sing.	5. Dogs bark.
3. Vines grow.	6. Children play.

Direction.—Select the subject and predicate in these sentences according to the following:

MODEL.

"Boys study" is a declarative * sentence. The noun *boy* is the *subject*, because it is the part about which something is asserted; the verb *study* is the *predicate*, because it asserts something of the subject.

48. In these sentences, *boys* and *birds* and *vines* in general are spoken of; i. e., *any* boys, *any* birds, *any* vines. But we may wish to speak of a *particular* kind of boys, or birds, or vines. To do this, we must use some word with each of these nouns that will show *what* particular kind is meant; thus:

---

* The designation "simple sentence" is deferred until pupils are ready to take up compound sentences, as the term "simple" will be better understood when the term *compound* is used in contrast with it.

ADJECTIVES.

1. *Good* boys study.
2. *Little* birds sing.
3. *These* vines grow.
4. *Weary* people sleep.
5. *Ugly* dogs bark.
6. *Happy* children play.

49. Such words as *good, little, these, weary, ugly,* and *happy,* used with nouns to *describe* or *limit* their meaning, are called **adjectives**.

Explanation.—The adjective *good* describes boys by showing the *kind* of boys spoken of. *Good* also *limits* [confines] boys to the class called *good. These* does *not* describe; it only *limits* by pointing out.

50. Adjectives *describe* when they tell what *kind* of a person or thing is meant; as, *honest* man; *sweet* apple.

51. Some adjectives *limit* nouns without describing them; they simply *point out*; as, *this* book; *that* hat; *these* books; *those* hats; *the* boy; *some* apples.

52. Other adjectives *limit* nouns by *expressing number*; as, *two* men; *twenty-five* dollars; *first* boy.

Explanation.—The expression *good boys* does not mean the same as *boys* used alone; nor does the expression *these vines* mean the same as *vines* used alone; therefore, *good* used with *boys,* or *these* used with *vines, changes* or *varies* the meaning of these nouns.

53. The word *modify* means to *change somewhat*; therefore, *good* and *these* modify the nouns with which they are used.

54. An *adjective* is a **modifier**; this is its *sentence name*.

Some adjectives describe.
Some adjectives limit by pointing out.
Other adjectives limit by expressing number.
All adjectives *modify*.

Direction.—In the following sentences, tell which adjectives *describe, point out,* or *express number*; also tell what each modifies:

1. Bad boys fight.
2. One flower wilted.
3. Five stars appeared.
4. That man sings.
5. Industrious people work.
6. Seven boys recited.
7. Wholesome food nourishes.
8. Some people quarrel.

55. Definition.—An adjective is a word used to describe or limit the meaning of a noun.

Questions.—1. In the sentence, "Little birds sing," what part of speech is *little*? 2. When do adjectives describe? 3. How may adjectives *limit*, without describing? 4. Give an example. 5. What does the word *modify* mean? 6. How do adjectives *modify* nouns? 7. What is an adjective?

XVI.—MODIFIED SUBJECT.

1. The good boys obeyed.
2. That large ship sank.
3. Those men smoke.
4. Some dogs growl.
5. Beautiful flowers decay.
6. The sick child died.

Explanation.—In sentence 1, the simple subject *boys* is modified by the adjective *the*, and also by the adjective *good*.

Questions.—What is the simple subject in sentence 2 modified by? In 3, 4, 5, 6? Mention the predicate in each sentence.

56. *Nouns* and *verbs* are the two most important parts of speech, because sentences can be formed with these alone. Hence, the *simple subject* and the *simple predicate* are called the **principal parts** of a sentence. They are often called the **principal elements**.

57. Definition.—An **element** is *one* of the parts of which anything is composed.

58. Words used to modify the principal elements of a sentence are called *dependent elements*. **Adjectives** are, therefore, **dependent elements**.

Direction.—Mention the principal, and also the dependent, elements in the following sentences:

1. The old wooden clock stopped.
2. Warm air rises.
3. That beautiful bird died.
4. Those yellow flowers faded.

59. Definition.—The *simple subject*, taken *with all its modifiers*, is called the **modified* subject**.

---

* The *modified subject* is sometimes called the *logical subject*. The *simple subject* is sometimes called the *grammatical subject*.

DESCRIPTIVE AND LIMITING ADJECTIVES.

Note.—In sentence 1, above, the *simple* subject is the noun *clock*; the *modified* subject is *the old wooden clock.*

Direction.—Write a subject, modified by one or more adjectives, for each of these verbs: *lie, cheat, cry, talk, sing.*

Questions.—1. What is the simple subject in 2? 2. The modified subject? 3. What is the simple subject in 3? 4. The modified subject? 5. What is the simple subject in 4? 6. The modified subject? 7. What is an element? 8. What are the principal elements in a sentence? 9. What is a dependent element? 10. What is an adjective? 11. Is an adjective a principal, or a dependent, element? 12. What kind of element is a simple subject? 13. A simple predicate? 14. What general use, or office, do adjectives have in a sentence? 15. In what three ways do adjectives modify? 16. What is a modified subject? 17. By what other name is it known? 18. By what other name is the simple subject sometimes known?

XVII.—DESCRIPTIVE AND LIMITING ADJECTIVES.

60. Definition.—A **descriptive adjective** is one that describes or qualifies the meaning of the noun with which it is used.

Descriptive adjectives indicate the *quality* that is possessed by the thing named by the noun. When we speak of a *sweet apple*, the adjective *sweet* indicates the quality of the apple; that is, *sweet* shows that the apple possesses the *quality* called *sweetness.* Descriptive adjectives show *color, size, kind*; as, *white* horse; *large* house; *gentle* lamb.

61. Definition.—A **limiting adjective** merely limits or restricts the application of a noun with which it is used.

Limiting adjectives show *which* things, *how many* things, *quantity* of things; as, *the* book; *this* river; *that* mountain; *five* houses; *several* stores; *much* sugar; *some* bread.

Direction.—Select the descriptive, and also the limiting, adjectives in the following sentences, and tell what each adjective shows:

1. Healthy children grow.
2. The sun shines.
3. Both men returned.
4. Much rain fell.
5. Ugly dogs bite.
6. Foolish boys smoke.
7. Those little girls laughed.
8. Three ladies sang.
9. That old clock stopped.
10. Cold air descends.
11. Warm air rises.
12. Several carriages passed.

ANALYSIS OF SENTENCES.

Direction.—Write two sentences containing descriptive adjectives, and three containing limiting adjectives.

Questions.—1. What is an adjective? 2. What is a descriptive adjective? 3. What do descriptive adjectives express? 4. What is a limiting adjective? 5. What do limiting adjectives express? 6. What is the *general* or *sentence* name of any kind of an adjective?

Direction.—Draw a part of speech diagram (see page 13), and write all the words in these twelve sentences in their proper columns.

XVIII.—ANALYSIS.

62. Analysis, in grammar, is the separating of a sentence into its elements.

Direction.—Analyze the following sentences according to the model here given:

Remark.—The analysis of sentences is greatly helpful to the learner, in enabling him to punctuate properly. It will also aid him in reading, for we should read by phrases and clauses.

1. All good boys study.

63. Model.—"All good boys study" is a declarative sentence; *declarative*, because it asserts a fact. The modified subject is *all good boys*; the simple predicate is the verb *study*. The simple subject *boys* is modified by the adjectives *all* and *good*.

Sentences for Analysis.

1. The weary little child slept.
2. Profane men swear.
3. Wicked boys steal.
4. Some insects sting.
5. The old locomotive whistled.
6. Four men rode.
7. Several men walked.
8. Industrious men prosper.
9. Most animals swim.
10. The light snow drifted.

Questions.—1. Which nouns in these sentences are singular? 2. Which are plural? 3. What is analysis? 4. What is meant by the *simple* subject? 5. What is meant by *modified* subject? 6. What is a descriptive adjective? 7. A limiting adjective? 8. What is an element? 9. What is a principal element? 10. A dependent element? 11. What is the general office of an adjective? 12. With what part of speech are adjectives used?

13. By what other name is the modified subject known? 14. What is an interrogative sentence? 15. A declarative sentence? 16. An imperative sentence? 17. When are quotation marks used? 18. What are quotation marks? 19. When should the first word of a quotation *not* begin with a capital letter?

XIX.—COMPOSITION WRITING.

64. To Teachers.—We learn to use language by *attempting* to use it. Although composition writing should go hand in hand with instruction in grammar, yet the former must be largely separate from the latter until sufficient progress shall have been made by the pupil to enable him to understand *how* to correct the errors pointed out by the teacher.

The object, in composition writing, should be to develop the perception, the memory, and the imagination, as well as to teach the child to use language. Indeed, to aid the child in acquiring ideas is fully as important as to teach him the use of words.

In carrying out this object, the child should be directed to observe carefully the things with which he comes in contact in his daily life; such as *flowers, fruits, trees, architecture, scenery, pictures*, etc., so that he may be able to describe them at least with tolerable accuracy. In the description of pictures, the imagination is cultivated rather than the perception; besides, pictures give an erroneous idea of size, and no idea of weight and sound. Pictures, therefore, should not be used as *subjects for compositions* to the exclusion of others, nor too often in alternation with them. The memory should be brought into exercise by the narration of events, and, indeed, the teacher should use every means available to bring all the powers of the mind into active exercise.

As pictures can be easily obtained, none are here given. The directions, and the material for description and narration in the composition exercises, should not be considered exhaustive, but rather as suggestive; nor are they necessarily to be taken exactly in the order given.

Special Directions.—In the lower grammar grades, compositions should *seldom* be given for a home exercise, and *never* unless the subject has been worked up according to directions given farther on. *It is very important* that compositions should be carefully corrected (or errors indicated), that they should be returned to pupils for revision, again examined by the teacher to see if pupils have made the proper changes, and then carefully re-written. It is not the *number* of compositions, but *the care* with which they *are written* and *re-written* that will insure success.

XX.—COMPOSITION LESSONS.

65. General Direction.—Before trying to describe an object, the different points for description should be selected in some regular order. These points may be brought out by asking questions about the object to be described. Ask questions about different points suggested by examining the object, or, if unobtainable, by talking about it, getting as great a variety of answers as possible, and giving all necessary help in forming answers; then make an orderly arrangement of the points to be described.

Direction.—Taking "oranges" for description, ask the following questions, and then examine with the class the "Topical Outline" here given. Require pupils to read the composition written from the outline, calling attention to the fact that the description follows the order of the points as they are arranged, and also that the paragraphs correspond to the divisions of the *outline*.

ORANGES.

Questions.—1. What are oranges? 2. In what kind of climate do they flourish? 3. Where are they obtained? 4. What is their average size? 5. Their shape? 6. Their color? 7. What name is given to the outside of an orange? 8. What, to the inside parts? 9. What are they used for? 10. How do they taste?

TOPICAL OUTLINE.

Description of oranges.
- What they are.
- Climate where raised.
- Where obtained.
- General appearance.
  - Size.
  - Shape.
  - Color.
- Parts.
  - Peel: rough, oily.
  - Pulp: soft, juicy, sweet.
  - Seeds: numerous, in center.
  - Cells: tough, contain seeds.
- Use: Food, uncooked.

Direction.—For the next lesson, write the *outline* on the blackboard, and, after asking the questions given above, require the class to produce a composition which need not be an exact reproduction of the model in this lesson.

ORANGES.

Oranges are a kind of fruit raised in a warm climate in different countries. We obtain oranges from the southern parts of Europe and of the United States, and also from the West Indies.

In size, oranges average a little larger than apples. They are nearly round, and when ripe are of a deep yellow color.

The outside of an orange is called the rind, or peel. The inside consists of the pulp and seeds; and the seeds are inclosed in a tough substance called cells.

Oranges are used for food, and are generally very sweet and juicy. Sometimes, however, they are quite sour to the taste, especially when eaten before they are fully ripe.

CHERRIES.

Questions.—1. What are they? 2. How do they grow? 3. How does a cherry tree look when in full bloom? 4. Which appears first, the blossom or the fruit? 5. What is the size of cherries? 6. Their shape? 7. Their color? 8. How do wild cherries compare in size with those that are cultivated? 9. Is the skin of a cherry tough or tender? 10. Is the pulp hard or soft, sweet or sour? 11. Does the cherry contain more than one seed? 12. For what are cherries used? 13. Are they eaten when unripe?

TOPICAL OUTLINE.

Description of cherries.
- What they are.
- How they grow.
- General appearance.
  - Size: hazel-nut.
  - Shape: nearly round.
  - Color: various.
- Kinds: Wild, cultivated.
- Parts.
  - Skin: thin, tender.
  - Pulp: soft, juicy, sweet, bitter.
  - Seed: single stones.
- Use: Food, when ripe, cooked or uncooked.

XXI.—ADJECTIVES.—ARTICLES.

66. The little words *the*, *an*, and *a* are really adjectives, because they are used with nouns, to limit them; most grammarians, however, give them another name—*articles*.

ADJECTIVES.—ARTICLES.

67. *The* is called the *definite* article because it points out some particular object or objects. *Definite* means *particular.*

68. *An* and *a* are called *indefinite* articles because they do *not* point out any particular object. *In*definite means *not* particular (*in* = *not*).

A is *an** with the *n* omitted.

69. In this book, *the, an,* and *a* are called adjectives.

70. It is necessary to learn when to use *a,* and when to use *an.* If one should say, "*A* orange dropped," or "*An* cow bellowed," it would sound strange; but, "*An* ox bellowed" is correct, and so is "*A* cow eats grass."

A and *an* mean *one.* They are used only with singular nouns. *The* may be used with either singular or plural nouns.

An is used before words beginning with a *vowel sound.*

A is used before words beginning with a *consonant sound.*

A vowel is a letter that can be sounded alone in a word or syllable. A consonant is a letter that can be sounded in a word or syllable only in connection with a vowel.

71. The *vowels* are *a, e, i, o, u*; also *w* and *y,* when not before a vowel *sounded* in the same syllable; as, vie*w*, new*ly*, b*y*, *e*we. All the other letters are consonants.

In *ewe, w* comes before the vowel *e,* but the *e* is not sounded; therefore, *w* in ewe is a vowel.

W and *y,* before a vowel sounded in the same syllable, are consonants; as, *w*et, *w*het, s*w*ing, re-*w*ard, *y*outh, un-*y*ield-ing.

72. Words beginning with silent *h,* begin with a vowel sound; therefore we say, "*an* hour"; "*an* honorable man."

Some writers use *an* before a word beginning with *h* not silent, when such word is not accented on the first syllable; as, "An historical essay."

Questions.—1. What are *w* and *y* when they begin words? 2. When they end words? 3. What is *w* in ewe? 4. Why? 5. When is *a* used? 6. When is *an* used? 7. When are *w* and *y* consonants?

---

*An and *a* are contractions of the Anglo-Saxon word *ane,* meaning *one.* Afterward the *e* was dropped, and *an* was used before words beginning with vowels and consonants. For the sake of ease in speaking, the *n* was finally dropped before words beginning with consonant sounds, leaving *an* before vowel sounds only.

XXII.—PROPER USE OF A AND AN.

Direction.—After giving pupils a thorough review on the sounds of the vowels* and consonants, require them to select from the following words those that begin with a vowel sound: *Honest, hungry, herb, husband, house, honor, hour.*

73. The words *union, eulogy, unit,* and *ewe,* begin with the consonant sound of *y*; therefore we say, *a* union, *a* eulogy, *a* unit, etc.

74. *One* begins with the consonant sound of *w* [*wŭn*]; therefore we say, such *a* one, *a* one-horse chaise, *a* one-sided view.

Direction.—Require pupils to give the reason for the use of *a* or *an* in each of the following sentences; then analyze them, calling *a* and *an* adjectives:

1. An hour passed.
2. A dark cloud arose.
3. An honest man prospers.
4. A useful clerk resigned.
5. An ugly dog barked.
6. An owl hooted.
7. A gray owl hooted.
8. A young child creeps.
9. An old clock stopped.
10. A little child cried.
11. An onion decayed.
12. A star appeared.
13. An apple dropped.
14. An old vessel sank.
15. A prisoner escaped.
16. An eagle screamed.

Questions.—1. In sentence 1, why is *an* used? 2. In 4, why is *a* used? 3. In 8, why is *an* used? 4. To which of the eight parts of speech do *the, an,* and *a* belong? 5. By what other name are they sometimes known? 6. Before what words is *a* used? 7. Before what words is *an* used? 8. With what sound does *useful* begin? 9. Is it correct to say, "an united country"? 10. Is it correct to say, "a honest man"? 11. What is *y* in *yellow,* and what is *w* in *plow*?

---

* A vowel is a letter that represents an unobstructed sound; i. e., a vowel can be sounded without bringing the parts of the mouth into contact to interrupt the stream of air from the lungs. A vowel can be used *alone* as a syllable [70]. (For the different sounds of each vowel, see a *Speller* or *Reader.*)

A consonant is a letter that represents an obstructed sound; i. e., a consonant cannot be sounded without bringing the parts of the mouth into contact. A consonant cannot be used alone as a syllable.

The union of *two* vowels in one sound is called a *diphthong*; as *oi* in *voice.* The union of *three* vowels in one syllable is called a *triphthong*; as *eau* in *beauty.*

Direction.—Supply *a* or *an* in each of the following unfinished sentences:

1. —— young robin chirped.
2. —— angry storm arose.
3. —— swallow twittered.
4. —— one-horse wagon passed.
5. —— honest merchant thrives.
6. —— heavy beam fell.
7. —— united country prospers.
8. —— humorous man lectured.

Review Questions.—1. Which are the two most important parts of speech, and why? 2. What is a sentence? 3. How many words are required to form the simplest kind of a sentence? 4. What part of speech may be the subject of a sentence? 5. By what may the subject be modified? 6. What is an element? 7. What kind of element is an adjective? 8. Which are the principal elements in a sentence? 9. What is a simple subject? 10. What is a modified subject? 11. May a subject have more than one modifier? 12. Before what words is *a* used? 13. What is the meaning of *a*? 14. Why is *w* or *y* a consonant when it begins a word or syllable? 15. Why is *w* a vowel in *view*? 16. Which of the letters can be used alone as a syllable?

XXIII.—SYNTHESIS.*

75. Direction.—Combine each of the following sets of statements into a single sentence:

1. This girl is ambitious.
She wrote a composition.
The composition was excellent.

2. This boy is little.
He found a knife.
The knife was new.

Model.—This ambitious girl wrote an excellent composition.

3. That boy plays.
He plays games.
He always plays fairly.

4. Mary sings.
She sings songs.
She sings them delightfully.

5. That dog is ugly.
He bit a little girl.
He bit her severely.

6. This dog is faithful.
He saved a child.
The child was drowning.

7. That little child laughs.
She laughs heartily.
She does so always.

8. The swan swims.
It swims gracefully.
It does so always.

---

* *Synthesis* is the *putting together* of words to form a sentence. It is the opposite of analysis.

ADVERBS.—MODIFIED PREDICATE. 27

Direction.—Ask the following questions, as directed in the last composition lesson. After forming the topical outline, any of the minor points may be checked off, if it is thought best, to shorten the composition.

APPLES.

Questions.—1. What are they? 2. How do they grow? 3. Do the trees blossom? 4. What is the color of the blossoms? 5. What is the appearance of an apple orchard in full bloom? 6. Which appear first, the blossoms or the fruit? 7. Are all apples of the same color? 8. How many kinds of apples can you mention? 9. Is the pulp soft or hard; sweet, sour, or neutral? 10. How are the seeds arranged? 11. For what are apples used?

TOPICAL OUTLINE.

Heads: What they are.—How they grow.—When they ripen. Shape.—Size.—Color.—Skin.—Pulp.—Seeds.—Use.

Shape: Somewhat round.
Color: Red, yellow, green, mixed, striped.
Skin: Thin, tough, tender.
Pulp: Mellow, when ripe; juicy, dry, sweet, sour, neutral.
Seeds: Surround the core; inclosed in cells.
Use: Food, cooked or raw. Cider, vinegar.

XXIV.—MODIFIED PREDICATE.

1. Good boys study.
2. Little birds sing.
3. These vines grow.
4. Weary people sleep.

76. In sentence 1, all that is stated of "Good boys" is the fact that they *study*; in 2, all that is stated of "Little birds" is that they *sing*; in 3, all that is stated of "These vines" is that they *grow*. But we may wish to state something more than these simple facts, and this may be done by using some word or words to *modify* the meaning of each verb; as,

1. Good boys study *diligently*.
2. Little birds sing *sweetly*.
3. These vines grow *rapidly*.
4. Weary people sleep *soundly*.
5. Weary people *sometimes* sleep soundly.

77. Such words as *diligently, sweetly, rapidly, soundly,* and *sometimes,* used to modify the meaning of verbs, are called

adverbs because they are *added* to verbs [used *with* verbs] *to modify* their meaning.

Questions.—1. In sentence 5, above, what is the simple subject? 2. By what is it modified? 3. What is the simple predicate, or verb? 4. By what is it modified?

Explanation.—The adjective *weary*, in sentence 5, modifies the simple subject *people*; therefore, "Weary people" is called the *modified subject*. The verb *sleep* does not make the *whole* assertion about "Weary people"; the *entire* assertion is "sometimes sleep soundly." The verb *sleep* is modified by the adverbs *sometimes* and *soundly*; therefore, "sometimes sleep soundly" is often called the *modified predicate*. But it is, perhaps, better to call the *modified subject* the **entire subject**, and the *modified predicate* the **entire predicate**, because the word *entire* better conveys the idea of *wholeness*, and is at the same time smoother in sound. It is also better to call the verb in the predicate the **predicate-verb**.

78. The *verb* in a sentence is the *entire predicate* when alone it makes a complete assertion about the subject; as, "Fishes *swim*." But when other words are used with the verb to make the whole assertion, the *verb* is the *principal word* in the predicate, and is called the **predicate-verb**; "The full moon *sometimes* shines *brightly*."

Direction.—Select the *entire subject* and the *entire predicate* in each of the five preceding sentences; also, the *simple subject* and the *predicate-verb*, mentioning the modifiers of each. Fill out the following unfinished sentences by inserting *subjects, predicate-verbs, adjectives,* and *adverbs* in the blank spaces, and mention the part of speech of each word inserted:

1. —— fire —— brightly.
2. —— boys laughed ——.
3. Little birds —— sing ——.
4. Careful —— write ——.
5. —— beasts —— ravenously.
6. The stars —— shine ——.

Questions.—1. What does an adverb modify? 2. Is an adverb a principal or a dependent element? 3. Which are the principal elements in the sentence, "These vines grow rapidly"? 4. Which are the dependent elements? 5. What is the *entire predicate* in this sentence? 6. The entire subject? 7. What part of speech is a dependent element when used with a subject? 8. When used with a predicate-verb? 9. When is a *predicate-verb* the *entire predicate*? 10. How does the verb rank in the predicate when other words are used with it to make the whole assertion?

XXV.—ADVERBS.—ANALYSIS.

Direction.—Mention the entire predicate in each of the following sentences, and tell what each predicate-verb is modified by:

1. Some birds fly *swiftly*.
2. The fishermen landed *here*.
3. The pleasure-party landed *yonder*.
4. Some flowers *always* bloom *early*.

Explanation.—In sentence 1, the adverb *swiftly* is used to show *how* "Some birds fly." In 2, the adverb *here* is used to show *where* "The fishermen landed." In 4, the adverbs *always* and *early* are used to show *when* "Some flowers bloom."

79. The three special uses of the adverbs in these four sentences are to show *how*, *where*, and *when* actions are performed; but their *general* use is to *modify*.

Questions.—1. What does the adverb show in each of these four sentences? 2. What part of speech does each modify? 3. What three different uses do these adverbs have? 4. What do adjectives modify? 5. What do they tell about nouns? 6. Can more than one adverb modify the same verb? 7. What is meant by the entire subject? 8. Entire predicate? 9. What is the subject of a sentence? 10. What is the predicate of a sentence? 11. When is the predicate-verb the whole predicate? 12. What is a noun? 13. What is a verb?

Model for Analysis.

1. Industrious people generally rise early.

80. This is a declarative sentence. The entire subject is "Industrious people"; the entire predicate is "generally rise early." The simple subject *people* is modified by the adjective *industrious*; the predicate-verb *rise* is modified by the adverbs *generally* and *early*.

Sentences for Analysis.

(For models for written analysis, see 120.)

1. The weary wanderers finally returned.
2. A snail moves slowly.
3. An old horse generally trots slowly.
4. Small children often cry violently.

ANALYSIS.

5. The great noisy crowd often shouted lustily.
6. The strong west wind changed suddenly.
7. The pleasant holidays soon passed away.
8. The full moon sometimes shines brightly.
9. Those young ladies skate gracefully.
10. The white, fleecy clouds floated rapidly away.

Direction.—State the particular use of each adjective and adverb in the preceding sentences.

81. An adverb is sometimes placed before and sometimes after the verb that it modifies, as in sentences 1 and 2 above. When two adverbs are used to modify the same verb, as in 3, 4, 5, etc., one of them should usually be placed *before* the verb and the other *after* it in such a way as to make the best sense. It would sound awkward to say, "An old horse trots *generally slowly*," or even "*slowly* trots *generally*." Sometimes (not often, however,) the sense is better expressed when two adverbs are written together, as "rapidly away" in sentence 10.

82. Office, or Relation.—In the sentence, "Good boys study diligently," the noun *boys* is the *simple subject*; this is its *office*, or *relation*, in the sentence. The word *good* is used to modify *boys*; *good*, therefore, performs an *adjective* office. The word *study* performs the office of *predicate-verb* in the sentence. The word *diligently* modifies the verb *study*; therefore it performs an *adverbial* office.

83. Definition.—The **office** or **relation** of a word is its *use* in a sentence.

XXVI.—SECONDARY MODIFIER.

1. That beautiful swan swims gracefully.
2. That *exceedingly* beautiful swan swims *very* gracefully.

Explanation.—In sentence 2, the word *exceedingly* modifies the adjective *beautiful* by intensifying its meaning; and the word *very* modifies the adverb *gracefully* in the same way.

84. A word used to modify an adjective or an adverb is an *adverb*.

ADVERBS.

85. Definition.—An adverb, when it modifies a *verb* [principal element], is called a **primary modifier**.

86. Definition.—An adverb, when it modifies an *adjective* or an *adverb* [dependent element], is called a **secondary modifier**.

87. Definition.—An adverb is a word used to modify the meaning of a verb, an adjective, or another adverb.

88. Some words are used *only* as *adverbs*; as, *often, soon, away, sometimes*.

89. Some words are *sometimes adverbs* and *sometimes adjectives*; as, *fast, late, early*. I have a *fast* horse. This horse travels *fast*.

90. Many adjectives become adverbs by adding **ly**; as, sweet, sweet**ly**; slow, slow**ly**; violent, violent**ly**.

91. Some *nouns* by adding **ly** become *adjectives*; as, man, man**ly**; friend, friend**ly**. Such adjectives as these must not be mistaken for adverbs. The use of a word determines its *part of speech*. **Not** is called a *negative* adverb because it expresses a *negation*, or *denial*.

Model for Analysis.

1. That exceedingly beautiful swan swims very gracefully.

92. This is a declarative sentence. The entire subject is "That exceedingly beautiful swan"; the entire predicate is "swims very gracefully." The simple subject *swan* is modified by the adjective *beautiful*, and *beautiful*, itself, is modified by the adverb *exceedingly*. The predicate-verb *swims* is modified by the adverb *gracefully*, and *gracefully*, itself, is modified by the adverb *very*.

Direction.—Before using the following sentences for analysis, dictate them for writing, *omitting the secondary modifiers*; then, assigning those modifiers for the several sentences, re-write, inserting them where they belong.

Sentences for Analysis.

1. The fire burns very brightly.
2. That dreadfully tedious journey finally ended.
3. That inconsiderate man acted too hastily.
4. The extremely hot weather finally passed away.
5. A terrible accident happened quite recently.
6. Those boys came back very soon.

XXVII.—RELATED IDEAS.

93. Definition.—A sentence is a combination of words so arranged as to make complete sense.

But words are not strung together at random to express a thought. Only ideas that are related to each other can be put together, and words must be properly arranged to express these ideas.

Direction.—Arrange the words in the first eight of the following sentences so that they will make complete sense, and, in the ninth and tenth, use subjects that will be properly related to the ideas expressed by the verbs:

1. Blow the severely often winds cold.
2. Quickly some always move people.
3. Often suddenly die men intemperate.
4. The away fleecy floated white rapidly clouds.
5. People quietly seldom nervous sit.
6. Ugly barked large a furiously dog.
7. The quickly boy naughty ran little away.
8. Rapidly little flew the away bird beautiful.
9. The mud smiled pleasantly.
10. The dog laughed heartily.

Review Questions.—1. What is an adverb? 2. What kind of element is an adverb? 3. What three parts of speech may an adverb modify? 4. What is the *modified subject*? 5. What is a *predicate-verb*? 6. What is the meaning of the term *predicate*? 7. When is the verb the whole or *entire* predicate in a sentence? 8. How should adverbs generally be placed when two of them modify the same verb in a sentence? 9. What position does a *single* adverb occupy in a sentence? 10. What is analysis in grammar? 11. What is the subject of a sentence? 12. What is the predicate? 13. What is a *primary* modifier? 14. What is a *secondary* modifier? 15. What is a sentence? 16. Why are the eight collections of words standing first on this page not sentences? 17. What kind of ideas can be put together to form sentences? 18. Why do 9 and 10 not make sense? 19. What words are used *only* as *adverbs*? 20. What words are sometimes adjectives and sometimes adverbs? 21. Mention five *adjectives* that may be changed to *adverbs* by adding *ly*. 22. Mention five *nouns* that may be changed to *adjectives* by adding *ly*. 23. How do we determine to what part of speech any word in a sentence belongs? 24. What is meant by the *office* of a word in a sentence?

XXVIII.—COMPOSITION LESSON.

94. Direction.—The teacher may call upon a pupil to read the first of the following paragraphs, cautioning all to observe closely the punctuation, and to see if the reader makes the proper pauses where the points occur. Then request other pupils to read the second paragraph (or the teacher may do so), and to make the proper period-pauses as nearly as they may be able to make them.

After judicious practice of this kind, require all pupils to copy the other paragraphs, and place periods or interrogation points where they should occur. Most pupils will soon acquire skill in breaking up solid paragraphs into sentences, if properly drilled in this way or in any other that may suggest itself to the judicious and inventive teacher.

1. Flowers have habits, or ways of acting, just as people have. For example, all flowers naturally turn toward the light, as if they loved it. This can be seen by watching plants that are standing near a window. If the pots are allowed always to stand in the same position, the flowers will all be bent toward the light. By turning the pots around a little every day while the blossoms are opening, the flowers can be made to look in different directions.

2. The splendid flower, called the night-blooming cereus, opens only once it lets its beauty be seen but for a few hours, and then it fades and dies it is a very rare flower, and few people ever have an opportunity of seeing it those who have seen it watch for its opening with great eagerness this flower generally opens very late in the evening and is closed again in a few hours.

3. Some people do not observe the habits of flowers how many people know that the blossom of the dandelion closes at night and opens again in the morning the gaudy tulip has the same habit as the dandelion most flowers, however, never close their petals after they have once blossomed. The chrysanthemum blooms late in autumn there are many new and beautiful varieties of this flower, which has now become very popular at the yearly exhibition, the chrysanthemum can be seen in large numbers and in great variety the study of flowers is very interesting.

Direction.—For another lesson, copy the first paragraph on the blackboard in solid form, omitting periods and capitals only, and require pupils to copy and supply all omissions. Select other exercises of the same kind from the reading-lessons. Do not be afraid of too much practice of this kind.

XXIX.—CONJUNCTIONS.—SIMPLE AND COMPOUND SENTENCES.

1. The parrot whistled.
2. The swallow twittered.
3. The parrot whistled **and** the swallow twittered.
4. Some insects fly.
5. The flea hops.
6. Some insects fly, **but** the flea hops.

Questions.—Sentence 1 is a *single* statement. Is sentence 2 a single statement? Are 4, 5, and 6 single statements? How many of these six sentences are single statements?

95. Definition.—A **simple sentence** is a single statement, and contains but one subject and one predicate.

Explanation.—Each of the sentences 3 and 6 contains two simple statements. The two statements in 3 are joined by the word *and*, and those in 6 by *but*.

96. Such sentences as 3 and 6 are called **compound sentences**, and the words **and** and **but** are called **conjunctions**.

97. Definition.—A compound sentence is one that consists of two or more simple sentences connected together.

98. Each separate statement in a compound sentence is called a *member*.

Explanation.—In sentence 6, "Some insects fly" is the first member and "the flea hops" is the second member. The conjunction *but* is the connecting word.

99. Definition.—A word used to join sentences together is called a **conjunction**.

The conjunctions in most common use are *and, but, or,* and *nor*.

Questions.—1. How many single statements in 6? 2. What word connects the statements? 3. What part of speech is *but*? 4. What kind of sentence is 2, and why? 5. Is 3, and why? 6. What is the second member in 3? 7. The first member? 8. The connective? 9. What is a simple sentence? 10. What is a compound sentence? 11. A member? 12. A conjunction?

XXX.—ANALYSIS OF COMPOUND SENTENCES.

100. Only sentences that contain related thoughts can be connected to form a compound sentence. The following sentences, therefore, are not properly constructed:

1. The gentle wind blew softly, and some men cheat.
2. Some men deal fairly, and the boat sailed slowly.
3. The moon shone brightly, but other flowers bloom late.
4. Some flowers bloom early, and the sleigh-bells rang merrily.
5. Some men build houses, and the sun again shone brightly.
6. The rain finally ceased, and other men build ships.

Questions.—1. Why should the second member of sentence 1 be connected with the first member of sentence 2? 2. How may these sentences be arranged so as to make good sense? 3. Arrange them properly.

Models for Analysis.

1. Some small birds sing very sweetly.

101. This is a *simple* declarative sentence. The entire subject is "Some small birds," and the entire predicate is "sing very sweetly." The simple subject *birds* is modified by the adjectives *some* and *small*. The predicate-verb *sing* is modified by the adverb *sweetly*, and sweetly *itself* is modified by the adverb *very*.

2. The cold wind blew furiously, and the waves dashed high.

This is a *compound* declarative sentence consisting of two members connected by the conjunction *and*. In the first member, "The cold wind blew furiously," the simple subject *wind* is modified by the adjectives *the* and *cold*; the predicate-verb *blew* is modified by the adverb *furiously*. In the second member, "the waves dashed high," the simple subject *waves* is modified by the adjective *the*; the predicate-verb *dashed* is modified by the adverb *high*.

Remark.—This abbreviated model saves time, and is therefore better at this stage of the pupil's progress. The full analysis may be required, however, at the teacher's discretion.

102. Comma Rule.—The members of a compound sentence are usually separated by a comma when the second statement follows as a consequence of the condition expressed in the first.

COMPOSITION.

Sentences for Analysis.

1. The policeman ran rapidly, but the thief finally escaped.
2. The gentle wind blew softly, and the boat sailed slowly along.
3. The sun shone brightly, and the clouds floated slowly away.
4. The stars twinkle, but the planets shine steadily.
5. Men live, and men die, but God lives forever.

Explanation.—Sentence 5 is a compound sentence consisting of three members. The first and second members are connected by the conjunction *and*; the second and third members, by the conjunction *but*.

Direction.—Dictate these five sentences for a lesson in punctuation; also, write three compound sentences containing only the elements already learned.

XXXI.—SYNTHESIS.

103. Direction.—Combine the following statements as in the preceding composition lesson:

1. I see a man.
He is on a bridge.
The bridge is over a brook.

2. We gathered some berries.
They were in a field.
The field was across the river.

Model.—We gathered some berries in the field across the river.

3. Birds are found in South America.
There are many kinds of them.
They are beautiful.

4. The boys ran.
They ran around the corner.
They ran rapidly.

5. We found a nest.
It was a robin's nest.
It was full of eggs.
It was in an apple-tree.

6. Mary received a prize.
It was for good scholarship.
She received it yesterday.
It was beautiful.

Direction.—For the first lesson in the following exercise, examine the questions with the class, giving all necessary information; compare the questions with the topical outline, and this with the written composition on the next page; then write the questions on the blackboard, and require pupils, with books closed, to form a topical outline. For a second lesson, write the questions on the blackboard, and require pupils to form an outline on their slates; then to examine the exercise, and, from their own outline, or from that in the book, to write a composition.

CUCUMBERS.

Questions.—1. What are cucumbers? 2. How do they grow? 3. What is their general appearance? 4. What are the names of the parts? 5. Are there different kinds? 6. For what are they used? 7. Which appears first, the blossom or the cucumber?

Topical Outline.

Cucumbers.
- What they are.
- How they grow.
- When blossoms appear.
- Appearance.
  - Size: two to ten inches long.
  - Shape: round like a banana.
  - Color: green, cream; orange when ripe.
- Parts.
  - Skin: rough, spines.
  - Pulp: crisp near the skin; soft in center.
  - Seeds: form part of pulpy center.
- Use: Food, green and raw, as a salad.

XXXII.—COMPOSITION LESSON.

CUCUMBERS.

104. Cucumbers are a kind of vegetable or fruit that grows in the garden, on running vines, like the melon. The little cucumber first appears, bearing on its end a little bud, which soon bursts into a blossom. Blossoms without cucumbers also appear, but these wither and drop off soon after their pollen has fertilized the other flowers. This peculiarity is also true of melons, pumpkins, and squashes. The blossoms of the different kinds of fruit that grow on trees, appear before the fruit.

Cucumbers vary in size from two inches to ten, five being about the average length of most kinds. They are, in form, something like the banana. They are generally of a dark green color, but some are nearly the color of cream. When fully ripe, they are of a dark orange color, and are then unfit for food.

The skin is rough, little elevations ending in sharp, black spines, being scattered quite thickly over the surface, except at the stem end. The pulp, in the center, is soft and full of seeds.

The only part of the cucumber fit to be eaten is the seedy pulp, the hard crisp part near the skin being more or less indigestible.

WATERMELONS.

Questions.—1. When and where do they grow? 2. From what place is the early supply derived? 3. What different shapes have you noticed? 4. Is the rind of all melons of the same color? 5. Are the pulp and seeds of the same color in all? 6. In what part of the pulp do the seeds grow? 7. Do the seeds of the nutmeg melon occupy a similar position? Are melons eaten raw or cooked? What is the taste, or flavor?

TOPICAL OUTLINE.

Heads: Where produced.—Shape.—Rind.—Pulp.—Seeds.
Produced: Temperate climates, on vines.
Shape: Oval, short or longer, round.
Rind: Dark green, light green, striped, thick or thin.
Pulp: Pale red, deep red, yellow, soft, sweet, very juicy.
Seeds: Black, brown, white, tipped with black, surround the core.

XXXIII.—TRANSITIVE VERBS.—OBJECT COMPLEMENT.

Remark.—We have learned that there must be a *subject* and a *verb* in every simple sentence; that the verb alone sometimes expresses all we wish to say about the subject; that adverbs are sometimes used with the verb to express the whole thought about the subject. We shall now learn that it often becomes necessary to use a noun with the predicate-verb to make the sense complete.

105. When we say, "Wolves howl," the sense is complete—no question is suggested by the sentence. But when we say—

1. Wolves catch ———.
2. Honest men dislike ———.

the sense is plainly incomplete in each case, and the questions arise, "catch *what*?" "dislike *what* or *whom*?" If we add a *noun* to each to fill out or *complete* the meaning of the verb, the sentences will stand thus:

1. Wolves catch *lambs*.
2. Honest men dislike *rogues*.

Explanation.—The noun *lambs* completes the meaning of the predicate-verb *catch* by representing the *receiver* of the action.

106. A verb that requires the addition of a noun to represent the receiver of an action is called a **transitive verb**, and the added noun is called the *object* of the verb. The added noun is also called the **object complement,** because whatever *completes* may be called a *complement.*

The word *transitive* [Lat. *trans-it-us*] means *passing over*; and in the sentence, "Wolves catch lambs," the action expressed by the verb *catch* passes over from the subject *wolves* to the object *lambs.* The object *lambs receives* the action; that is, the *object* is acted *upon.*

In the sentences "Wolves howl" and "Children sleep," the verbs *howl* and *sleep* do not require the addition of an object to complete the sense. Such verbs are called **intransitive verbs.** [*In*-transitive = *not* transitive.] *Sleep* in this sentence denotes *state* or *condition.*

Questions.—1. What is a transitive verb? 2. An intransitive verb? 3. What is an *object complement*? 4. Why is it so called? 5. Does *sleep* denote *action*?

XXXIV.—TRANSITIVE VERBS.

107. Definition.—A transitive* verb is one that expresses an act done by one person or thing to another.

108. Definition.—An intransitive verb is one that denotes *state* or *condition*, or expresses an action *not* requiring an object to complete its meaning.

109. When the action expressed by a verb is confined to the subject, the verb is *intransitive.*

110. A *transitive* verb expresses an action that goes beyond the subject [the actor], and affects some other person or thing called the *object*; that is, the use of a transitive verb brings into the sentence the *names* of *two* different persons or things—*one*, the name of the *actor*, and the *other*, the name of the *recipient* of the action.

111. Definition.—The object complement of a verb is that part of the predicate of a sentence which represents the *receiver* of the action.

---

* Transitive verbs are sometimes called *incomplete* verbs. Those intransitive verbs that express action, are sometimes called *complete* verbs [see 106 and 108].

OBJECT COMPLEMENT.

Direction.—In the following sentences, determine which contain transitive verbs, which intransitive, and tell why. Mention the *object complement* in each sentence where one occurs. Change into interrogative sentences by using *do, did, does, have,* or *has,* for the introductory word of each.

1. Bees fly rapidly.
2. Bees make honey.
3. Wolves howl fearfully.
4. Wolves eat lambs.
5. The hawk flew slowly.
6. The hawk caught a fish.
7. Brutus stabbed Cæsar.
8. The hunter shot a large deer.
9. California produces gold.
10. That girl skates gracefully.
11. Some roses bloom early.
12. The farmer carted the hay.
13. Those men work hard.
14. This tree bears sweet apples.
15. The rain fell abundantly.
16. The rain moistened the ground.

Questions.—1. What is the meaning of the word transitive? 2. What is a transitive verb? 3. What is the relation of the object to the action? 4. What is the relation of the subject to the action? 5. What is the subject sometimes called? 6. What is an intransitive verb? 7. What kind of verb requires the use of an object complement?

XXXV.—OBJECT COMPLEMENT.

Direction.—Fill out the following sentences by adding object complements to the transitive verbs, and adverbs to the intransitive verbs:

1. Horses draw ——.
2. Some merchants lose ——.
3. Water flows ——.
4. Farmers raise ——.
5. The lion roared ——.
6. Carpenters build ——.
7. Some people act ——.
8. William saw ——.
9. The boy listened ——.
10. Some trees bear ——.
11. John found ——.
12. The thieves fled ——.
13. The farmer mowed ——.
14. The visitors arrived ——.

Direction.—Re-write these sentences, and add to what is already written the following adverbs where they will fit best: *often, sometimes, quickly.* Also use the following adjectives with the object complements: *heavy, good, the, wild, fine, large, excellent.*

112. The **principal parts** of a sentence are the **subject** and the **predicate.** The *principal word* in the *predicate* is the *predicate-verb,* and the *object* ranks next in importance.

The *object complement* * is one of the principal parts of the *predicate*, but *not* a principal part of the sentence as a whole. In a sentence containing a transitive verb, the predicate-verb and its complement, with all their modifiers, form the *entire predicate*.

Direction.—Mention the principal parts of the following sentences in the order here given: 1. Entire subject. 2. Entire predicate. 3. Predicate-verb. 4. Object complement.

1. A rich gentleman built a beautiful house.
2. This industrious boy received a suitable reward.
3. The warm sun gradually dissolved the frozen snow.
4. The hurricane destroyed a large barn.
5. The heavy wind blew the vessel along.
6. The gentle wind blew steadily.
7. The little boy quickly threw the flowers away.
8. Many wild beasts inhabit Africa.
9. Thrifty vines covered the little porch.
10. Sweet odors filled the balmy air.

XXXVI.—ANALYSIS.

Direction.—Select the simple subject, predicate-verb, and object complement in the following sentences; then analyze according to the following:

Model for Analysis.

1. An old sailor soon mended the ragged sail.

113. This is a *simple* declarative sentence. The entire subject is "An old sailor." The entire predicate is "soon mended the ragged sail." The simple subject *sailor* is modified by the adjectives *an* and *old*. The predicate-verb *mended* is modified by the adverb *soon* and completed by the object complement *sail*, which is modified by the adjectives *the* and *ragged*.

---

* The object complement is really a *dependent* element, as it limits [confines] the action expressed by the verb to itself. Taking this view of it, some authors say that in the sentence, "The firemen quickly brought the ladders," the predicate-verb *brought* is *modified* by the adverb *quickly*, and is *limited* by the object *ladders*. [In complex sentences the object clause is considered a dependent element.]

Sentences for Analysis.

1. Most children like melons.
2. The early bird catches the worm.
3. Deep rivers flow silently.
4. That severe storm injured the crops.
5. Some trees bear excellent fruit.
6. The golden sunset lighted the eastern hills.
7. The Romans destroyed Jerusalem.
8. Mary bought a ripe, juicy peach.
9. Galileo invented the telescope.
10. The loose windows rattled constantly.
11. The gentle rain refreshes the thirsty flowers.
12. Washington defeated Cornwallis.
13. The dusky blacksmith shod the restive horse.
14. The happy boys started quite early.
15. The fisherman caught an extremely fine trout.
16. A soft answer turneth away wrath.
17. Some men build houses, and other men build ships.
18. The men carried guns, but the boys carried brooms.
19. Some very good artists occasionally paint poor pictures.

Direction.—Mention the singular and the plural nouns in these sentences. In 2, 6, and 15, state what relation each word holds in the sentence in which it occurs [82].

XXXVII.—SAME VERB TRANSITIVE OR INTRANSITIVE.

114. The same word may be a transitive verb in one sentence and an intransitive verb in another; as,

1. Henry studies intelligently [in general].
2. Henry studies his difficult *lessons* very thoroughly.

Explanation.—The verb *studies* in the first sentence expresses the action in a general way; in the second sentence, *studies* expresses an action limited to something particular—"lessons."

115. When a verb, generally transitive, is used in an intransitive sense, it should be considered *intransitive* in parsing.

Direction.—Mention the transitive, and also the intransitive, use of each verb in the following sentences:

OBJECTS OF KINDRED MEANING. 43

1. Mary writes carefully.
2. Henry writes excellent compositions.
3. That man speaks four languages.
4. That child speaks correctly.
5. Some people eat too rapidly.
6. Lions eat raw flesh.
7. That lady reads well.
8. Mary reads poetry well.

XXXVIII.—OBJECTS OF KINDRED MEANING.

116. Some verbs, generally intransitive, may take an object complement expressing an idea similar to that expressed by the verb itself. Such objects are called *objects of kindred meaning*, some of which are found in the following sentences:

1. This man *lives* a happy *life*.
2. That man *died* a happy *death*.
3. The boy *ran* a *race*.
4. That wicked boy *swore* a horrible *oath*.
5. The visitors *looked* a last *look*.
6. The lady *sang* a beautiful *song*.

Question.—What is meant by an object of kindred meaning?

Interrogative and Imperative Sentences.

117. In an interrogative sentence, the subject stands after the verb, or after one of its parts [18, 301].

1. Has this *village* a bank?
2. Will *James* return soon?

118. In an imperative sentence, the subject is seldom expressed.

1. (   ) Shut the door.
2. (*You*) shut the door.

Direction.—Determine which of the following sentences is declarative, interrogative, imperative, or exclamatory. Give reasons for punctuation; mention the subject in each; analyze each:

1. Have animals reason?
2. Bring the long oars.
3. Has John any bait?
4. Take the box away.
5. How dreadfully the thunder rolls!
6. The heavy engine drew a long train.
7. The farmer raised the grain, but the speculator made the money.

XXXIX.—SYNTHESIS.

119. Direction.—Combine the statements in the following sets of sentences by using as connectives between each couplet *and*, *or*, *nor*, *if*, *but*, *because*, or *therefore*, making two combinations for each when it is possible. To make a second combination, the second sentence may be taken first. Any word may be changed, or may be entirely omitted, to avoid repetition; as,

1. George was late at school.
2. George did not start in time.

Combination 1.—George was late at school because he did not start in time.

Combination 2.—George did not start in time, therefore he was late at school.

1. Industry leads to wealth.
   Laziness leads to poverty.
2. The garden is well cultivated.
   The garden will produce flowers in abundance.
3. Will Henry do the errand?
   Will Charles do it instead of Henry?
4. Mary used her books shamefully.
   Susan preserved her books with care.
5. William will arrive in time.
   Charles will be here late.
6. The price of wheat is low.
   There was a plentiful crop last year.
7. Mary is as tall as her sister.
   She is not so tall as her brother.
8. Ella skates gracefully.
   Mary does not skate so well.
9. Eight cents were divided *between* the *two* brothers.
   Twelve cents were divided *among* the *three* sisters.

Note.—Notice that *between* is used in speaking of *two* persons, and *among*, in speaking of *three* or more than three.

Direction.—Fill the blanks by inserting *between* or *among* in the following:

ANALYSIS.

1. There are six books on the table; you will find yours —— them.
2. Take your seat —— those —— boys.
3. He divided the apples —— his four companions.

Questions.—1. What is the difference in meaning when I say, "You will find the peach on the shelf between the pears," and "You will find the peach among the pears"? 2. When should *between* be used? 2. When should *among* be used?

XL.—MODELS FOR WRITTEN ANALYSIS.

120. A very old sailor soon mended the ragged sail.

Class...............	Simple declarative.
Entire subject........	A very old sailor.
Entire predicate......	Soon mended the ragged sail.
Simple subject........	*Sailor*, modified by the adjectives *the* and *old*; and *old* is modified by the adverb *very*.
Predicate-verb........	*Mended*, modified by the adverb *soon*.
Object...............	*Sail*, modified by the adjectives *the* and *ragged*.

2. God made the country and man made the town.

Class..................	Compound declarative.
First member..........	God made the country.
Second member.........	Man made the town.
Connective.............	**And.**
Simp. sub., first mem....	*God*, unmodified.
Predicate-verb..........	*Made*, unmodified.
Object.................	*Country*, modified by the adjective *the*.
Simp. sub., second mem..	*Man*, unmodified.
Predicate-verb..........	*Made*, unmodified.
Object.................	*Town*, modified by the adjective *the*.

Direction.—Use a few of the sentences on the preceding pages, for written analysis, both as a home lesson and as a school exercise. Break up the following paragraph into sentences, using periods and exclamation points:

As we roam about the fields and woods, it is pleasant to see, here and there, a flower flowers are like familiar friends whom we love to meet a little girl finding a wild violet exclaimed How glad I am to see you again it is a long time since I saw you, and you look as pretty as ever how much we should miss flowers if they did not come every year.

XLI.—DIAGRAMMING.

121. There are various opinions as to the benefit to be derived from diagramming sentences. As a *method* of *imparting* instruction, it is of importance *mainly* as a means of calling the special attention of the learner to the work he *must perform*; for, a knowledge of the structure of a sentence must precede the act of diagramming. By requiring an occasional use of this method of analysis, the teacher is enabled readily to discover the special defects in the knowledge of each pupil, as it affords a convenient form of work to be examined; but the systems of diagramming in general use so *distort* the sentence as to *prevent* a rapid examination.

While the system here presented may not be quite so readily applied to the most intricately involved sentences as other methods, yet it is more easily applied to simple sentences, and also to compound and complex sentences as far as any system is of special importance; and besides, it affords a much more convenient form of work for examination. [See 777].

Directions.—Mark the subject *word*   1.
           Mark the *predicate-verb*   2.
           Mark the *object complement* o. c.

Join *modifying* to *principal elements* by lines, as below.

Join *as one* two or more adjectives or adverbs standing together and modifying the same word.

Underline a conjunction connecting *members*, with *one* line; connecting *words*, with *two* lines.

Use paper wide enough to contain the whole sentence on one line.

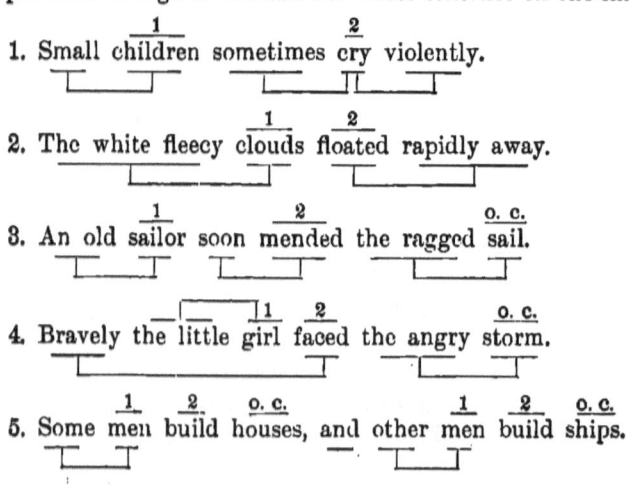

XLII.—PROPER NOUNS.

122. All things, animate and inanimate, may be separated into groups or classes.

Men, women, boys, girls, etc., are names of different classes of persons. *Man, boy,* or *girl* is the name of a single one of a class. *Dogs, horses, elephants,* etc., are names of different classes of animals. *Robins, thrushes, orioles,* etc., are names of different classes of birds. *Cities, streets, parks, islands,* etc., are names of different classes of places. *Trees, rocks, flowers, days,* etc., are names of different classes of things.

Direction.—Examine the two following sentences, and notice the names used for the subject and the object in sentence 1, and corresponding names in sentence 2:

    1. A man discovered a country.
    2. Columbus discovered America.

Questions.—1. Does *man* show what *particular* person is meant? 2. Does *country* show what *particular* part of the earth is meant? 3. What does *Columbus* show? 4. *America?*

123. *Man* is a name that belongs to *any one* of a whole class. *Man* is a *common* noun; *common* means belonging *to many*, or *to all alike*. But each *man* has a special name *given* to him for *his own* to *distinguish* him from others of the same class. The word *proper* means *one's own*; *Columbus* is a **proper noun**.

Direction.—Select the common nouns and the corresponding proper nouns, in each set of the following sentences:

1. The dog bit a girl.
2. Carlo bit Mary.

1. A boy visited a city.
2. John Smith visited Chicago.

1. The tree died.
2. The oak died.
3. The Charter Oak died.

1. Last month passed rapidly.
2. Last August passed rapidly.

1. A man wrote a book.
2. Milton wrote "Paradise Lost."

1. A man purchased an elephant.
2. Barnum purchased Jumbo.
3. A bee stung Henry.

124. Proper nouns may be—

1. The names of persons; as, Lincoln, Grant, Bryant.
2. Names of countries, islands, rivers, places, and objects of special note; as, America, the Bermudas, Gulf of Mexico, City Hall, Central Park.

XLIII.—PROPER NOUNS.—CAPITAL LETTERS.

125. A *common* noun is the name of a *whole* class:

Girls, boys, books, trees.

A common noun is the name of any *one* of a class:

Girl, boy, book, tree.

126. A **proper noun** is a **special name** *given* to a particular *one* of a class to distinguish it from others of the same kind; as, *Mary, George, Columbus, John Smith, "Paradise Lost," Monday, January, Good Friday.*

Note.—Such names as "John Smith" and "Paradise Lost" are called *compound* proper nouns. Some authors call them *complex* proper nouns.

127. Definition.—A common noun is the name of a *whole* class of objects or things, or of *any one* of a class.

128. Definition.—A proper noun is a *special* name given to a *particular one* of a class.

129. A proper noun is often used as an *adjective*; as, The *Albany* boat has arrived. Sometimes there is a change made in the ending; as, America protects American citizens. A proper noun, when used as an adjective, is called a **proper adjective**, and the capital letter is retained.

130. Capital Letter Rule.—Every proper noun and every proper adjective must begin with a capital letter.

131. Capital Letter Rule.—Every name of the Deity must begin with a capital letter; as, *God*, the *Almighty*, the *Most High*, the *Supreme Being, Jehovah.*

Direction.—Write the following proper nouns in one column, and the common nouns in another:

Boy, chair, william, city, brooklyn, street, broadway, table, dog, fido, book, girl, susan, mountains, alps, new york, liverpool, river, nile, animal, elephant, london, boston, bird, robin, tuesday, august.

Questions.—1. Is *boy* a class name? 2. Is *cousin*? 3. Is *trees*? 4. Is *Susan*? 5. Why is *dog* a common noun? 6. Why is a dog called Rover? 7. Why is one person called John, and another, James? 8. What is a proper noun? 9. A common noun? 10. What is a proper adjective?

ABBREVIATION. 49

XLIV.—ABBREVIATION OF NOUNS.

132. In writing proper nouns, *Joseph* is sometimes written *Jos.*; *Geo.* is written for *George*; *Alf.* for *Alfred*; *N. Y.* for *New York*; *Esq.* for *Esquire*.

This shortening of nouns is called *abbreviation*, and a period should be placed at the end of a word thus shortened, to mark the abbreviation. Common nouns are also thus abbreviated; as, *gram.* for grammar.

133. Punctuation Rule.—A period should be used to mark an abbreviation.

134. Sometimes nouns are abbreviated by using one or more of the first letters and adding the last; as, Wm. for William; Jas. for James; Chas. for Charles; Robt. for Robert; Pa. for Pennsylvania; Ga. for Georgia; Fla. for Florida; Ia. for Iowa; La. for Louisiana; Me. for Maine; Md. for Maryland; Ky. for Kentucky; recd. for received; recpt. for receipt; yrs. for years; wk. for week; St. for street or saint; Dr. for doctor or debtor.

135. Sometimes a selection of letters is made, and sometimes all but the first letter are cut off; as, *Mo.* for Missouri; *mts.* for mountains; *P. O.* for post-office; *U. S.* for United States; *G. B.* Winthrop for George Benton Winthrop. *No.* for number, *oz.* for ounce, and *bbl.* for barrel are arbitrary abbreviations; that is, they follow no rule.

136. The following abbreviations are in general use in writing:

Mr.	for Mister.	Co.	for	County or Company.
Mrs.	" Mistress.	M. D.	"	Doctor of Medicine.
Jr.	" Junior.	D. D.	"	Doctor of Divinity.
Rev.	" Reverend.	U. S. A.	"	United States of America.
Gen.	" General.	M. C.	"	Member of Congress.
Col.	" Colonel.	U. S. N.	"	United States Navy.
Com.	" Commodore.	MS.	"	Manuscript.
Ave.	" Avenue.	i. e.	"	*id est* = that is.

Direction.—Write as many sentences as may be deemed necessary containing properly abbreviated nouns that are names of the months and of the days of the week, and nouns used as commercial terms, etc.

XLV.—COMPOSITION LESSON.

137. Direction.—Dictate the following sentences, and require pupils to be particular in the use of capital letters, and to give the reason for the correct use of each. Justify the use of abbreviation and quotation marks:

1. A tall young man shot a beautiful bird.
2. A snake frightened John fearfully.
3. Geo. Hollis found a new knife.
4. The sun dried the green grass.
5. That ugly dog bit Susan severely.
6. The elephant ate some peanuts.
7. Five little girls met Robert yesterday.
8. John's teacher said, "Never be unemployed."
9. Mary whipped Rover dreadfully.
10. The teacher reproved Jos. Sanford.
11. Will the steamer soon reach Albany?
12. Some Americans visited Italy.
13. The Portuguese discovered the Azores.
14. England exports English manufactures.
15. The girls exclaimed, "What a beautiful sunset!"
16. Thackeray says, "A good woman is the loveliest flower that blooms under heaven."

Direction. After these sentences have been written, use the first seven as a lesson in analysis.

Note.—In sentence 13, "Portuguese" is the name of *one* particular *race* of people, and "Azores" is the name of *one* particular *group* of islands; they are therefore *proper nouns*.

Review Questions.—1. What is meant by the abbreviation of a noun? 2. What is used to mark an abbreviation? 3. In what way are the nouns abbreviated in 132? 4. How are they abbreviated in 134? 5. In 135?

Direction.—Copy the following *original composition*, correcting the spelling, and the wrong use of capital letters and of periods, etc., and give the reason for each correction:

Their are a great many animals throughout the world of various sizes and colors the most powerful land animals ever known are the Elephant Rhinoserus. Lion and Tiger. belong. to torrid zone. the natives of the temperate and most useful to man. are the Horse. Ox. Sheep and goat. The largest marine animals as the Whale and Walrus. belong mostly to the Frigid Zone. their are a great many smaller animals not mentioned.

XLVI.—ARRANGEMENT OF ADVERBS.

138. Place adverbs where they will most clearly modify the word intended to be modified, having regard also to the sound. An adverb should seldom stand between a verb and its object.

Direction.—Improve the following sentences by changing the position of the adverbs in italics:

1. I understand your statement *fully*.
2. Industrious people *rapidly* acquire wealth sometimes.
3. The prisoner watched the judge's face *anxiously*.
4. He makes such mistakes *generally*.
5. That careless boy makes *always* mistakes.
6. Beautiful leaves covered *entirely* the ground.
7. A strong wind swept *away* the troublesome mosquitoes.

Remark.—*Away* (as in 7) may stand between a verb and its object.

139. An adverb sometimes introduces a sentence:

1. Slowly the sun melted the frozen snow.
2. Bravely the little lad faced the angry storm.

COMPOSITION LESSON.

Direction.—Fill out the following unfinished sentences by using the words here given—as many words in each as there are dashes:

Always, make, cultivate, hasty, citizens, beautiful, farmers, some, obey, vegetables, bitter, other, gold, coal.

1. Florists —— —— flowers.
2. —— mines produce ——.
3. —— mines produce ——.
4. Many —— raise early ——.
5. Good —— —— the laws.
6. —— words often make —— enemies.

Review Questions.—1. What other name is sometimes given to *transitive* verbs? 2. What name is given to the noun used to complete the meaning of a transitive verb? 3. Which is the most important word in the predicate? 4. Which is next in importance? 5. What position should an adverb seldom occupy in a sentence? 6. Where should an adverb be placed in a sentence? 7. Mention the different positions that an adverb may occupy.

XLVII.—LETTER WRITING.

(DATE OR HEADING.)
Fabyan House, N. H.,
(ADDRESS.) *July 24, 1888.*
My dear Mother, (BODY OF LETTER.)
Father and I have had a very pleasant time since we left home. We arrived at the Fabyan House yesterday. The scenery along the route to this place was so delightful that we did not even think of being tired.

This morning we had a ride up Mt. Washington on the mountain railway. The engine and cars are queer-looking things, and they seem to crawl up instead of running ^like *a common train.*

The top of this mountain is all rocks piled on rocks, except just a little space where the Tip Top House stands. From the piazza one can see, on a clear day, most of New Hampshire and even into Maine on one side, and into Vermont on the other; and there are ever so many lakes scattered all over as far as one can see.

I will write again after I have been to other places and have seen something more that will interest you.

(SUBSCRIPTION.)
Your affectionate son,
William Herbert.

Directions for Letter Writing.—A page of a written letter should have only two margins—one of an inch and a half at the top of the sheet, and the other three quarters of an inch at the left of the body of the letter.

The address, also each paragraph, should begin on a line half an inch to the right of the letter-margin.

A short letter of less than a page should have as much blank space above the heading as below the subscription.

All numbers in a letter or in an ordinary composition should be expressed in writing, excepting those indicating the time of day [9 o'clock], or the day of the month and the year [June 10, 1887].

A comma should separate the parts of the date, or heading; the address from the body of the letter; the parts of the subscription; also the parts of the superscription on the envelope.

Questions.—1. How many margins should there be on a page of a written letter? 2. What comes first in writing a letter? 3. Where should it be written? 4. What comes second? 5. Where should the address begin? 6. Where should a paragraph begin? 7. What comes third? 8. Where should the body of the letter begin? 9. How many parts to the subscription? 10. How should they be placed? 11. How should the space be divided in a letter of less than a page? 12. Where should commas be used?

Explanation.—At the end of the second line in the body of the letter there is placed a little mark (-) called a *hyphen*; also at the end of the seventh line.

140. Rule.—A **hyphen** is placed at the end of a line to connect a *syllable* of a word written partly on that line, with a *syllable* on the next.

Explanation.—There is an omission of the word *like* in the seventh line, and a mark (∧) called a *caret* is placed below the line under the space where the omission occurs.

141. Rule.—In writing, when a word is omitted, a caret is used to denote the omission, and the omitted word is written between the lines above the mark.

Questions.—1. When should a hyphen be used? 2. Where is the omitted word to be placed? 3. Where is the hyphen placed?

Direction.—After *making* corrections a few times, teachers should simply *indicate*, by certain marks, the errors made in writing letters and ordinary compositions. Pupils should be required to re-write their compositions, correcting the errors from the indications.

(SUPERSCRIPTION.)

Mr. Nelson J. Smith,
124 Franklin St.,
New York.

XLVIII.—PRONOUNS.

1. A little girl told the driver that the driver had dropped the driver's whip.

2. A little girl told the driver that *he* had dropped *his* whip.

Explanation.—Sentence 1 is an awkward expression, because the noun *driver* is repeated unpleasantly. In sentence 2, the words *he* and *his* are used instead of the noun *driver*, thus preventing disagreeable repetition.

142. Such words as **he** and **his**, used *instead* of nouns, are called **pronouns** [pro = *for*; pro-noun = *for*-noun, or *instead of a noun*].

143. Definition.—A pronoun is a word used instead of a noun.

1. *I* laughed heartily.
2. *You* laughed also.
3. *We* witnessed a laughable occurrence.
4. The man tried, but the man failed.
5. The man tried, but *he* failed.
6. That little boy found a knife, but *he* soon lost *it*.
7. The lady started, but *she* soon returned.
8. The boys tried hard, and *they* finally succeeded.
9. James picked some green apples, but *he* soon threw *them* away.

Explanation.—In sentence 1, the pronoun *I* is used instead of the name of the person speaking. In 2, *you* is used instead of the names of the persons spoken to. In 5, 6, 7, 8, and 9, the pronouns *he, she, it, they*, and *them* are used instead of the names of the persons and things spoken of, to prevent repetition.

144. The noun *man* (in 5) is called the **antecedent** of *he*, because *man* is the noun which *goes before* he, and for which *he* stands [cedent = *going*; ante = *before*]. In sentences 1 and 2, *I* and *you* have no antecedents, *I* simply *representing* the person speaking, and *you* representing the persons spoken to.

145. Definition.—The noun for which a pronoun stands is called its **antecedent**.

146. The pronouns *I, thou, he, she*, and *it* stand for singular nouns; *we, you, they*, and *them*, for plural nouns.

CONTRACTED COMPOUND SENTENCES. 55

Direction.—Select the pronoun in each of the nine preceding sentences, and tell whether it simply *represents* a noun or stands for an antecedent to prevent repetition. Analyze each sentence. Write three compound sentences, each containing a singular pronoun in the second member; also three others, each containing a plural pronoun.

Questions.—1. What is a pronoun? 2. Why are pronouns used? 3. What is an antecedent? 4. What does the word *antecedent* mean? 5. Which of the pronouns in the preceding sentences are singular, and which are plural? 6. Which pronouns stand for the person or persons speaking? 7. Which, for the persons spoken to? 8. Which, for the person or persons spoken of?

XLIX.—CONTRACTED COMPOUND SENTENCES.

1. Robins sing sweetly and thrushes sing sweetly.
2. Robins and thrushes sing sweetly [contracted].

147. Subjects connected.—In 1, the two predicates being alike, disagreeable repetition may be avoided by connecting the two subjects by *and*, and using only one of the predicates. Sentence 2 is a *simple sentence* with a *compound subject*.

148. Predicates connected.—To avoid repetition of the subject or of the object, predicates are often connected:

1. The farmer watered the horse, and he fed the horse.
2. The farmer watered the horse, and he fed the cow.
3. The farmer watered and fed the horse [contracted].
4. The farmer watered the horse and fed the cow [contracted].

Explanation.—In the sentence, "Robins and thrushes sing sweetly," although there are two subjects, only a single statement is made; therefore it is only a *simple sentence*. But in the sentence, "The farmer watered and fed the horse," two statements are made; therefore some call it a compound sentence, and supply the subject *he* in the second member, in analysis and parsing. Others call it a simple sentence with a compound predicate. The latter is preferable, unless the members are made long by the use of modifying words, phrases, and clauses. Sentence 2 (second set) is contracted by simply omitting the pronoun *he*.

149. Objects connected.—Object complements are also connected to avoid repetition of the subject and verb, as in sentence 2 of the following:

1. The fisherman caught a trout and he caught a bass.
2. The fisherman caught a trout and a bass [contracted].
3. The carpenter built a house and a barn.
4. She and I played a duet yesterday.
5. Those boys treated you and me meanly yesterday.
6. Productive fields and shady groves dotted the valleys and hills.

Explanation.—Sentence 2 is a *simple* sentence with a compound object. Sentence 6 is *simple* with a *compound subject* and a *compound object*.

150. Two or more connected subjects make a *compound subject*. Two or more connected predicates make a *compound predicate*. Two or more connected objects make a *compound object*.

Questions.—1. What is the subject in sentence 3? 2. Is it simple or compound? 3. What is the subject in 4? Is it simple or compound? 4. Why are sentences abbreviated? 5. How is the first sentence in this lesson abbreviated? 6. What is a compound subject? 7. What is a compound object?

Direction.—Expand each of 2, 3, 4, 5 into a compound sentence and 6 into two compound sentences, using pronouns for subjects in the second members. Analyze each sentence.

151. Adverbs and Adjectives connected.—To avoid repetition, adverbs and adjectives are frequently connected:

1. The blind man walked slowly, and he walked carefully.
2. The merchant had a large business, and he had a prosperous business.
3. The blind man walked slowly and carefully [contracted].
4. That merchant had a large and prosperous business [contracted].

152. The primary use of the conjunction is to connect *sentences*. But it is also used to connect *words* as parts of an abbreviated compound sentence.

Model for Analysis.

1. Two men and three boys slowly ascended the lofty mountain.

153. This is a simple declarative sentence containing the compound subject, "Two men and three boys." The simple part *men* is modified by the adjective *two*, and the simple part *boys* is modified by the adjective *three*. [Analyze the predicate as before].

Model for Analysis.

1. The careful farmer thoroughly prepares the soil and sows good seed.

154. This is a simple declarative sentence with a compound predicate. The entire subject is "The careful farmer"; the entire predicate is "thoroughly prepares the soil and sows good seed." The simple subject *farmer* is modified by the adjectives *the* and *careful*. The predicate-verbs are *prepares* and *sows*, connected by the conjunction *and*. *Prepares* is modified by the adverb *thoroughly*, and completed by its object complement *soil*, which is modified by the adjective *the*. *Sows* is completed by its object complement *seed*, which is modified by the adjective *good*.

DIAGRAMS.

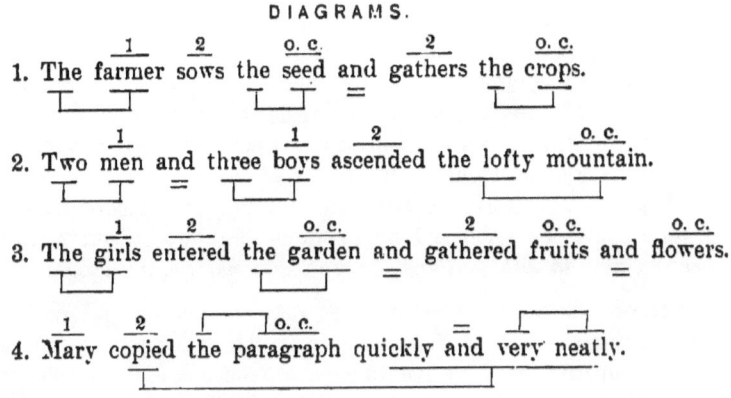

1. The farmer sows the seed and gathers the crops.
2. Two men and three boys ascended the lofty mountain.
3. The girls entered the garden and gathered fruits and flowers.
4. Mary copied the paragraph quickly and very neatly.

Note.—In 4, *and* has the lines drawn *over* it, to avoid a confusion of lines below. After sufficient practice, an *article* standing next to a noun need not be joined to it.

Sentences for Analysis.

1. Exercise and temperance strengthen the constitution.
2. Make friends and keep them.
3. The fire consumed the old church and the new theatre.
4. The lightning struck the barn and killed a valuable horse.

Questions.—1. When a sentence contains two or more connected subjects, what is it called? 2. What is it called when it contains two or more connected predicates? 3. How does it happen that *words* are connected by conjunctions?

L.—SYNTHESIS AND PUNCTUATION.

155. SEPARATE STATEMENTS.

1. The lark sings sweetly.
The nightingale sings sweetly.
2. This boy studies diligently.
He recites correctly.
He improves rapidly.
3. Glass is hard.
It is brittle.
It is smooth.
It is transparent.

COMBINED.

1. The *lark* and the *nightingale* sing sweetly.
2. This boy studies diligently, recites correctly, and improves rapidly.
3. Glass is *hard, brittle, smooth,* and *transparent.*
(*a*) The hard, brittle glass is smooth and transparent.

Explanation.—In the first of the combined sentences, only two nouns are used in succession, and, being connected by the conjunction *and*, they do not require a comma to separate them. But *three or more words* of the same part of speech used *in succession* (as in 2 and in the first combination of 3) make a *series* of words, and they must be separated by commas when the connective between any two of them is omitted. *Two adjectives* without a connective, as *hard* and *brittle* in the second combination of 3, should also be separated by a comma; but two adjectives *having a connective*, as "*smooth* and *transparent*," do *not* require a comma.

Questions.—1. Why is a comma used between *studies* and *recites* in 2? 2. Why to separate the italicized words in 3? 3. Why to separate *hard* and *brittle* in (*a*)? 4. Why *not* to separate *smooth* and *transparent*? 5. What word is omitted between *hard* and *brittle*?

Direction.—Combine each of the following sets of statements into a single sentence, making two combinations for each of 3 and 6 (the same as in 3 above), and punctuate properly:

1. My father went to Niagara.
My mother went to Niagara.
My sister went also.
2. Large apples covered the ground.
Ripe apples covered the ground.
Yellow apples covered the ground.
3. The water was smooth.
It was clear.
It was cold.
It was deep.
4. This lady sings finely.
She plays correctly.
She fingers admirably.
5. James caught a trout.
He caught a bass.
He caught a pickerel.
6. The storm was short.
The storm was sudden.
It was severe.
It was very destructive.

LI.—COMPOUND WORDS.

156. We learned [140] that the hyphen is used to join a syllable of a word that is partly written on one line, with a syllable written on the next line. We shall now see that the hyphen has another use—that of joining two distinct words together (generally for the purpose of abbreviation), thus forming a compound word; as, *grass-plot* [plot of grass]; *pin-cushion* [cushion for pins].

157. The following words are compound: Ice-house, down-fall, life-blood, linsey-woolsey, commander-in-chief, iron-gray, tea-chest, two-thirds, twenty-six, key-hole, eye-tooth, father-in-law, touch-me-not.

Direction.—Dictate a few of the preceding compound words to be used in sentences.

158. Definition.—A **compound word** is one that is composed of two or more words connected by the hyphen.

159. When a compound word is a noun, it is called a *compound noun*. When a compound word is an adjective, it is called a *compound adjective*.

160. Some compounds have become permanent; that is, they are written as one word without the hyphen; as, *schoolmate, backwoodsman, watchman, runaway*.

161. Compound proper nouns do not require the hyphen; as, New York, Charter Oak.

Questions.—1. What is a compound word? 2. How is a permanent compound word written? 3. How are compound proper nouns written? 4. What two uses of the hyphen are mentioned in this lesson? 5. What is a compound sentence? 6. Compound subject? 7. What are the elements in each? 8. What is the connective in each? 9. What are the elements of a compound word? 10. What is the connective in a compound word?

Sentences for Analysis.

1. The farmer drove an iron-gray horse.
2. The gardener trimmed the grass-plot neatly.
3. The Niagara Falls make a tremendous noise.
4. Twenty-four grains make one pennyweight.
5. The subject naturally precedes the predicate-verb.

LII.—GENDER OF NOUNS.—INFLECTION.

162. So far, we have considered, mainly, the *use* of words in a sentence [syntax]. We come now to speak more particularly of the different *forms* that words assume to vary their meaning, or to suit their relations to each other in a sentence. The noun *boy* is changed to *boys* to vary the meaning. *Hero* is changed to *heroine*; *long*, to *longer*. "The boys talk" becomes "The boy talks," to suit the use of the *verb* with the singular subject *boy*. This change in the ending of a word, either to vary its meaning or to adapt the form of one word to that of another, is called **inflection** [etymology].

Note.—The classification of the words in the language into the different parts of speech [p. 13] is the first part of etymology. The second part treats of the *changes* in the *form* of words.

163. Every noun is the name of some being of the *male sex* or of the *female sex*, or of some thing which is assumed to be without sex.

1. A heedless *boy* broke a costly window.
2. A little *girl* soiled the new *book*.
3. A strong *man* lifted a heavy box.
4. A stately woman entered the room.
5. The lion growled fiercely.
6. The lioness seized her prey.
7. John shot a beautiful bird.
8. Mary embroidered a pretty cushion.

Explanation.—In sentence 1, the noun *boy* denotes the male sex, and in 2, the noun *girl* denotes the female sex; but the noun *book* makes no suggestion of sex.

Questions.—Which sex does each of the following nouns denote? *Man, woman, lion, lioness, John, Mary, cushion, uncle, window, book.*

164. Nouns denoting the **male sex** are said to be of the **masculine gender**. The pronouns *he*, *his*, and *him* are *masculine*.

165. Nouns denoting the **female sex** are said to be of the **feminine gender**. The pronouns *she* and *her* are *feminine*.

Direction.—Mention the gender of each noun and pronoun in the eight preceding sentences. Analyze.

166. Nouns that do **not** denote **either sex** are said to be of the **neuter gender**; i. e., of *neither* gender. The pronouns *it* and *its* are neuter.

167. The word *neuter* means *neither*. Although there is no *neuter sex*, yet we may properly speak of a *neuter gender*, this being simply a grammatical term applied to the *names* of things without life.

168. Sex refers to the **objects themselves**; gender refers **only** to **words**.

169. Definition.—**Gender** is a difference in the *form* of words by which *sex* is distinguished.

170. If the gender of such nouns as *parent, teacher, cousin*, etc. (which may suggest either of the sexes), can not be inferred from the context, it is better to say, in parsing, that they are *either masculine or feminine gender*.

Questions.—What is meant by the term *gender*? 2. What is the difference in the meaning of the terms *sex* and *gender*? 3. What does the word *neuter* mean? 4. Of what gender are *he, she, it, him, her*?

LIII.—GENDER FORMS.

171. The *gender* of nouns is distinguished in *three ways*:

	Masculine.	Feminine.
1. By a change of form:	Tiger, Count, Jew, Hero,	tigress. countess. Jewess. heroine.
2. By the use of different words:	Man, Father, Boy, Bachelor,	woman. mother. girl. maid.
3. By prefixing or affixing another word, making a compound:	*Man*-servant, *He*-goat, *Mr.* Brown, Step-*son*,	*maid*-servant. *she*-goat. *Mrs.* Brown. step-*daughter*.

Direction.—Arrange the following nouns under the three different heads just given:

GENDER.—PERSONIFICATION.

Duke, duchess; miss, master; empress, emperor; marquis, marchioness; negress, negro; drake, duck; male, female; king, queen; husband, wife; peacock, peahen; lad, lass; sir, madam; papa, mamma; wizard, witch; groom, bride; administrator, administratrix; lady, gentleman; gander, goose; Paul, Pauline; baron, baroness; lord, lady; cock-sparrow, hen-sparrow; widow, widower; hart, roe; Joseph, Josephine; he-bear, she-bear; brother, sister; doctor, doctress; belle, beau; rooster, hen; steer, heifer; czar, czarina; uncle, aunt; youth, maiden; nephew, niece; stag, hind; fox, vixen*; sultan, sultana; archduke, archduchess; male-child, female-child; testator, testatrix; slovern, slattern; monk, nun.

172. In each pair of such nouns as *count, countess*; *Paul, Pauline*; *shepherd, shepherdess*, there are different forms of the *same* word to denote gender. *Some* nouns, then, have *gender forms*.

173. Some *pronouns* indicate gender by their form. *He* indicates the *masculine*, *she* the *feminine*, and *it* the *neuter*, gender.

LIV.—GENDER.—PERSONIFICATION.

174. Nouns that are names of small animals, or of those whose sex is unknown or unimportant, are generally considered to be neuter; as,

 1. I wounded the *deer*, but *it* escaped.
 2. He hurt the *child*, and *it* cried.
 3. The *bee* stung the child, and then *it* flew away.

175. A **pronoun** must be of the **same gender** as its **antecedent**; i. e., *he*, *his*, and *him* must be used for masculine nouns; *she* and *her* for feminine nouns; *it* and *its* for neuter nouns. In the three preceding sentences, the gender of *deer*, *bee*, and *child* are unknown; therefore the neuter pronoun *it* is used to represent each of them.

176. The chief importance of gender, in grammar, lies in the correct use of the pronouns *he*, *she*, and *it*, and their variations.

---

* Vixen is the old feminine of *fox* (once pronounced *vox* in some parts of England).

GENDER.—PERSONIFICATION. 63

177. When animals are regarded as possessing masculine qualities or characteristics, although the sex may be unknown, they are represented by *he*, *his*, or *him*; when they possess feminine qualities, they are represented by *she* or *her*; as,
1. The *lion* meets *his* foe boldly.
2. The *nightingale* sang *her* sweetest song.
3. The *fox* eluded *his* pursuers.
4. The *panther* steals upon *her* prey.

Personified Objects.

178. Things without life are said to be *personified* when they are spoken to, or spoken of, as persons, or living beings. Nouns that are names of *personified* objects are regarded as either masculine or feminine, and the pronouns standing for such nouns must be masculine or feminine; as,
1. The sun displays *his* splendor.
2. The moon arose; *her* silvery light revealed a charming scene.

179. The following names of *things personified* are *masculine*: The *sun, time, winter, death, war*. They convey the idea of *strength, power, awe,* or *grandeur*.

180. The following are considered feminine: The *moon*, a *ship*, *earth*, *night, spring*. They convey the idea of *beauty* or *weakness*.

181. *Personified nouns* expressing *masculine characteristics* are masculine; those expressing *feminine characteristics*, feminine.

182. When personification is strongly marked, the noun personified should begin with a capital letter; as,
1. "Then comes *spring*, bringing warmth and life" [not strongly marked].
2. "Come, gentle Spring! ethereal mildness, come!" [strongly marked].

LV.—PERSON FORMS.

183. Nouns, standing for intelligent beings, are the names of persons speaking (or writing), of persons spoken to, or of persons or things spoken of. In speaking or writing, however, a person seldom uses his own name; yet a name is sometimes so used, as will be seen in the first of the following sentences:

    1. I, *John*, saw these things.
    2. John, you have a bad cold.
    3. He saw John yesterday.
    4. She lost a book, and John found it.

Explanation.—In sentence 1, *I* and *John* are used to represent the *speaker*. In 2, *John* and *you* are used to represent the *person spoken to*. In 3, *he* and *John* are used to represent the *persons spoken of*. In 4, *she* and *John* are used to represent the *persons* spoken of, and *it* represents the *thing* spoken of. There is *no* difference in the *form* of the noun *John* to show whether it represents the speaker, the hearer, or the person spoken of; but there *are* different forms of *pronouns* to show these three distinctions; viz., *I*, representing the *first* person; *you*, the *second*; *he*, *she*, and *it*, the *third*.

184. *Nouns*, then, do not change their forms to denote the different persons. *Most pronouns*, however, *have person forms*.

185. Definition.—Person is the *use* or *form* of a noun or pronoun to distinguish the *speaker*, the person *spoken to*, or the person or thing *spoken of*. [*Use* of nouns; *use* and *form* of pronouns.]

186. The *first person* denotes the *speaker*.

187. The *second person* denotes the person *spoken to* [hearer].

188. The *third person* denotes the person or thing *spoken of*.

Direction.—Name the person of each noun and pronoun in the following sentences; also name the gender and number of each; name the antecedent of each pronoun:

    1. I found a watch, and Charles claimed it.
    2. William found a knife, but he soon lost it.
    3. You hurt Jane, and she cried bitterly.

Questions.—1. What is person? 2. How many persons have nouns and pronouns? 3. What is the first person? 4. The second person? 5. The third person? 6. Do nouns have special forms to distinguish person? 7. Do pronouns? 8. When is a pronoun in the first person? 9. When is a noun in the first person? Second? Third?

LVI.—FORMATION OF THE PLURAL OF NOUNS.

1. Chair, chairs.
2. Book, books.
3. Orange, oranges.
4. Apple, apples.

Questions.—1. How many of these eight nouns are singular? 2. How many are plural? 3. How does *chair* differ in meaning from *chairs*? 4. *Book*, from *books*? 5. What is the difference in spelling? 6. How many of these words mean more than one?

189. Common nouns, with few exceptions, have **two forms** to indicate number—a **singular** and a **plural** *form*.

190. The *singular* form of a noun stands for a *single thing*, and is called the *singular number*.

191. The *plural* form of a noun stands for *more than one thing*, and is called the *plural number*.

192. Definition.—Number is that *form* of a word which shows whether the word refers to *one thing*, or to *more than one*.

193. General Rule.—Most nouns form their plural number by adding **s** to the singular form.

Direction.—Write, or spell orally, the plural of the following nouns, according to the *general rule*:

House, roof, dog, cow, turkey, pencil, piano, tree, solo, monkey, bundle, star, planet, cap, letter.

194. To form the plural of nouns not coming under the general rule, *four special rules* are given, requiring the addition of *es*, and *two* of these rules require a *change* in the *terminal letter* or *letters* before *es* is added.

195. Special Rule 1.—Nouns ending in *ch*, *sh*, *x*, *z*, and *s* form their plurals by adding *es* to the singular form.

Note.—The sound of *s* does not easily unite with these five terminations; therefore *es* is added, making another syllable.

Direction.—Write, or spell orally, the plural of the following nouns, and give the reasons:

Hand, boy, dish, tree, box, desk, bush, gas, peach, pear, table, church, flower, chestnut, match, crutch, brush, topaz, fox, kiss.

Remark.—In giving reasons, any short form may be used. The following is suggested: *Hand* adds *s* according to the general rule. *Dish* ends in *sh*; therefore *es* is added.

Questions.—1. What is meant by number? 2. What is the singular number? 3. The plural number? 4. How is the plural of nouns generally formed? 5. What nouns require the addition of *es* to form their plural number? 6. Why do nouns ending in *ch*, *sh*, etc., add *es* to form their plural?

196. Special Rule 2.—Nouns ending in *o*, not preceded by a vowel, form their plurals by adding *es* to the singular; as, *negro, negroes.*

When the *o* is preceded by a vowel, only *s* is added.

Direction.—Write, or spell orally, the plural of the following nouns, noticing that in eight of them the final *o* is preceded by a vowel:

Hero, mosquito, cameo, cargo, bamboo, echo, calico, embryo, embargo, grotto, cuckoo, folio, innuendo, portfolio, motto, trio, mulatto, tornado, seraglio, potato, volcano.

Exceptions.—The following nouns are exceptions to this rule:

Albino, canto, domino, fresco, halo, junto, lasso, memento, octavo, piano, portico, proviso, quarto, salvo, sirocco, solo, stiletto, tyro, zero.

197. Special Rule 3.—Nouns ending in *y*, not preceded by a vowel, form their plurals by adding *es*, the *y* being changed into *i*; as, *city, cities.*

When the *y* is preceded by a vowel, only *s* is added, and the *y* is not changed; as, *toy, toys.*

Direction.—Write, or spell orally, the plural of the following nouns, and give reasons:

Fancy, daisy, lady, jockey, candy, journey, berry, lily, joy, way, hobby, donkey, victory, turkey, bounty, country.

198. Special Rule 4.—The following nouns ending in *f* or *fe* form their plurals by adding *es*, *f* or *fe* being changed into *v*; as,

Loaf, *loaves*; life, *lives*; wife, *wives*; knife, *knives*; thief, *thieves*; beef, *beeves*; calf, *calves*; half, *halves*; elf, *elves*; self, *selves*; shelf, *shelves*; wolf, *wolves*; staff, *staves* (or *staffs*); wharf, *wharves* (or *wharfs*).

COMPOSITION. 67

Other nouns ending in *f* or *fe* follow the general rule in forming their plurals.

Questions.—1. What is special rule 2 ? 2. Special rules 3 and 4 ? 3. Why does *hero* become *heroes* in the plural? 4. Why do *turkey, candy,* and *knife* become *turkeys, candies,* and *knives,* in the plural?

LVII.—COMPOSITION LESSON.

199. Until the learner has acquired considerable knowledge of principles, the correction of compositions must be more or less arbitrary. But pupils may now learn to understand the proper use of *is* and *are, was* and *were, has* and *have,* with subjects having a singular or a plural meaning, by observing carefully the statements in the next two paragraphs.

200. When we make a statement about *one* person or thing, requiring any of the verbs mentioned above, *am, is, was,* or *has* [singular forms] should be used; i. e., a *singular subject* requires a *singular verb.*

201. When we make a statement about *more than one* person or thing, *are, were,* or *have* [plural forms] should be used; i. e., a *plural subject* requires a *plural verb.*

Direction.—Fill each blank space in the following exercise with *am, is, are, was, were, has,* or *have,* and give the reason for each choice of a word:

    1. This orange —— ripe and juicy.
    2. These birds —— good singers.
    3. New York and Philadelphia —— large cities.
    4. The girls —— been to school to-day.
    5. My cousin and I —— been to the park.
    6. There —— a peach and a pear in the basket.
    7. The stars —— shining bright this evening.
    8. John and William —— the lunch-basket.
    9. There —— four of us in the party yesterday.
    10. —— father and mother gone to New York?
    11. I —— very sick this morning.

Direction.—Combine each of the following sets of statements into a single sentence, changing the form of the verb to conform to the directions given above:

1. New York has a fine harbor.
Portland has a fine harbor.
2. The rose is a beautiful flower.
The lily is a beautiful flower.
3. His hat was found in the boat.
His coat was found in the boat.
4. Has that boy brought the bait?
Has the other boy brought the oars?

Direction.—In the following sentences, change the plural subjects to the singular form and the singular subjects to the plural form, making the necessary changes in the verbs and in other words:

1. The slates need cleaning.
2. Those boys go to school early.
3. His books were soiled.
4. That boy has a gun.
5. Ducks dive for food.
6. This boy smokes cigars.
7. Saplings become large trees.
8. Bobolinks lead a merry life.

LVIII.—IRREGULAR PLURALS.

202. Irregular Plurals.—A few nouns form their plural number irregularly, some by a change in one or more vowels, and others by adding *en*, either with or without other changes in the word; as,

Singular.	Plural.	Singular.	Plural.
1. man,	men.	5. tooth,	teeth.
2. woman,	women.	6. goose,	geese.
3. child,	children.	7. mouse,	mice.
4. ox,	oxen.	8. louse,	lice.

203. Plural of Letters and Figures.—The plural number of letters and figures is formed by adding the apostrophe and *s*; as, Dot your *i*'s and cross your *t*'s and add the *9*'s correctly. But a noun representing a *written* number, forms its plural in the regular way; as, Count by twos, fives, and tens.

Direction.—Write the plurals of the following nouns, and give reasons:

Board, pulley, baby, lily, street, grief, fife, cherry, church, journey, cameo, cliff, octavo, box, cargo, potato, monkey, calf, zero, loaf, money, jockey, hoof, ox, mouse, wife, handkerchief, 7, q, 5, 0, d.

Review Questions.—1. What is meant by number, in grammar? 2. How many numbers are there? 3. What is the singular number? 4.

NUMBER OF NOUNS. 69

What is the plural? 5. What is the general rule for forming the plural of nouns? 6. How many special rules are given? 7. What is added to form the plural under the special rules? 8. To which of the special rules are there quite a large number of exceptions? 9. Why does *daisy* add *es* to form the plural, while turkey adds only *s*? 10. When the final letter of a word is not preceded by a vowel, what is it preceded by? 11. Name the vowels. 12. What kind of plurals are *men* and *oxen* called?

LIX.—OTHER FACTS ABOUT NUMBER.

Remark.—This and the two following lessons may be deferred until *verb-forms* have been learned, especially the last parts of lessons sixty and sixty-one.

204. Always Plural.—Some nouns that are the names of things consisting of a number of parts, or forming a pair, are always plural in form, and generally in meaning:

Scissors, tongs, shears, pincers, manners, billiards, snuffers, bellows, ashes, clothes, trousers, thanks, riches, tidings, vespers, eaves, goods, vitals, entrails, dregs, victuals, annals, assets, nuptials, measles, mumps, hysterics, compasses.

205. Plural in Form, Singular in Meaning.—Other nouns are always plural in form, but are generally singular in meaning:

Amends, news, odds, gallows, pains (care), tidings, politics, ethics, physics, optics, mathematics, series, means.

206. No Plural Form.—Some nouns have only one form for both numbers:

Sheep, deer, swine, grouse, heathen, vermin, moose, trout, salmon, mackerel, herring, cannon.

207. Always Singular.—Some nouns are always singular both in form and meaning:

Courage, rhetoric, architecture, furniture, cider, milk, pitch, rye, wheat, lead, flax, pride, patience, music, gold.

208. The Plural of Compounds.—Most compound nouns form their plurals by adding *s* to the principal part of the word:

Father-in-law, *fathers*-in-law ; eye-tooth, eye-*teeth* ; commander-in-chief, *commanders*-in-chief ; ox-cart, ox-*carts* ; step-mother, step-*mothers* ; mouse-trap, mouse-*traps* ; court-martial, *courts*-martial.

209. Compounds ending in *full*, and those in which the descriptive part is not very obvious, form the plural by adding *s* to the end of the word :

Spoonful, *spoonfuls* ; cupful, *cupfuls* ; runaway, *runaways* ; forget-me-not, forget-me-*nots* ; piano-forte, piano-*fortes* ; jack-a-lantern, jack-a-*lanterns* ; tête-à-tête, tête-à-*têtes* ; camera-obscura, camera-*obscuras*.

Remark.—Any quantity measured by a cup or a spoon should be spoken of as *cupfuls* or *spoonfuls*. *Cups full* is not a compound. This expression denotes a number of cups, each being full. It is *not* correct to say, "She put three *cupsful* of jelly into the dish."

210. A few compounds have both parts made plural :

Man-servant, *men-servants* ; woman-servant, *women-servants* ; knight-templar, *knights-templars*.

Questions.—1. What is the singular of shears, news, sheep? 2. Plural of *wheat*? 3. Of cupful? 4. Of runaway? 5. Of woman-servant?

LX.—PLURALS OF PROPER AND FOREIGN NOUNS.

211. The Plural of Proper Nouns.—Proper nouns form their plurals in the same way as common nouns of similar endings. When *titles* are used with proper names, the custom is to pluralize either the title or the name; as, " The Misses Brown, or the Miss Browns."

212. That the title *only* should be made plural, is apparent for the following reasons :

1. No other form will answer in certain cases ; as, "Senators Ferry and Morrill."

2. Such awkward expressions as the following would be avoided : " The Miss Wilkinses," " The Miss Collinses."

3. If the titles of such singular nouns as *Field* and *Fields*, *Young* and *Youngs*, are pluralized, no confusion can arise as to the spelling of the singular. But, " The two Miss Fields" may mean two ladies by the name

of Field, or of Fields. No mistake could occur, however, should we write "The two Misses Field" or "The two Misses Fields."

213. Foreign Plurals.—Some foreign nouns retain their native plurals. The ending *is* becomes *es* in the plural; the ending *ex* or *ix* becomes *ices*; *um* or *on* becomes *a*; *us* becomes *i*; as,

Axis, *axes*; analysis, *analyses*; basis, *bases*; crisis, *crises*; ellipsis, *ellipses*; oasis, *oases*; phasis, *phases*; hypothesis, *hypotheses*; appendix, *appendices*; vortex, *vortices*; vertex, *vertices*; aquarium, *aquaria*; datum, *data*; erratum, *errata*; effluvium, *effluvia*; phenomenon, *phenomena*; alumnus, *alumni*.

214. Various Plurals.—Beau, *beaux*; genus, *genera*; bandit, *banditti*; seraph, *seraphim*; cherub, *cherubim*; stamen, *stamina*.

Remark.—*Beau, bandit, seraph, cherub,* and *stamen* also form plurals by the general rule; as, *beau, beaus.*

215. Abstract nouns,* as such, have no plural form; as, *beauty, pride, ambition, hope, hardness, goodness, whiteness, knowledge, virtue, youth, heat, grandeur, industry, poverty.*

When used in the plural such nouns are class names; as,
1. We all admire *beauty* [abstract noun].
2. These sisters are famous *beauties* [common noun].

Questions.—1. What is the singular of *goods, bellows, mathematics*? 2. What is the plural of *deer, handful, furniture, woman-servant, touch-me-not*? 3. Mention five nouns having only the plural form. 4. Five having only the singular form. 5. Five having the plural form, but are singular in meaning. 6. Five having only one form for both numbers. 7. Give the plural of five compound nouns. 8. Give the plural of three foreign nouns. 9. How would you speak of two sisters by the name of *Youngs*? 10. What is the plural of *basis, analysis, vertex, aquarium, bandit*? 11. How is the plural of letters and figures formed?

---

* An abstract noun is the name of a quality, an action, or a state of being; as, sweetness, darkness; relief, deception; peace, infancy. *Abstract* means *drawn from*, and when we speak of *beauty* we have in mind a quality *not* connected with any particular person or thing; but when we speak of *famous beauties* the quality is associated with some particular persons.

LXI.—DOUBLE PLURALS.

216. Some nouns have two plurals of different meanings:

1. brother, brothers (by birth), brethren (of the same society).
2. die, dies (stamp for coining), dice (for playing games).
3. fish,* fishes (number), fish (quantity).
4. genius, geniuses (human beings), genii (imaginary beings—spirits).
5. head, heads (belonging to the body), head (of cattle).
6. index, indexes (tables of contents), indices (algebraic signs).
7. pea, peas (number), pease (quantity).
8. penny, pennies (coins), pence (amount).
9. shot, shots (number of discharges), shot (number of balls).
10. sail, sails (pieces of canvas), sail (number of vessels).
11. staff, staffs (military term), staffs } (sticks, or canes). staves }

(The remainder of this lesson may be omitted till further progress has been made.)

Direction.—Give the reason for the form of the verb used in each of the following sentences, but do not use the sentences for analysis until further progress has been made:

1. Great pains was taken with his education.
2. The sheep produces wool.
3. The sheep are in the pasture.
4. The deer is a beautiful animal.
5. Deer are beautiful animals.
6. A rare species of flower grows in our garden.
7. Some beautiful species of flowers grow wild in the woods.
8. The news is encouraging.
9. The salmon is an excellent fish for food.
10. Salmon are scarce this year.
11. Mathematics is his favorite study.

217. Some nouns, always plural in form, are used as either singular or plural, according as the mind is conscious of the thing as a whole, or as composed of parts:

---

* The names of several kinds of fish, such as *herring*, *mackerel*, and *trout*, are used by some writers in the same way.

1. This *species* of bird *inhabits* South America.
2. These *species* of birds inhabit South America.
3. The means employed was not sufficient.
4. All the means at command were necessary.

Direction.—Give the reason for the form of the verb used in each of the four preceding sentences.

Review Questions.—1. What is meant by the singular form of nouns? 2. By the plural form? 3. What is the general rule for forming the plural of nouns? 4. What suffix besides *s* is used to form the plural of most nouns not coming under the general rule? 5. How many special rules are given requiring the addition of *es* to form the plural? 6. Which letters of the alphabet are vowels? 7. Which are consonants? 8. How is the plural of *attorney* formed, and why? 9. Of *berry*, and why? 10. How is the plural of *calico* formed, and why? 11. Of *cameo*, and why? 12. How is the plural of a letter or a figure formed? 13. What is the custom for forming the plural of proper nouns when titles are used? 14. How is the plural of tooth formed?

LXII.—COLLECTIVE NOUNS.

1. Cane, canes.
2. Lamp, lamps.
3. Flock, flocks.
4. Crowd, crowds.

Questions.—1. Does the singular form *cane* stand for one or more than one? 2. Does *lamp*? 3. Does *flock*? 4. Does *crowd*?

218. The singular form of most nouns stands for only a single thing; but there are a few nouns, like *flock* and *crowd*, that stand for more than one thing of the same kind, even in the singular form. Such nouns are called **collective nouns**.

219. Definition.—A **collective noun** is one, which, in its singular form, denotes a collection of objects of the same kind.

Direction.—Select the collective nouns found among the following names: Hammer, herd, letters, swarm, army, rug, class, nails, family, coat, assembly, multitude, mountains, pair, bevy, jury, congregation, committee, peasantry, society.

Direction.—Use the sentences in this lesson for analysis after answers to questions have been learned, and other directions have been followed.

COLLECTIVE NOUNS.

220. A *collective noun* names a collection of *living beings*; as, *jury, society, herd, swarm.*

The name of a *collection* of objects *without life* is *not* a collective noun; as, *pile, heap, mass, clothing, baggage, furniture, hosiery, finery, machinery.* These are merely common nouns.

221. A collective noun is neuter when reference is made to the individuals of the collection as *one whole*; as,

This teacher has a large *class*; I must divide *it*.

But when the individuals of the collection are referred to separately, the noun takes the gender of the individuals composing the collection.

Direction.—Observe carefully the following sentences and determine whether, in the use of each collective noun, reference is made to the collection as *a whole*, or whether the individuals of the collection are referred to separately:

1. Every *congregation* likes *its* own minister best.
2. The congregation used their hymn-books.
3. The sewing society elected its officers yesterday.
4. The army followed their leader.
5. The army fought bravely, but its commander fell.

Explanation.—In the preceding sentences, *congregation* (in 1) is neuter, and is properly represented by the neuter pronoun *it*. In 2, *congregation* and *their* may be called *either masculine* or *feminine*, as both sexes may be considered to compose the collection. In 3, *society* and *its* are both considered neuter, and (in 4) *army* and *their* are both *masculine*.

222. When a collective noun in the singular form is taken in a plural sense, it is sometimes called a *noun of multitude*; as, "The *congregation* used *their* hymn-books."

223. Most collective nouns have a regular plural form; as, *committees, armies, classes, families, congregations.* These plural forms are in the neuter gender.

Questions.—1. What is a collective noun? 2. Why is *army* a collective noun? 3. What is the plural of army? 4. Have collective nouns regular plural forms? 5. Why is clothing *not* a collective noun? 6. Is *machinery* a collective noun? 7. Why is committee a collective noun? 8. What is the gender of *armies, families*?

Direction.—Select the collective nouns and the pronouns used to represent them, and tell their gender:

    1. The army began its march.
    2. The jury rendered their verdict.
    3. Every generation has its peculiarities.

LXIII.—COMPOSITION LESSON.

THE HOUSE IN THE MEADOW.

It stands in a sunny meadow,
  The house, so mossy and brown,
With its cumbrous old stone chimneys,
  And the gray roof sloping down.

The trees throw their green arms around it—
  The trees a century old—
And the winds go chanting through them,
  And the sunbeams drop their gold.

The cowslips spring in the marshes,
  The roses bloom on the hill,
And beside the brook in the pasture
  The herds go feeding at will.
            —*Louise Chandler Moulton.*

224. Direction.—Ask four questions about the first verse, three questions about the second, and four about the third. Finish the following incomplete topical outline, and write a prose composition, giving the sense contained in the poem.

                TOPICAL OUTLINE.

Description of "The House in the Meadow."
- Location—
- General appearance.
- Near surroundings.
- Distant surroundings.

Sentences for Analysis.

1. The nightingale sang her sweetest song.
2. The small but courageous band finally drove back the enemy.
3. Rainy weather and muddy roads prevented further progress.
4. The feathery snow-flakes soon covered the valleys and hills.
5. The merry party entered the garden and gathered fruits and flowers.
6. She copied the paragraph quickly and very neatly.
7. A large black Newfoundland dog saved a drowning child.
8. This little twig bore that large red apple.

LXIV.—RELATION FORMS OF NOUNS.

225. We have learned that nouns change their *form* to indicate *gender* and *number*. We have also learned that a noun may hold the relation of *subject* or *object* of a verb. We shall now learn that a noun often holds another relation in a sentence, and that this *relation* causes the noun to change its form:

1. Dishonest *men* often cheat honest *men*.
2. This *man* falsely accused an innocent *man*.
3. That *man's* horse travels very fast.
4. The *children's* father arrived yesterday.
5. That *boy's* mother treats him very kindly.
6. The *boys'* mother treats them very kindly.
7. A wicked boy stole *Charles's* hat.

Explanation.—The plural noun *men* (in sentence 1) is of the same form both as subject and object. *Man* (in 2), as subject and object, is of the same form; but *man* (in 3) is used to denote ownership, or possession,* and its form is changed by adding the apostrophe and *s* ['*s*] to indicate the possession. *Children* (in 4) and *boy* (in 5) add '*s* for the same reason. The plural noun *boys* ends in *s* when ownership is not denoted; therefore, in 6, *boys'* has only the apostrophe added, to indicate possession. In 7, the singular *proper* noun *Charles*, ending in *s*, adds '*s*. In "Socrates's death," the second *s* need not be sounded, if the ear be offended.

226. Rule.—*Any noun* not ending in *s* must add the apostrophe and *s* ['*s*] to denote possession.

---

* The horse can not be the "man's horse" unless he owns or possesses the animal; therefore "man's" denotes possession. *Man's* limits [modifies] *horse* like an adjective.

RELATION FORMS OF NOUNS.

227. Rule.—A *plural noun* already ending in *s* must add *only* the apostrophe ['] to denote possession.

228. Rule.—*Singular proper nouns* ending in *s*, take the full possessive sign [*'s*] to denote possession.

Questions.—1. Why does *man's* (in 3) have a form different from *man* in 2? 2. Why does *children's* (in 4) take the **apostrophe** and **s**? 3. Why does **boys'** (in 6) take only the **apostrophe**? 4. Why does **Charles's** (in 7) take the full possessive sign? 5. Has *boy's* (in 5) the full sign? 6. What are the rules for the sign of possession? 7. Give the possessive plural of *girl* and of *woman*? 8. Why are the plural possessive forms of these two nouns different? 9. Spell the possessive form of *George, girls, aunt, cousins, uncle*. 10. Is "the Adams's reception" correct? 11. Write the seven sentences in this lesson correctly.

LXV.—RELATION FORMS OF NOUNS.

229. A noun has *two forms* in each number to distinguish its relation to other words in a sentence—the *name form*, used as *subject* or *object*, and a *form to denote possession*.

The *name form* of a noun (the form used simply as the *name* of anything apart from a sentence) is its *subject form*. In *English*, the object complement has not a form of its own, but takes the subject form.

	Sing.	Plural.	Sing.	Plural.	Sing.	Plural.
Subject forms:	Man,	men.	Boy,	boys.	Cousin,	cousins.
Possessive forms:	Man's,	men's.	Boy's,	boys'.	Cousin's,	cousins'.
Forms used for obj.:	Man,	men.	Boy,	boys.	Cousin,	cousins.

Questions.—1. Why is the apostrophe placed *before* the *s* in *men's* to mark the possessive form? 2. Why is the apostrophe in *boys'* placed *after* the *s* to mark the *plural* possessive? 3. In what respect does the object form differ from the subject form of a noun?

Direction.—Write the following nouns in a column, and their plurals in a corresponding column on the right; then add the correct possessive sign to each word: *cousin, father, lady, man, brother, gentleman, servant, woman, fly, fox, child, baby, ox, ship, pupil, teacher, Wednesday*.

Direction.—Write correctly from dictation the following pairs of sentences, the noun being singular in the first, and plural in the second.

State the reason for writing the possessive forms of the similar nouns in each pair:

1. I heard the pupil's lessons.
2. I heard the pupils' lessons.
1. The lady's trunks arrived.
2. The ladies' trunks arrived.
1. The boy's father returned.
2. The boys' father returned.
1. She upset the baby's carriage.
2. She upset the babies' carriage.

1. I found the child's shoes.
2. I found the children's shoes.
1. He took the physician's advice.
2. He took the physicians' advice.
1. The man's business prospered.
2. The men's business prospered.
1. We saw the fox's burrow.
2. We saw the foxes' burrow.

230. The possessive form of a noun is sometimes called its adjective form, because its use is like that of an adjective—to modify the noun with which it is used.

231. The apostrophe is used to indicate the omission of one or more letters; as, *I'll* for *I will*; *we'll* for *we will*; *o'er* for *over*; *ne'er* for *never*; *o'clock* for *of the clock*. The apostrophe is also used to form the plurals of letters and figures; as, "Dot your *i's* and cross your *t's*, and write your *7's* and *9's* neatly."

LXVI.—PERSONAL PRONOUNS.

232. The five pronouns, *I, you, he, she,* and *it,* and their plurals, are called **personal pronouns**; and special forms are used to denote each of the three persons [186–7–8].

	Singular.	Plural.
First person forms:	I,	we.
Second person forms:	You (thou),	you (ye).
Third person forms:	He, she, it,	they.

Note.—*Thou* and *ye* are the "old style" singular and plural forms of the second person.

233. Definition.—A *personal* pronoun is one that personates a noun; i. e., stands directly for it. It shows by its form whether it denotes the *speaker*, the *hearer*, or the *person* or *thing spoken of*.

234. You, formerly used only in the plural, is now used in speaking to *one* person or to *more than one;* but *you,* when used as a subject, always requires a *plural* verb.

235. He, she, and **it** are called gender pronouns because they show gender by their form—*he* being masculine; *she,* feminine; and *it,* neuter.

236. It represents objects without sex, or those whose sex is unknown or unimportant.

Questions.—1. What is a personal pronoun? 2. Mention the five singular personal pronouns. 3. Which is the pronoun of the first person, and what is its plural? 4. Which are the second person forms, singular and plural? 5. Which are the third person forms, singular and plural? 6. Which are the gender pronouns? 7. What are *thou* and *ye?*

LXVII.—RELATION FORMS.

237. *Two* of the five personal pronouns, *I* and *he,* have *three* forms in each number to distinguish their relations to other words in a sentence—a *subject form,* a *possessive form,* and an *object form* ; as,

	(1st Per.)		(2d Per.)	(3d Per.)	
	Sing.	Plural.	S. or P.	Singular.	Plural.
Subject forms:	**I,**	**we.**	**You.**	**He,** she, it,	**they.**
Possessive forms:	**My,**	**our.**	**Your.**	**His,** her, its,	**their.**
Object forms:	**Me,**	**us.**	**You.**	**Him,** her, it,	**them.**

Directions.—Ask the following questions and require answers, pupils having books open at the lesson. Then write the pronouns promiscuously on the blackboard, and require pupils to point out the pronouns in answer to the same (or other) questions, books being closed.

Questions.—1. Which are the *subject* forms of the first person? 2. Second person? 3. Third person? 4. Which are the *singular* subject forms? 5. *Plural* subject forms? 6. Which are the *singular* and the *plural* possessive forms? 7. The *singular* and the *plural* object forms? 8. Which are the object forms of the first person? 9. Of the second person? 10. Of the third person? 11. What are the three different relation forms of *I* in the *singular,* and also in the *plural?* 12. What are the three different *relation* forms of *he* in the *singular,* and also in the *plural?* 13. Which three pronouns have the *same plural forms?* 14. Which three pronouns have each the same form for *two* different relations? 15. Which *two* pronouns have their singular *subject* forms like their *object* forms? 15. Which pronoun has its singular *adjective* form like its *object* form?

PRONOUNS.—RELATION FORMS.

238. In using pronouns in sentences, care must be taken to use the correct forms for *subjects*, for *objects*, and *to denote possession*. Do not confound the pronoun *their* with the adverb *there*, nor use the pronoun *them* for the adjective *these*, or *those*.

Direction.—Supply the correct forms of the pronoun of the first person, singular, in the first four of the following sentences, and the correct form of a pronoun of the third person, singular, in 5 and 6; also use in 7, 8, 9, 10, and 11 the correct *adjective form* of some pronoun, or an adjective or adverb mentioned in [238].

1. Mary and —— visited Central Park.
2. An ugly dog followed John and ——.
3. James and —— found a bird's nest.
4. Mother just called you and ——.
5. —— and I generally sit together.
6. Father will need James and —— soon.
7. —— brother planted —— potatoes.
8. Susan gathered —— beautiful flowers.
9. The boys soiled —— new clothes.
10. I looked ——, but I could not find the book.
11. —— trunks came yesterday.

239. A pronoun used as the subject of a verb must have the *subject form*.

240. A pronoun used as the object complement of a verb must have the *object form*.

241. A noun or pronoun used to denote possession must have the *possessive form*.

Direction.—Tell the *gender*, *person*, *number*, and *relation* of the nouns in the following sentences. Tell why each pronoun has its particular form in regard to gender. *Justify* the use of each pronoun on account of its relation. Mention the antecedent of each pronoun:

1. He deserves a reprimand. 2. We saw him yesterday. 3. Mary found a bird's egg, but she carelessly broke it. 4. The cow eats grass, and then she lies down and chews her cud. 5. You soiled your new book. 6. The boys started, but they soon returned. 7. We found some wild strawberries and we picked them.

LXVIII.—RELATION FORMS OF NOUNS AND PRONOUNS.

Direction.—Write the following sentences, using the possessive sign properly; determine the number of each noun by the pronoun following it; justify the use of each pronoun in regard to form:
1. The boys mother reproved them sharply. 2. The boys mother reproved him sharply. 3. The girls teacher detained her yesterday. 4. The girls teacher detained them yesterday. 5. A poor boy found the ladys watch. 6. The ladies baggage finally arrived. 7. The farmers horse ran away. 8. The farmers association met yesterday. 9. The thief stole Charles watch. 10. John lost his new knife.

Model for Analysis.

1. My youngest brother broke the old gardener's rake.

242. This is a simple declarative sentence. The entire subject is "my youngest brother." The entire predicate is "broke the old gardener's rake." The simple subject *brother* is modified by the possessive pronoun *my* and the adjective *youngest*. The predicate-verb *broke* is completed by the object complement *rake*, which is modified by the possessive noun *gardener's*; and the noun *gardener's* is modified by the adjectives *the* and *old*.

Review Questions.—1. How are nouns written to indicate number? 2. Do all nouns add *s* or *es* to indicate the plural? 3. What other forms have nouns besides number-forms? 4. In how many relations may nouns and pronouns be used in a sentence? 5. Do nouns have a special form for each relation? 6. Do pronouns? 7. In which relation does a noun *not* have a form of its own? 8. Do pronouns add letters to indicate number? 9. Do pronouns add the apostrophe and *s* to indicate possession? 10. Which is the adjective form of a pronoun?

LXIX.—RELATIONS OF WORDS AND PARSING.

1. That old farmer's son generally raises good crops.

243. Every word in this sentence is used in a certain relation to some other word in it; i. e., every word *performs* a certain *office* in the sentence. *Son* and *raises* hold the relation to each other of *subject* and *predicate-verb*; and the noun *crops* holds the relation of *object* of the verb *raises*. *That, old, farmer's,* and *good* hold the relation of *adjective modifiers* of the nouns with which they are used; and *generally* holds the relation of *adverbial modifier* of *raises*.

PARSING.

244. Parsing.—*Parsing* * a word is giving an orderly statement of its grammatical use in a sentence (oral parsing 281).

Direction.—After analyzing the sentences at the bottom of the page, parse them according to the following model:

245. MODEL FOR WRITTEN PARSING.

Word.	Class.	Gender.	Person.	Number.	Relation form.	Office.
The	lim. adj.					modifies *boys*
dutiful	des. adj.					modifies *boys*
boys	com. noun	masc.	3d	plur.	subject	subj. of *obeyed*
obeyed	trans. verb					predicate-verb
their	pers. pron.	masc.	3d	plur.	possessive	modifies *father's*
father's	com. noun	masc.	3d	sing.	possessive	mod. *instruction*
instruction	com. noun	neuter	3d	sing.	object	object of *obeyed*
and	conj.					con. two mem.
he	pers. pron.	masc.	3d	sing.	subject	subj. of *praised*
praised	trans. verb					predicate-verb
them	pers. pron.	masc.	3d	plur.	objective	object of *praised*
very	adverb					modifies *highly*
highly	adverb					modifies *praised*

Sentences for Analysis and Parsing.

1. William's companion soon caught two very beautiful butterflies.
2. The gentle rain moistened the thirsty earth.
3. John's father met us yesterday.
4. My uncle met our party very cordially.
5. Some pupils write very good compositions.
6. We often resolve but we seldom fulfill.
7. The warm sun soon melted the ice and snow.
8. The moon arose, and her silvery light displayed a charming scene.
9. Loudly the thunder rolled and brightly the lightning flashed.
10. The dutiful boys obeyed their father's instruction, and he praised them very highly.

---

* The real object in parsing is to discover whether the words in a sentence are properly used in their several relations, in regard to form, etc. Another object is to develope the mental faculties.

LXX.—SYNTHESIS.

246. Direction.—Combine the following disconnected statements into a connected narrative. First, *with the class*, compare the narrative given below with the separate statements. Then write the statements on the blackboard, and require pupils to write from them a narrative, not necessarily like the one below:

>It was a bright morning in July.
>We prepared for a sail across the bay.
>There were ten ladies and gentlemen in the party.
>There was a fine breeze. We soon crossed the bay.
>On the way over a lady lost her hat.
>The captain put the boat about; sailed close to the hat.
>One of the party reached it; pulled it out of the water.
>It soon dried; was as good as ever.
>We landed on a beautiful beach. It was sandy.
>From this point, across to the ocean, it was three miles.
>We engaged a man to take us across.
>He prepared his team. We ate our lunch under the trees.
>Only two gentlemen attempted to bathe in the ocean.
>A large wave came sweeping in.
>One tried to ride the wave by swimming.
>The wave broke before he reached its crest.
>It turned him over backward.
>He struck on the beach, lying on his back.
>It was a laughable sight.
>It did not hurt him.

Combined.

On a bright morning in July, a party of ten ladies and gentlemen prepared for a sail across the bay, and for a ride from the landing across to the ocean, a distance of three miles. A fine breeze soon carried us to the other side of the bay. On the way over, one of the ladies lost her sun-hat overboard; but the captain quickly put the boat about, and, sailing close to the hat, one of the party reached it and pulled it out of the water. It was soon dried and was as good as ever.

After landing on a beautiful sandy beach, we engaged a man to drive us over to the ocean. While he was preparing his team, we ate our lunch in the shade of the trees. On our arrival at the ocean, we found the waves so very high that only two gentlemen ventured to take a bath. While they were bathing, one of them, seeing a very large wave sweeping toward him, attempted to surmount it by swimming; but the wave, breaking before he reached its crest, threw him over toward the beach. He struck on his back unhurt, where he lay for a moment presenting a very laughable appearance.

LXXI.—CASES.—DECLENSION.

247. The different forms of a pronoun showing its use as subject or object, or in denoting possession [ownership], are called its **cases**.

248. The *subject form* of a pronoun is its *nominative case*.

249. The *possessive form* of a pronoun is its *possessive case*.

250. The *object form* of a pronoun is its *objective case*.

251. A *noun* has only *two* different forms to indicate its uses in a sentence—a *subject* [or name] *form* and a *possessive form*; yet a noun is considered to have *three* cases, corresponding with its uses as *subject* and *object*, and as *denoting possession*.

252. Definition.—Case in grammar is that *form* of a noun or pronoun which shows its *relation* to some other word in a sentence.

253. Definition.—The **nominative case** is the form of a noun or pronoun required, when it is the *subject* of a verb.

254. Definition.—The **possessive case** is the form of a noun or pronoun required, when it is used to denote *possession, origin,* or *fitness* [260].

255. Definition.—The **objective case** is the form of a noun or pronoun required, when it is the *object* of a verb.

Note.—There is no distinct *form* of a noun as an object complement; yet its *use* as an object entitles it *to be considered* as being in the objective case.

Remark.—We have now seen that nouns and pronouns are *inflected* to show gender, number, and case.

CASES OF NOUNS AND PRONOUNS.

256. Rules for Construction.

Rule 1.—A *noun* or a *pronoun* used as the **subject** of a verb must be in the **nominative case.**

Rule 2.—A *noun* or a *pronoun* used to modify another noun by denoting *possession, origin,* or *fitness,* must be in the **possessive case.**

Rule 3.—A *noun* or a *pronoun* used as the **object** of a transitive verb must be in the **objective case.**

257. Declension.—The following arrangement of the case-forms of the pronoun is called **declension:**

	SINGULAR.		PLURAL.
Nom. case	I,	Nom. case	We,
Poss. case	My (or mine),	Poss. case	Our (or ours),
Obj. case	Me.	Obj. case	Us.

(Or more briefly)

	SINGULAR.		PLURAL.
Nom.	I,	Nom.	We,
Poss.	My (or mine),	Poss.	Our (or ours),
Obj.	Me.	Obj.	Us.

Remark.—A pronoun is said to be *declined* when its cases are given in both numbers.

Questions.—1. How many case-forms has the pronoun *I* in the singular number? 2. In the plural number? 3. Which case is used for the subject in a sentence? 4. Which for the object? 5. To denote possession? 6. What is case? 7. Nominative case? 8. Possessive case? 9. Objective case? 10. For how many purposes are nouns and pronouns inflected? 11. When is a pronoun declined?

258. Direction.—Mention the pronouns in the following sentences and justify the use of each as to form. Write the parsing of two or more of these sentences according to the following model, noticing that "Case" is used for a heading in place of "Relation Form"; as in the model previously given [245].

1. I soiled my new coat, and my mother scolded me.
2. Our teacher helped us yesterday, and we now understand our lesson.

3. He ran very fast, but his companion soon overtook him.
4. General Lincoln's forces desperately assaulted the enemy's works.
5. The enemy drove back the American forces.

Explanation.—In sentence 1, *I* has no antecedent; it simply *represents* the person speaking. *My* and *me* have *I* for their antecedent.

MODEL FOR WRITTEN PARSING.

Word.	Class.	Gender.	Person.	Number.	Case.	Office.

LXXII.—DECLENSION OF NOUNS.

SINGULAR.		PLURAL.	
Nom.	boy,	Nom.	boys,
Poss.	boy's,	Poss.	boys',
Obj.	boy.	Obj.	boys.

SINGULAR.		PLURAL.	
Nom.	man,	Nom.	men,
Poss.	man's,	Poss.	men's,
Obj.	man.	Obj.	men.

SINGULAR.		PLURAL.	
Nom.	lady,	Nom.	ladies,
Poss.	lady's,	Poss.	ladies',
Obj.	lady.	Obj.	ladies.

259. Definition.—The **declension** of a noun or a pronoun is the naming of its cases in both numbers.

260. Nouns in the possessive case do not always express ownership; they sometimes express *source* or *fitness*; as, "The *sun's* rays warm the earth" [source]. "We saw some *ladies'* shoes" [shoes suitable or *fit* for ladies]. "They keep *Colt's* revolvers" [source—revolvers made by Colt].

Questions.—1. Do all nouns in the possessive case express possession? 2. What do they sometimes express? 3. Decline *boy, man, lady.* 4. What parts of speech may an antecedent be? 5. Decline *girl, fly, John.* 6. What is declension?

LXXIII.—DECLENSION OF PERSONAL PRONOUNS.

261. The five personal pronouns have the following variations:

First Person, I.

		SINGULAR.		PLURAL.
Masculine	Nom.	I,	Nom.	we,
or	Poss.	my (or mine),	Poss.	our (ours),
Feminine.	Obj.	me.	Obj.	us.

Second Person, You (thou).

		SINGULAR.		PLURAL.
Masculine	Nom.	you,	Nom.	you,
or	Poss.	your (yours),	Poss.	your (yours),
Feminine.	Obj.	you.	Obj.	you.

Third Person, He, She, It.

SINGULAR.

Masculine.	Nom.	he,		
	Poss.	his,		
	Obj.	him.		PLURAL.
Feminine.	Nom.	she,	Nom.	they,
	Poss.	her (hers),	Poss.	their (theirs),
	Obj.	her.	Obj.	them.
Neuter.	Nom.	it,		
	Poss.	its,		
	Obj.	it.		

262. The following is the *old* method of declining the pronoun of the second person, which should be carefully compared with the method in *present* use, as given above:

	SINGULAR.		PLURAL.
Nom.	thou,	Nom.	ye, or you,
Poss.	thy (thine),	Poss.	your (yours),
Obj.	thee.	Obj.	you.

263. These ancient forms are now used *orally* only by the Friends, and in religious services. They are found in poetry, in the Bible, and in other ancient writings. *Thou* as a *subject* requires a form of verb different from that required by *you*; as, "You *shall* go," "Thou *shalt* not steal."

RELATIONS OF PRONOUNS.

LXXIV.—USE OF PRONOUN FORMS.

1. *You* and *I* had a splendid visit.
2. That ugly dog followed *you* and *I* yesterday [incorrect].

Explanation.—In sentence 1, *you* and *I* are both subject forms, and are correctly used. Because *you* and *I* are correctly associated together as subjects, some make the mistake of using them together as objects. *You* is both a *subject form* and an *object form*, but *I* is a *subject form* only.

264. No mistake can occur in using *nouns* as subjects and objects, because the same form of a noun is used in both these relations; but there are six of the *personal pronouns* used as *subjects* that *change* their *form* when used as *objects*.

265. These six pronouns are *I, thou, he, she, we,* and *they,* which, used as objects, change to *me, thee, him, her, us,* and *them*.

Direction.—Complete the following sentences by inserting the correct relation forms of the pronouns indicated in the brackets at the end of each line, and give the reason for your choice of each [see 256]:

1. —— and —— picked the berries [3d fem., and 1st—both sing.].
2. Mother scolded —— and —— yesterday [3d sing. fem., and 1st].
3. —— and —— caught twenty fish [3d sing. mas., and 2d plu.].
4. Father called —— and —— [2d plu., and 3d fem., sing.].
5. I saw —— and —— yesterday [2d plu., and 3d plu., mas.].
6. —— mother dresses —— becomingly [3d sing., fem.—both].
7. Did —— recite —— lessons correctly [2d plu.—both]?
8. Did —— mean —— and —— [2d sing., 3d sing., fem., and 1st sing.]?

266. Pronouns may be modified by adjectives, but an adjective always follows the pronoun to which it relates.

1. He looks *weary*.
2. She feels *sick*.
3. We found him *asleep*.

Questions.—1. Which pronouns are always used for subjects? 2. Which always for objects? 3. Which pronouns have the same form for both subject and object? 4. Which pronoun has only one form for the possessive, and the objective case? 5. Why is there no difficulty in using any noun as subject or object? 6. Decline the five personal pronouns.

LXXV.—CONTRACTION OF WORDS.

267. In familiar conversation and writing, an expression like *I will* is contracted into *I'll* for the sake of brevity, and also to avoid unnecessary formality. In poetry it is often necessary to make these contractions to lessen the number of syllables in a line.

Allowable Contractions.

268. *I've* for *I have*; *they'll* for *they will*; *don't* for *do not*; *he's* for *he is* or *he has*; *we've* for *we have*; *doesn't* for *does not*; *isn't* for *is not*; *'tis* for *it is*; *can't* for *can not*; *o'er* for *over*; *ne'er* for *never*; *o'clock* for *of (the) clock*.

Improper Contractions.

269. *Ain't* and *'tain't* should never be used. Do not use *don't* for *does not*. "He *don't* know" is incorrect. *Aren't* for *are not* is sometimes used, but "*They're* not going" is better than "They *aren't* going."

Direction.—Re-write the following sentences, making all the proper contractions possible:

They are not coming. We have found them. He does not know. We do not know. I have heard from home. They will be sorry. They do not hear. He is going away. It is for you I am anxious. I have finished my letter. He has traveled over land and sea. He will go to-morrow. It is seven of the clock.

Review Questions.—1. What is a sentence? 2. What is the natural order of the principal parts of a sentence? 3. Is this order always observed in the construction of sentences? 4. Is a transitive verb a complete or an incomplete verb? 5. What is an object complement? 6. What is an imperative sentence? 7. An exclamatory sentence? 8. An interrogative sentence? 9. What is meant by the *entire subject*? 10. When is the verb in a sentence the *entire predicate*? 11. What is a secondary modifier? 12. What is a compound sentence? 13. What is a conjunction? 14. Use the verb *reads* as a *transitive* verb; also as an *intransitive* verb? 15. What is a proper noun? 16. What is the difference between *gender* and *sex*? 17. What are the rules for forming the possessive case of nouns? 18. What two contractions are not allowable? 19. When is *don't* a proper contraction? 20. When is *don't* an improper contraction? 21. What is parsing? 22. What is stated in the foot-note, on p. 82, in reference to parsing?

LXXVI.—PRONOUNS AND THEIR ANTECEDENTS.

We have learned [145] that "the noun for which a pronoun stands is called its antecedent." We have also learned [144] that a personal pronoun is often used without an antecedent, and that an *antecedent* may be either a *noun* or *another pronoun*.

270. In using a personal pronoun, care must be taken to select the proper pronoun according to the following rule:

271. Rule for Construction.—A pronoun must be in the same *gender*, *person*, and *number* as its antecedent.

    1. The *spider* again repaired *its* fragile web.
    2. Every *man* knows *his* own business best.

Explanation.—In sentence 1, the antecedent *spider*, being *neuter, third, singular*, is properly represented by the pronoun *its*, which is also *neuter, third, singular*. In 2, the antecedent *man* being *masculine, third, singular*, is properly represented by the pronoun *his*, which is also *masculine, third, singular*.

Direction.—Use the proper pronoun in the blank spaces in the following, and give the reason for its use:

    1. A studious girl recites —— lessons correctly.
    2. Every soldier received —— rations.
    3. The little bird carefully lined —— tiny nest.

272. Rule for Construction.—A pronoun must be plural when it represents two or more antecedents connected by *and*; as,

    1. The *cat* and the *dog* ate *their* dinner together.

Note.—If the antecedents so connected are only different names for the same person or thing, the pronoun must be singular; as, That eminent *statesman* and *orator* delighted *his* hearers.

273. Rule for Construction.—A pronoun must be singular when it represents two or more *singular* antecedents connected by *or* or *nor*; as,

    1. Neither *James* nor *William* has done *his* work correctly.

Note.—If one of the antecedents is plural, the pronoun must be plural, and the plural antecedent should stand nearest the pronoun; as, Either James or his younger *brothers* will help *their* father.

Questions.—1. What is an antecedent? 2. What two parts of speech may be antecedents? 3. In what three respects must a pronoun represent its antecedent? 4. Give the reason for the use of the pronouns in the sentences illustrating the other rules in this lesson. 5. Repeat these rules.

LXXVII.—PRONOUNS AND THEIR ANTECEDENTS.

The whole, or any part of this lesson, may be omitted until further progress shall have been made. The lesson should be learned by comparing with the text the sentences given for completion.

274. A pronoun, representing two or more antecedents of *different* persons, must be in the first person if either antecedent is in the first person; if neither antecedent is in the first person the pronoun must be in the second person; as,

    1. *John* and *I* like *our* presents.
    2. *You* and *John* do *your* work very neatly.

275. A pronoun representing a collective noun conveying the idea of *unity* [221], must be in the singular number; as,

    1. This teacher has a large *class*; I must divide *it*.
    2. Every *congregation* likes *its* own minister best.

276. When two or more personal pronouns are used in connection, the second person should precede the others, and the third person should precede the first; as, *You* and *I*. *You* and *he*. *She* and *I*.

277. Usage has fixed upon *he* and its variations to represent an antecedent whose gender is doubtful; as,

    1. Every *person* must take care of *himself*.
    2. Every *one* should love *his* own country.

Direction.—Complete the following sentences by inserting the correct form of pronoun in each, giving a reason for each insertion. These sentences should not now be given for analysis:

1. Every boy must use —— own books. 2. Mary and Susan have recited —— lessons. 3. William or Henry has lost —— books. 4. Either Julia or her sisters will assist —— mother. 5. Every class must take —— proper position. 6. The girls must obey —— teacher. 7. Every one should make —— useful. 8. Every person occasionally loses —— temper.

9. The jury rendered —— verdict. 10. When —— want —— knife or —— pencil —— can have ——. 11. —— and ——- will go to the fair. 12. —— and —— came in late this morning. 13. Neither Mary nor Susan offered —— assistance. 14. You know that every one has —— own troubles. 15. If any one thinks it is easy to recite a poem in public, let —— try it.

278. Care must be taken in using a pronoun when the antecedent is composed of two singular nouns of different genders; as,

1. When any *boy* or *girl* wishes to leave *their* seat, *they* must get permission to do so. [Incorrect—*their* and *they* are in the wrong number.]

2. When any *boy* or *girl* wishes to leave *his* or *her* seat, *he* or *she* must get permission to do so. [*Number* and *gender* correct, but very awkward.]

3. When boys or girls wish to leave *their* seats, *they* must get permission to do so. [Correct.]

LXXVIII.—QUOTATIONS.—DIRECT AND INDIRECT.

279. There are **two kinds** of **quotations**:

1. The **direct,** containing the *exact words* of the speaker or writer; as, "Dickens's works," said he, "are very interesting."

2. The **indirect,** containing the *substance* of the words of the speaker or writer; as, He said that Dickens's works are very interesting.

280. The indirect quotation does not require quotation marks, nor to be set off by commas; as,

1. My teacher said that I must remain. 2. My father said I must return early. 3. He declared that he would execute the contract faithfully.

Direction.—Dictate the following sentences to be written, pupils being required to use commas and quotation marks correctly:

1. Holmes says, "Sin has many tools, but a lie is a handle that fits them all."

2. "Sing to me, dearest nightingale," said a shepherd to the silent songstress.

3. Goldsmith says, "People seldom improve when they have no other model but themselves to copy after."

4. The willow said to the oak, "I am more graceful than thou."
5. Shenstone says, "Long sentences in short compositions are like large rooms in little houses."
6. "Let me make the ballads of a nation," said Fletcher, "and I care not who makes the laws."

Note.—When a quotation is divided by the insertion of other words (as in sentence 6), each division should be enclosed by quotation marks.

Direction.—Punctuate the two following sentences by using commas and quotation marks, so that in the first sentence the *witness* shall do the saying, and, in the second, *Plato* shall do the saying:

1. The prisoner said the witness is a convicted thief.
2. A boy says Plato is the most vicious of all wild beasts.

LXXIX.—ORAL PARSING.

281. Remarks on Parsing.—Routine parsing is often carried to such an extreme as seriously to interfere with the object that should ever be uppermost in teaching grammar, viz., *speaking* and *writing correctly*. After pupils have become familiar with the routine of parsing the different parts of speech, the most of the time generally devoted to a parsing lesson should be used in simply *mentioning* the parts of speech and their *relations* in the sentence, and giving the reasons for the *relation forms* when there are any. Only a few pupils should be required, during one lesson, to parse words in detail. More time will thus be secured for analysis and synthesis of sentences.

How to parse Personal Pronouns.

282. A personal pronoun is parsed by stating the five particulars that have been learned about it:

1. The **class**—*personal*, and why.
2. The **gender**—*masculine, feminine*, or *neuter*, and why.
3. The **person**—*first, second*, or *third*, and why.
4. The **number**—*singular* or *plural*, and why.
5. The **case**—*nominative, possessive*, or *objective*, and why.

Remarks.—Pronouns of the first and second persons may be in either the masculine or the feminine gender.

Personal pronouns are so often used without antecedents that it is perhaps better not to mention their agreement in parsing. The rules of syntax may be given or may be omitted. These *rules* are for *construction*, primarily, rather than for parsing [271].

    1. He knows me.
    2. I found his book.

283. Parsing Models.—*He* is a *personal pronoun*; in the *masculine* gender, because it represents a person of the *male* kind; in the *third* person, because it denotes the person *spoken of*; in the *singular* number, because it denotes but *one*; in the *nominative* case, because it is the *subject* of the verb *knows* [256, 1].

Note.—This model, in its details, should be discontinued as soon as pupils are familiar with the distinctions.

Abbreviated Models.—*He* is a personal pronoun, masculine gender, third person, singular number, nominative case, being the subject of the verb *knows*. Or, briefer and better—

He is a *personal pronoun, masculine, third, singular, nominative,* being the *subject* of the verb *knows*.

Me is a *personal pronoun, third, singular, objective,* being the *object* of the transitive verb *knows* [256, 3].

I is a *personal pronoun, first, singular, nominative,* being the *subject* of the verb *found*.

His is a personal pronoun, *masculine, third, singular, possessive,* and *modifies* the noun *book* [256, 2].

How to parse Nouns.

    1. John quickly gathered some delicious grapes.
    2. William's brother helped John.

284. Parsing Models.—*John* is a proper noun, masculine, third, singular, *nominative,* being the *subject* of the verb *gathered.*

Grapes is a common noun, neuter, third, plural, *objective,* being the *object* of the transitive verb *gathered.*

William's is a proper noun, masculine, third, singular, *possessive,* and *modifies* the noun *brother.*

How to parse Adjectives and Adverbs.

285. Parsing Models.—*Some* is a limiting adjective and modifies the noun *grapes.*

Delicious is a descriptive adjective, and modifies the noun *grapes.*

Quickly is an adverb, and modifies the verb *gathered.*

Direction.—Parse orally the *nouns, pronouns, adjectives,* and *adverbs* in the following sentences:

1. We soon reached the African coast.
2. Some pupils write very good compositions.
3. A majestic oak shaded the beautiful lawn.
4. The dutiful boys obeyed their father's instruction, and he praised them very highly.

286. Parsing Model.—*And* (in 4) is a conjunction, and connects the two members of the compound sentence. [Mention the members separately.]

LXXX.—DOUBLE POSSESSIVE FORMS.—INDEFINITE IT.—COMPOUND PERSONAL PRONOUNS.

287. The possessive forms, *mine, thine, ours, yours, hers,* and *theirs* are seldom now used except when the name of the thing possessed is omitted. They are generally considered as standing for the possessor and the thing possessed; as, "John ate his orange, you ate *yours* [your orange], and I ate *mine* [my orange]." These pronouns are thus disposed of by some grammarians.

In regard to the peculiar constructions, "a friend of mine," "that head of yours," "this heart of mine," and "this wicked world of ours" (in none of which does the pronoun properly represent the possessor and the thing possessed), these grammarians supply the word *possessing*; as, "this heart of *mine* [my possessing]. But this method of disposing of these pronouns is considered, by many, unsatisfactory.

288. The forms, **mine** and **thine,** formerly used *with* nouns as possessive modifiers, have become *absolved* [freed] from such use, and are now used *alone* in the sense of nouns; they may, therefore, be called **absolute possessive pronouns.** For the sake of uniformity, it is better to call all of these double possessive forms (when unaccompanied by nouns) *absolute possessive pronouns*, having the *nominative* and *objective* relations of nouns.

289. *Mine* and *thine* are still used as possessive modifiers in poetry and in the *solemn style*; as, "I shaded *mine* eyes one day."—J. Ingelow. "Time writes no wrinkle on *thine* azure brow."—Byron. "*Mine* enemies speak evil of me."—Bible.

RELATIVE PRONOUNS.

290. Indefinite It.—*It* often denotes simply a state or condition of things; as, "It rains"; "It snows"; "It thunders." Used in this way *it* has no antecedent, and is said to be used *indefinitely*.

291. Compound Personal Pronouns.—The compound personal pronouns *myself, thyself, himself, herself,* and *itself,* and their plurals *ourselves, yourselves, themselves,* are formed by adding *self* to *my, thy, him, her,* and *it* for the singular, and *selves* to *our, your,* and *them* for the plural. These compound personal pronouns may be used either as subjects or objects, but never to denote possession.

Questions.—1. When are *mine, thine,* etc., used? 2. To what do some authors consider them equivalent? 3. What would they consider *ours* equivalent to in "This world of *ours*"? 4. What name is given to these pronouns in this lesson? 5. Considering them *absolute possessive pronouns,* parse all those found in [287]. 6. What name is given to *it* in "It rains"? 7. Show how the singular compound personal pronouns (mentioned above) are formed; also the plural compounds.

LXXXI.—RELATIVE PRONOUNS.

Note to Teachers.—No use of this lesson should be made here other than to aid pupils in the correct use of relative pronouns in speaking, and in writing compositions. The pronouns should not be parsed, nor should the sentences be analyzed:

1. I know the man *who* built this boat.
2. I have a horse *which* can trot very fast.
3. William returned the book *that* he borrowed.

Explanation.—In sentence 1, *who* is used instead of the noun *man*. In 2, *which* is used instead of the noun *horse*. In 3, *that* is used instead of the noun *book*. Therefore *who, which,* and *that* are pronouns.

292. The pronouns *who, which,* and *that* are called **relative pronouns**.

293. Who is used when the antecedent is the name of a *person*; as,

1. The *man* who just passed us built our house.
2. We have a *workman* who understands his business.

RELATIVE PRONOUNS.—COMPOSITION.

RELATION FORMS.

SINGULAR.		PLURAL.	
Nom.	Who,	Nom.	Who,
Poss.	Whose,	Poss.	Whose,
Obj.	Whom.	Obj.	Whom.

294. Which is used when the antecedent is either the name of an animal or of a thing; as,

1. The *buffalo*, which once roamed the prairies, has become very scarce.
2. The *figs* which we ate came in a very neat box.

295. That may be used in the place of either who or which; i. e., the relative *that* may be used instead of the name of a person, of an animal, or of a thing; as,

1. The *man* that rescued the child received a reward.
2. The *dog* that bit my brother died yesterday.
3. The *storm* that came so suddenly did much damage.

Direction.—Point out the *relative pronoun* and its *antecedent* in each of the preceding sentences.

Questions.—1. In speaking or writing, what nouns must the relative pronoun *who* represent? 2. What nouns must *which* represent? 3. What nouns may *that* represent? 4. Would it be correct to say, "The horse *who* ran away was soon caught"?

LXXXII.—SYNTHESIS.—NARRATIVE.

296. Direction.—Combine the following statements into a connected narrative. This may be practiced in parts, *orally*, and then *written* as a composition:

I was boarding at a mountain resort. I arose one morning. It was at seven o'clock. The morning was cool. It was pleasant. I prepared for breakfast. I ate my breakfast. I then started on a tramp. I went with my friend. We rowed across the lake. We landed on the opposite side. We determined to climb a mountain. This mountain was at a distance. The path ascended gradually to the foot of the mountain. The path lay beside a mossy brook. It was a beautiful brook. Fern-moss covered its sides. Fern-moss covered the rocks beside the path. We traveled nearly a mile. We then came to a spring of water. We stopped at the spring to eat our lunch. We were very thirsty. The water was very cold. The water was very refreshing. We resumed our journey. We soon reached the foot of the mountain. We ascended to the top. The view was grand, beautiful, indescribable. Mountain piled on mountain in one direction. Valley and hill spread out in another. We returned by the same path. The mossy brook was still very beautiful. It was very beautiful when we went. Our tramp was a delightful one.

LXXXIII.—VERBS.—TENSE.

297. Most verbs express action. All actions take place at some *time*. *Time* is naturally separated into *three* great divisions—*present time*, *past time*, and *future time*.

Direction.—Notice carefully the time expressed by the verb in each of the following sentences:

    1. This boy *writes* carefully.
    2. That boy *wrote* carefully.
    3. I *will write* carefully.
    4. You *shall write* carefully.

298. Each of these four sentences contains a different form of the verb *write*.

The form *writes*, in 1, shows that the boy is *now* performing the act; therefore *writes* denotes *present time*.

The form *wrote*, in 2, shows that the act is finished; therefore *wrote* denotes *past time*.

The forms *will write* and *shall write*, in 3 and 4, show that the acts are yet to be performed; therefore these two verbs express *future time*.

299. In 3, the verb *will* is used with *write* to *help* express *future* time, and the *two verbs combined* in this way form *one verb*. In 4, the verb *shall* is used for the same purpose.

300. *Shall* and *will* used in this way are called *auxiliary* verbs, because *auxiliary* means *helping*.

301. Of these two verbs *will write* and *shall write*, **write** is the **principal part** in each, *shall* and *will* being *auxiliaries*.

302. In grammar, the *time* of an action or event is called **tense**. *Tense* means *time*.

VERBS.—TENSE.

303. Tense is the grammatical form of a verb which distinguishes the *time* of an action or event.

304. The **present tense** expresses the action as now taking place.

305. The **past tense** expresses the action as finished and past.

306. The **future tense** expresses the action as yet to be performed.

Questions.—1. What are the three principal divisions of time? 2. When does a verb express present time? 3. Past time? 4. Future time? 5. What name is given to *will* and *shall* in the verbs *will see* and *shall see*? 6. In grammar, what *term* is used to mean *time*? 7. Can a verb be composed of more than *one* word? 8. What is *tense*? 9. Present tense? 10. Past tense? 11. Future tense? 12. What time does the form *write* show? 13. *Wrote*? 14. *Shall write*?

LXXXIV.—TENSE.

307. Definition.—A **verb** is a *word* used to assert something of its subject.

Direction.—Mention the tense of the verb in each of the following sentences. Also analyze and parse:

1. The army lustily cheered their leader.
2. The merry girls gathered some pretty wild flowers.
3. The policeman soon dispersed the noisy crowd.
4. That lazy boy works very slowly.
5. The young man soon squandered his father's property.
6. Twenty-four girls know this lesson perfectly.
7. Those girls shall go first.
8. The boys will know their lessons to-morrow.
9. The west wind blew gently.
10. The rain will cease soon.
11. This extremely hot weather will produce much sickness.

Direction.—Give the tense of each verb in these eleven sentences, and mention the *principal part* and the *auxiliary* of each verb in the future tense, according to the following model:

VERBS.—TENSE.

308. Model.—*Cheered*, in 1, is a transitive verb in the *past tense*. *Works*, in 4, is an intransitive verb in the *present tense*. *Will know*, in 8, is a transitive verb in the *future tense*; principal part *know*, auxiliary, *will* [300, 301].

Direction.—Complete the following sentences by inserting the correct *tense forms* of the verbs *come, see, sit, give, go, return*, using them in the order here given:

1. John —— home yesterday.
2. I —— him once last week.
3. I —— with the driver yesterday.
4. Father —— me a knife last week.
5. I —— to school to-morrow.
6. They —— next week.

LXXXV.—TENSE.

Direction.—The teacher will dictate the present tense of the following verbs, and require pupils to give the past tense.

309. Some of the verbs in the following list have *two* forms in the past tense; both forms are correct, but the one first given is preferable in each instance. We may say, " I *awoke* early," or " I *awaked* early "; but " I *awoke* early " is preferable. The *present-tense form* of a verb is called the **verb-root**.

PRESENT TENSE.	PAST TENSE.	PRESENT TENSE.	PAST TENSE.
Awake,	awoke (awaked).	Go,	went.
Blame,	blamed.	Have,	had.
Bleed,	bled.	Lie (to recline),	lay.
Bring,	brought.	Lay (to place),	laid.
Build,	built (builded).	Lose,	lost.
Burn,	burned (burnt).	Light,	lighted (lit).
Buy,	bought.	Ring,	rang (rung).
Catch,	caught.	Run,	ran (run).
Come,	came.	See,	saw.
Dig,	dug (digged).	Sit (to rest),	sat.
Do,	did.	Set (to place),	set.
Draw,	drew.	Slip,	slipped.
Dream,	dreamed (dreamt).	Sing,	sang (sung).
Drink,	drank.	Spill,	spilled (spilt).
Eat,	ate.	Spoil,	spoiled (spoilt).
Freeze,	froze.	Throw,	threw.

VERBS.—NUMBER. 101

310. *Do* (also *does*) and its past tense *did*, are used as auxiliaries in *emphatic* statements, and also in asking questions; as, "I *do try*," "*Does* he *try*?" in the present tense, and "He *did try*," in the past tense. *Try* is the *simple form* of the present tense, and *do try*, the *compound form*.

1. I generally fail, but I *do* try.
2. John hesitated, but he *did* go finally.
3. The man means well, but he *does* make such absurd remarks.
4. That horse *does* not* travel very fast.
5. How *do* blacksmiths weld iron?
6. How *does* the patient feel to-day?
7. When *did* Columbus discover America?

Questions.—1. What is the verb in sentence 1? 2. How is it formed? 3. What is the verb in 2? 4. How is it formed? 5. How are the verbs formed in 5, 6, and 7. 6. Mention the tense of the verb in each of the preceding sentences. 7. Read the first four of these sentences, using the *simple* form of the verb, not changing the tense.

LXXXVI.—NUMBER OF VERBS.—S-FORMS.

311. Verbs have *number forms* showing their use with singular and plural subjects; as,

1. The boy writes.
2. The boys write.
3. The boy pushes.
4. The boys push.
5. The girl plays.
6. The girls play.
7. She plays.
8. They play.
9. He writes.
10. They write.
11. I write.
12. We write.

Questions.—1. Is the subject, in sentence 1, singular or plural? In 3? In 5? In 7? In 9? 2. With what letter does the verb end in each of these five sentences? 3. Tell whether the subject is singular or plural in each of sentences 2, 4, 6, 8, 10, and 12. 4. Does the verb end in **s** in either of these six sentences?

Explanation.—By examining these twelve sentences we see that the verb-root adds **s**, only when the subject is singular. We see, too, that

---

* The adverb *not* often stands between the principal part of the verb and its auxiliary. In interrogative sentences the *subject* often stands between the verb and its auxiliary, as in 5, 6, and 7 [117].

VERBS.—NUMBER.

when the subject is plural, and also when *I* is the subject, no **s** is added to the verb-root.

312. S-form.— { **s** or **es** *added* to a **noun** makes it *plural*.
{ a verb with **s** or **es** *added*, is *singular*.

*Write*s, *push*es, and *play*s are, therefore, *singular* forms of the verb, and they must be used with singular subjects.

313. A verb in the present tense must be in the *s-form* when used with *any singular* subject except *I*. *Euphony* requires that *plural* subjects should *reject* the *s-form* of the verb.

There are, then, *two* forms of the simple verb *in the present tense*—the *s-form*, which is always singular, and the form without the **s**. This *latter* form is *plural* except in its use with the pronoun *I* as its subject; then it is called the singular *first-person form*, as in sentence 11 [811]. It follows, then, that the *singular form of a verb* must be used with a *singular subject*, and the *plural form* with a *plural subject*.

314. Verbs in the past tense have no *s-form*. The *same form* is used with both *singular* and *plural* subjects; as, " I played," " He played," " You played," " We played," " They played."

315. Verbs in the future tense have no *s-form*, the same form being used with both singular and plural subjects; as, " He will go," " They will go."

Questions.—1. Why is the form *writes* used in sentence 1? 2. The form *write* in 2? 3. *Plays* in 5? 4. *Play* in 6? 5. Why is the form *write* used in 11? 6. Which form of a verb in the present tense is always singular? 7. How many forms has a verb in the present tense? 8. Past tense? 9. What is the singular *first-person* form of a verb in the present tense?

LXXXVII.—SYNTHESIS.—AUTOBIOGRAPHY.

316. Direction.—Combine into a connected narrative by weaving two or more questions and answers into one sentence. The teacher should prepare as many exercises of this and of other kinds as are needful to develop in the pupil skill in the use of language.

VERBS.—AGREEMENT.

Where do you live? In Brooklyn, N. Y. What school do you attend? Grammar School No. 90. How long have you attended this school? Nearly four years. Where do you go during vacation? Sometimes to the White Mountains. Sometimes to the Adirondacks. Have you been to the top of Mount Washington? Yes, once last year, and once the year before. By what route did you go up? Once by the mountain railroad and once by the carriage route. Do these routes approach the top from the same side of the mountain? They approach from opposite sides. What was the state of the atmosphere? It was clear and cool last year. Could you see any part of the State of Maine? Yes, and also a part of Vermont and Massachusetts. Where do you expect to go next vacation? Father thinks strongly of going to Mount Desert Island. Where is this island situated? Near the coast of Maine. Which summer resort on this island do you like best. South West Harbor. Why do you like this place better than Bar Harbor? Because it is more quiet. Because a breeze reaches there from almost every direction, making it cooler. Do you intend to become a teacher? Yes, if father and mother will consent. Why do you wish to teach? Because I think I shall like it.

LXXXVIII.—AGREEMENT OF VERB AND SUBJECT.

Direction.—Justify the use of the form of the verb in each of the following sentences; then change each subject from singular to plural, or from plural to singular, and make the necessary change in the verb, but do not change its tense. Also make any necessary change in the form of any adjective to suit the change in the subject that it modifies:

1. The bee gathers honey.
2. Those* children laugh heartily.
3. That man acts strangely.
4. That boy walks rapidly.
5. I eat too rapidly.
6. She recites correctly.
7. You sew very neatly.
8. He deals honestly.

Direction.—Complete the following sentences by inserting the present-tense form of some verb in each, that will properly agree with its subject, giving the reason for each insertion:

1. Hogs —— acorns.
2. The boys —— marbles here.
3. All people —— mistakes sometimes.
4. The ox —— his cud.
5. That child —— too much noise.
6. Some rivers —— in very crooked channels.

---

* The adjective *this* has a plural *these*; *that*, a plural *those*. *This* and *that* are used only with singular nouns; *these* and *those*, only with plural nouns.

VERBS.—AGREEMENT.

317. Besides *do*,* *does*, *did*, *shall*, and *will*, we often use as auxiliaries *have*, *has*, *had*, *may*, *can*, *must*, *might*, *could*, *would*, and *should*—*has* and *does* being singular forms; as,

1. Mary *has learned* her lesson.
2. James *does* not *know* his lesson.
3. We *have seen* the new bridge.
4. We *might have seen* it before.

Explanation.—These words in italics in each sentence form *one verb*. In sentence 3, bridge is the object of the verb *have seen*, and (in 4) *it* is the object of the verb *might have seen*. *Might have* is the auxiliary, and *seen* the principal part of the verb.

Direction.—Distinguish the verbs in the following sentences, and mention the auxiliaries and principal part in each. Pupils should *not* now be required to give the tense of the compound forms, except of those having *shall* and *will* as auxiliaries. These compound forms are used alike with singular and plural subjects. Analyze each sentence:

1. The senator has made an excellent speech.
2. We might have lost this train.
3. My brother may have arrived to-day.
4. The sheriff should have arrested the thief.

LXXXIX.—AGREEMENT OF VERB AND SUBJECT.

318. We have seen that the *singular form* of a verb must be used with a *singular subject*, and that the *plural form* of a verb must be used with a *plural subject* [313]; as,

1. That swan *swims* gracefully.
2. Those swans *swim* gracefully.

319. You is always *plural* in its grammatical relations in a sentence, although often used in speaking to one person [234]; as,

1. *You* often *make* mistakes.
2. *You have* upset the ink-stand.

320. It has been shown [313] that *I* (although singular), when used as a subject, never takes the singular *s-form* of the verb, but, instead, takes the singular *first-person* form. This form is also used with plural subjects; as,

---

* *Do, does, did,* and *have, has, had,* are often used as principal verbs as well as for auxiliaries.

VERBS.—AGREEMENT.

1. I generally *eat* too fast.
2. He generally *eats* too fast.
3. I generally *eats* too fast [incorrect].

Explanation.—Sentence 3 is incorrect, for, although *I* and *eats* are both singular, and so agree in number, yet they do not agree in person because *eats* is *not* the singular *first-person* form [313]. In 2, *he* and *eats* agree in both person and number.

321. We see, then, that a verb has two different forms that must be considered in its use with a subject on account of *person* and *number*.

322. When the proper form of a verb is used with its subject, such a a verb is said to *agree* with its subject in *person* and *number*.

323. Rule for Construction.—A verb must agree with its subject in person and number.

Sentences for Parsing.

1. He generally *eats* too fast.
2. You *made* too much noise.
3. I always *eat* breakfast early.
4. The rain *will* soon *cease*.
5. You shall surely go.
6. I rise very early.
7. She feels her loss keenly.
8. The fire burns brightly.

324. Parsing Models.—*Eats* is an intransitive verb in the present tense, and agrees with its subject *he* in the *third* person and *singular* number [323].

Made is a transitive verb in the past tense, and agrees with its subject *you* in the second person and plural number [323, 234].

Eat is a transitive verb in the present tense, and agrees with its subject *I* in the first person, singular number [323, 313].

Will cease is an intransitive verb in the future tense—principal part *cease*, auxiliary *will*—and agrees with its subject *rain* in the third person and singular number [323].

Direction.—Parse the *verbs* (and other words) in the last four sentences.

Questions.—1. In what respects must a verb agree with its subject? 2. What form of a verb is always singular? 3. What disagreement is there between *verb* and *subject* in each of these sentences—"We keeps good groceries," "I keeps good groceries"? 4. When does a verb agree with its subject in person and number? 5. What is the rule for the agreement of *verb* and *subject*? 6. Which form of the verb must be used with the pronoun *I* as a subject? Which form with *you* as a subject?

XC.—SUBJECTS CONNECTED BY "AND."

325. A subject is sometimes *plural* in *meaning* when it is *not* plural in *form* [222]. When a *subject* is *plural* in meaning its *verb* must be *plural*.

326. Two or more singular subjects taken jointly (connected by *and*) form a *compound subject* whose meaning is generally plural. The assertion is made of *all* the subjects; as,

    1. William and Mary *row* the boat steadily.
    2. William, Mary, and Susan *row* the boat steadily.

327. Rule for Construction.—*Two or more singular subjects* connected by *and*, when they convey a plural meaning, require a *plural verb*.

328. When a *subject* is singular *in meaning* its *verb* must also be *singular*.

329. Sometimes two or more singular subjects connected by *and* are only different names for the same person or thing. Such a compound subject has a singular meaning and requires a singular verb, which agrees with each subject separately; as,

    1. That eminent philosopher and poet *has* many admirers.
    2. That eminent scholar and judicious critic *writes* the purest English.

330. The verbs *am*, *is*, and *was* are singular forms [200], and should be used with singular subjects in speaking and writing. *Are* and *were* are plural forms, and should be used with plural subjects [201].

Direction.—Use the correct form of one of the verbs just mentioned in each blank space in the following sentences:

1. The boys —— in a hurry.
2. Mary and Susan —— here yesterday.
3. —— he at the fair last week?
4. —— he and John here yesterday?
5. I —— going to New York.
6. She —— here last month.
7. —— you ready?
8. There —— Mary and Paul.

331. When two or more singular subjects are so connected that the verb evidently agrees with each subject separately, or with one to the exclusion of the others, or when they are preceded by *each*, *every*, or *no*, a singular verb is required; as,

1. His wit *pleases* me, his frankness, his courtesy.
2. John, and also James, *attends* school.
3. John, as well as James, *attends* school.
4. John, and not James, *attends* school.
5. Every tempest and every dew-drop *has* its mission.

Explanation.—In sentence 1, the singular verb *pleases* is correctly used, although there are three subjects connected by *and* [understood]. This manner of construction is used for the sake of force, or emphasis, and the verb is understood to each of the subjects *frankness* and *courtesy*. In 4, it is evident that *attends* agrees with *John* to the exclusion of *James* (only one person attends). "John, and not James, attends" = John attends, and James attends not.

Questions.—1. What kind of subjects require plural verbs? 2. When is a compound subject plural? 3. When do two or more singular subjects connected by *and* convey a singular meaning? 4. Tell which of these verbs are singular: *am, are, is, was, were*. 5. What kind of subjects are plural in meaning when they are not plural in form [326, 222]?

XCI.—SUBJECTS CONNECTED BY "OR" OR "NOR."

332. Two or more singular subjects connected by **or** or **nor** form a *compound subject* whose meaning is *singular*. The assertion is made of each subject separately; as,

1. He or his brother *has* the book.
2. He or his brother or his sister *has* the book.
3. He or his brother *have* the book [incorrect—why?].

333. Rule for Construction.—*Two or more singular subjects connected by or or nor have a singular meaning and require a singular verb.*

The different parts of a compound subject are taken *separately* [331] in their use with a verb when they are connected by *or, nor, and also, and too, and not, but not, if not, as well as*.

334. A *collective noun* in its singular form is *singular in meaning* when the collection is spoken of as a *whole*. Such a noun when used as a subject requires a singular verb; as,

1. That choir [as a body] *sings* well.

COMPOUND SUBJECT.

But when the *individuals* of the collection are in the mind of the speaker or writer, such a noun is *plural in meaning* and requires a *plural verb*; as,

    2. The choir [as individuals] respect their leader.

335. When a collective noun, used as a subject, is preceded by *this, that, each, every,* or *no,* reference is made to the collection as *one body.*

Direction.—Decide which of the two *verb forms,* in brackets, in the following sentences, is the correct one, and give the reason for your decision:

1. Patience and diligence [remove or removes] mountains.
2. My poverty, but not my will [consent or consents].
3. That able scholar and critic [have or has] a valuable library.
4. Each man, each woman, each child [know or knows] the hour.
5. Thy goodness [soothes or soothe] thy tenderness, and love.
6. All work and no play [make or makes] Jack a dull boy.
7. The crime, not the scaffold, [make or makes] the shame.
8. Each village and hamlet [has or have] their petty chief.
9. The father, as well as the son [enjoy or enjoys] the sport.
10. Every congregation [like or likes] their own minister best.
11. The Senate [have or has] only one session to-day.

XCII.—COMPOSITION LESSON.

336. Direction.—Copy the *first* paragraph and place periods and interrogation points where they belong. The remaining paragraphs should be used by giving at least one each week for punctuation.

Exercises in Punctuation.

    1. If the man should leap to the pavement below he would be instantly killed he could not go back already the smoke and heat and fire were close upon him despair was in his face what could he do the firemen quickly brought ladders but they were too short the longest of them would not reach half the distance it seemed as if nothing could save him he was finally rescued by the efforts of a colored boy do you not think this boy was brave

    2. In the early days of Massachusetts, when a man bought a coat, he perhaps exchanged a bear-skin for it if he wished for a barrel of molasses he might purchase it with a pile of pine boards musket-bullets were used

instead of farthings the indians had a sort of money called wampum which was made of clam-shells this strange sort of specie was taken in payment of debts by the settlers bank-bills had never been heard of

3. There once lived in France an old tinker he used to travel about the country, mending clocks and umbrellas this he had done for many years, and people used to expect him when his regular time came round at last the old man became too old to work, and finally died leaving his cane and bundle to his proud nephew, who would not accept the legacy when he afterward learned that the hollow cane contained bank-notes to the value of several thousands of dollars he repented of his folly, but it was too late.

XCIII.—NATURAL ORDER OF WORDS.

337. Most of the sentences used so far have been *declarative*. The *natural* order of the parts of a declarative sentence is: first, the *subject*, then the *predicate verb* followed by its *complement*. An *adjective* precedes its noun. An *adverb* stands before or after the verb, according to the sense or sound; and when it follows a transitive verb it generally follows the *object* also.

1. Cortes conquered Mexico.
2. *Some* flowers bloom *early*.
3. *Industrious* people *generally* succeed.
4. *Thrifty* trees produce fruit *abundantly*.

338. Position of Adjectives.—Adjectives *naturally* precede their nouns, yet they often follow them, especially in poetry; as,

1. Tobacco makes boys *sick*.
2. Mary found the fawn *asleep*.
3. Hard work makes people *weary*.
4. Attention held them *mute*.
5. The silent grove, the solemn shade,
 Proclaim the power *divine*.

339. Position of Adverbs.—An adverb generally either precedes or follows the verb according to the sound; but for the sake of emphasis it is often placed at the beginning of a sentence. It is frequently placed between an auxiliary and the principal part of a verb; as,

RHETORICAL ORDER OF WORDS.

1. Strong ships *sometimes* sink.
2. Some pupils learn *rapidly*.
3. *Carefully* she lifted the sleepy child.
4. The gardener planted his potatoes *early*.
5. The farmer planted his early potatoes *late*.
6. You should *always* obey your parents.

Direction.—Analyze the last six sentences in this lesson, and describe the position of each adverb. Describe the position of each adjective in all the sentences in this lesson, and mention the noun to which each adjective refers.

Questions.—1. What is the natural order of the parts of a sentence? 2. What is the position of the adverb in 1 of the last set of sentences? In 3? In 4? 3. In each of the other sentences? 4. What is the natural position of an adjective? 5. What other position may it occupy?

XCIV.—RHETORICAL ARRANGEMENT.

340. Position of the Subject.—Although the subject naturally precedes the verb, yet sentences are not always arranged in this way. We sometimes place *first* that which strikes us most forcibly, or that which we wish to make most impressive; as,

1. Down fell the whole *platform*.

It is plain, from this sentence, that the *falling* was uppermost in the mind of the beholder—not the *platform*. Arranged in the natural order of its parts, the sentence is much less expressive; as,

2. The whole platform fell down.

341. Position of the Object.—Sometimes the *object* stands between the subject and its verb, and sometimes it precedes both subject and verb; as,

1. "No busy hand the *food* prepares,
No soothing voice sweet *comfort* gives."
2. A lovelier *scene* I never saw.

342. This arrangement of the parts of a sentence out of their natural order is called the *inverted* or *rhetorical* order of words. It is also sometimes called *transposed* order. Even

ANALYTICAL PARSING.

when an *adverb* introduces a sentence the order is slightly inverted.

Direction.—Mention the words that are out of their natural order in the preceding sentences, and also in those following. Change rhetorical to natural order and notice the loss in force and beauty. Analyze and parse:

1. There* stood the poor old man.
2. Slowly and solemnly the soldiers left the grave.
3. A transient calm the happy scenes bestow.
4. No busy steps the grass-grown garden trod.
5. Full quickly flew the morning hours.
6. The stormy sea I do not fear.
7. So madly rushed the fiery steeds.
8. The bribe I scorn, and you I despise.
9. The rod I brought, but I forgot the bait.

Questions.—1. What two positions may a subject occupy in a sentence? 2. What three positions may an object complement occupy? 3. What do you understand by *rhetorical* order? 4. When is a sentence inverted?

XCV.—ANALYTICAL PARSING.

343. To Teachers.—The regular routine of analysis and parsing may be varied by using a combination of these two exercises, thus directing attention more especially to the *structure* of sentences and to the *forms* of the words that compose them [244 f. n.].

1. They soon found him.

344. Model.—This sentence is *simple, declarative, direct,*† the subject preceding its predicate-verb *found*. The subject *they* is properly used in the *nominative form*. *Soon* modifies the verb *found*. *Found* is in the *past tense form* to express *past time*. The object complement *him* has the proper *object* form.

2. So madly rushed the fiery steeds.

345. Model.—This sentence is simple, declarative, *inverted*, the predicate-verb *rushed* standing before its subject *steeds*. The adverb *so* modifies

---

* When the adverb *there* introduces a sentence, the subject follows the verb.

† When a sentence is arranged in the natural order of *subject, verb,* and *object*, it may be called *direct*. But when either of these parts is out of its natural order, the sentence is said to be *inverted* [342].

112 INTERROGATIVE ADJECTIVES AND ADVERBS.

the adverb *madly*. *Madly* has the proper *adverbial form* to modify the verb *rushed* [from adj. *mad*]. *Rushed* has the *past tense form* to express *past time*. The adjectives *the* and *fiery* modify the noun *steeds*. *Steeds* is the *name form*, and is properly used as a subject [229].

3. The stormy sea I do not fear.

346. Model.—This sentence is *simple, declarative, inverted*, the object complement *sea* standing before the predicate-verb *fear*. The adjectives *the* and *stormy* modify the noun *sea*. *Sea* is the proper form for the object complement, because a noun has no form for an object different from the *subject form*. The subject *I* has the proper *nominative* form. The predicate-verb *do fear* is used in the *emphatic present tense form* to express present time. The negative adverb *not* modifies *do fear*.

4. Me he released, but him he hanged.

347. Model.—This sentence is *compound, declarative, inverted* in both members, the object in each standing before the predicate-verb. The object complement *me* has the proper object form, and the subject *he* the proper *nominative form*. The verb *released* is used in the *past tense form* to express past time. The conjunction *but* connects the two members. In the second member, the object complement *him* has the proper *object form*, and the subject *he* has the proper *subject form*.

XCVI.—INTERROGATIVE ADJECTIVES AND ADVERBS.

1. Has John any money?
2. Will Mary return soon?
3. Do you like this cold weather?

Questions.—1. Are these declarative sentences? 2. What are they? 3. What is the subject in 1? 4. What is its position? 5. What is the object? 6. What is the subject in 2? 7. What is its position? 8. What is the subject in 3? 9. What is its position [117]?

348. The subject in an interrogative sentence generally follows the predicate-verb, or stands between the principal part of the verb and its auxiliary.

Direction.—Justify the use of the verb in the following sentences, and change the declarative sentences to the interrogative form; also change the interrogative sentences to declarative. Analyze and parse after reading the explanation below:

1. Some people have very poor memories.
2. The builder will soon finish the house.
3. Has Sarah's brother my cloak and umbrella?
4. **Whose** boat did you borrow?
5. **What** book has mother?
6. **Which** boy will open the window?
7. **When** will John's father return?
8. **How** will the miner crush the quartz?
9. **Why** did you start so soon?

Explanation.—*Whose, what,* and *which,* in 4, 5, and 6, are interrogative adjectives, because they are used in asking questions, as well as to modify the nouns with which they are used. *When, how,* and *why,* in 7, 8, and 9, are interrogative adverbs, because they are adverbs used in asking questions, as well as to modify the verbs in the sentences in which they are used.

349. Definition.—An **interrogative adjective** is an adjective used in asking a question.

The *interrogative adjectives* are *whose, what,* and *which.*

350. Definition.—An **interrogative adverb** is an adverb used in asking a question.

The *interrogative adverbs* are *how, where, when,* and *why.*

Questions.—1. What is an interrogative adjective? 2. Repeat the three interrogative adjectives. 3. What is an interrogative adverb? 4. Repeat them. 5. How do you parse an interrogative adjective [see explanation]? 6. How do you parse interrogative adverbs?

XCVII.—REVIEW BY SENTENCES.

351. The order and the extent of progress in the development of the sentence, so far, are seen at a glance by observing the following series of sentences:

1. Birds sing. [Simple subject and predicate.]
2. *Little* birds sing. [Adjective element.]
3. Little birds sing *sweetly.* [Adverbial element.]
4. Little birds sing *very* sweetly. [Secondary modifier.]
5. A furious storm arose, *but* the pilot still slept. [Conjunction and compound sentence.]

6. The early bird catches the *worm*. [Object complement.]
7. That ugly little dog bit *James* severely. [Proper noun.]
8. The boblincoln lives a merry *life*. [Object of kindred meaning.]
9. The fisherman rowed *rapidly* the boat. [Wrong position of adverbs.]
10. *I* caught a fine trout yesterday. [*General* use of pronouns.]
11. *Charles* and *Henry* rowed the boat. [Condensed compound.]
12. The farmer fed the *cows* and *horses*. [Objects connected.]
13. The captain lost a *large* and *valuable* cargo. [Adj. con.]
14. The man worked *faithfully* and *well*. [Adverbs connected.]
15. William *harnessed* and *drove* the team. [Verbs connected.]
16. The *ice-house* stands alone. [Compound word.]
17. The *moon* takes up *her* wondrous tale. [Gender, personification, person, number, case.]
18. *She* soiled *her* new dress and *her* mother scolded *her*. [Personal pronoun.]
19. The atmosphere surrounds the earth. [Tense, *present*.]
20. Benjamin Franklin learned a trade. [Tense, *past*.]
21. The carpenter *will finish* the house soon. [Tense, *future*.]
22. These boys *swim* nicely. That boy *swims* nicely. [Number of verbs.]
23. Oxen *chew* [not chews] the cud. [Agreement of verb with subject.]
24. No *home* have *I*. [Natural and rhetorical order of words.]
25. Opium makes people *dull*. [Position of adjectives.]
26. Will you pass the bread? [Interrogative sentence.]
27. *Which* road shall we take? [Interrogative adjective.]
28. *When* did you arrive? [Interrogative adverb.]

Direction.—These sentences, illustrating the progress of the learner, should be given as review lessons in analysis and parsing to test his knowledge, before taking up prepositions and prepositional phrases.

XCVIII.—SYNTHESIS.

352. Direction.—Combine the following into a connected description, using as connectives *therefore* in the section marked 1; *and* in part 2; *so* and *that* in part 3, striking out words in italics; *which* and *and* in part 4; *as* and *as* in the third and fourth lines of part 5; *through which* in 6; *but* in 7 and 8; any connective may be repeated and unnecessary words may be omitted, etc.

THE ELEPHANT.

1. The elephant is a large animal.
   He is a clumsy animal.
   He makes a very awkward appearance in traveling.

2. His neck is short and thick.
   He has a large head.
   He has a heavy head.
   He has a large, heavy body.
   He has stout legs.

3. His head and body are very heavy.
   On this account they require a short neck and stout legs to support them.

4. He has not a nose.
   He has a long, muscular arm instead.
   His arm is called a trunk.
   He uses this trunk like an arm and hand.
   He uses it for passing all kinds of food into his mouth.
   He uses it for other purposes.

5. At the end of the trunk is a curious lip-shaped muscle.
   This muscle is called a finger.
   With this finger he can pick up very small objects.
   He can pick up even a pin.

6. The nostrils are near this finger.
   He breathes through these nostrils.

7. He has long, heavy tusks.
   They are of solid ivory.
   He has them in a wild state.
   They are sawed off.
   This is done when he is captured.

8. The elephant is a docile animal.
   He is very much so.
   He sometimes becomes unmanageable.
   He becomes so when he is enraged.

Remark.—In the composition lessons already given, various methods of supplying material for thought have been *suggested*. More material of the same kind or of something different, that pupils can comprehend, should be furnished.

XCIX.—PREPOSITIONS.

353. *Adjectives* and *adverbs* are *single* words, and are therefore called *word*-modifiers. But single words are not always sufficient to express *adjective* and *adverbial* ideas. In the following sentences, another kind of modifier is used with which we can often express what we wish to say more smoothly and accurately than can be done by single words; as,

1. *Industrious* men labor *patiently*.
2. Men *of industry* labor *with patience*.
3. A man *of wisdom* will act *with prudence*.
4. The people listened *with close attention*.
5. The king wore a crown *of gold*.
6. The soldiers fought *with great bravery*.
7. Mary's father waited *for her*.

Explanation.—In sentence 2, the words *of industry* express the same idea as the single word *industrious* in 1; therefore the words *of industry*, taken as a whole, have an *adjective* use and modify the noun *men*. The words *with patience*, in 2, are used in place of *patiently* in 1; therefore, taken together, they modify the verb *labor* like an *adverb*.

354. These *groups of words* are called *phrases*, and the words *of*, *with*, and *for* (each forming a part of a phrase), are called prepositions,* because each has a *position before* the noun or pronoun in the phrase.

Direction.—In the seven preceding sentences, mention each word that is modified by a phrase, and tell whether such phrase performs an adjective or an adverbial office. Substitute a single word for each phrase, except for that in the last sentence.

355. Definition.—A **phrase** is any group of words not containing a verb and its subject, which, taken as a whole, performs the office of a single word.

356. The *noun* or *pronoun* following a preposition is called the *object* of the preposition, and it must be in the objective case, as in sentence 7.

357. Rule for Construction.—A *noun* or a *pronoun* which is the **object** of a **preposition** must be in the **objective case**.

---

* *Preposition* means *placed before* (Latin *pre* = before ; *positus* = placed).

PREPOSITIONAL PHRASE.

Questions.—1. In sentence 3, which phrase performs an adjective office, and why? 2. An adverbial office, and why? 3. What part of the phrase is *prudence*? 4. What part of speech is *with*, is *of*, is *for*? 5. Of what is the phrase composed in sentence 4? 6. Why is *her* (in 7) used instead of *she*? 7. What is a phrase? 8. Which case of a pronoun must be used as the object of a preposition? 9. Mention the preposition and its object in each phrase in these seven sentences.

C.—PREPOSITIONAL PHRASE.

358. Although a single word may often be substituted for a phrase, yet it often happens that no single word can be thus substituted; and this is true of the phrases in 3 to 8, inclusive, of the following sentences. Each phrase, however, performs the *office* of an *adjective* or of an *adverb*:

1. All men admire an act *of generosity*.
2. Groves *of oranges* lined the banks *of the river*.
3. The merchant hastened *to Chicago*.
4. The bright stars shone *above us*.
5. A man *with a long, white* beard walked slowly *over the lawn*.
6. The book *on the table* belongs *to me*.
7. The roses *by my window* bloom *in the spring*.
8. Heaven's light shone *on their path*.
9. The light *of heaven* shone *on their path*.
10. The light *of the sun* shone *through my window*.

Remark.—The prepositions *to, above, over, by, in, on,* and *through,* found in this lesson, do not occur in the previous one.

Direction.—Mention the word modified by each phrase in these ten sentences; mention the office of each phrase; the preposition and object in each, and the modifiers of the object. For the phrases in the first two sentences, substitute adjective *words*.

Explanation.—The preposition *on* (in 6) connects its object *table* with the noun *book*, and also shows the relation of *place* between them. The book is *on* the table—that is its *position*, or *place*. The preposition *to* (in sentence 3) shows the relation of *direction* between *hastened* and *Chicago*. In 9, *of* shows the relation of possession, and the phrase *of heaven* is used in place of the possessive noun *heaven's*.

359. The **possessive case** of a noun may often be more smoothly expressed by using the noun without the possessive sign, and placing the preposition *of* before it. *Socrates's death* is not so smooth an expression as *the death of Socrates.*

Direction.—Write five sentences containing nouns in the possessive case; then rewrite them and express possession by using the preposition *of* with an object. Define a phrase.

360. Definition.—**A prepositional phrase** is a group of words formed by a preposition and its object.

361. Definition.—**A preposition** is a connective word in a phrase showing the relation of its object to the word which the phrase modifies.

362. A preposition connects the principal word [object] in its phrase to the word which the phrase modifies, and also shows the relation existing between the words so connected.

In the sentence, "Roses grow in the garden," *in* shows the relation of *place* between *grow* and *garden.* The two words *grow* and *garden* in this sentence are called the *terms* of relation, *grow* being the *antecedent* term, and *garden* the *subsequent* term.

List of the Principal Prepositions.

aboard,	below,	for,	throughout,
about,	beneath,	from,	till,
above,	beside,	in,	to,
across,	besides,	into,	toward,
after,	between,	of,	towards,
against,	betwixt,	off,	under,
along,	beyond,	on,	underneath,
amid, amidst,	but (except),	over,	until,
among, amongst,	by,	past,	unto,
around,	concerning,	round,	up,
at,	down,	regarding,	upon,
athwart,	during,	save,	with,
before,	ere,	since,	within,
behind,	except,	through,	without.

Questions.—1. What is a phrase? 2. What is a prepositional phrase? 3. What is a preposition? 4. What twofold office does a preposition perform? 5. What is the *use* of a prepositional phrase in a sentence? 6. Of what is a prepositional phrase composed? 7. What is the principal word in a prepositional phrase? 8. What is the connective? 9. To what does a preposition connect its object? 10. Which term of relation is its object? 11. What is the other term of relation called? 12. What part of speech shows the relation existing between these two terms? 13. Can a single word be substituted for a phrase in every instance? 14. What relation does *on* show, in "The book lies *on* the table"? 15. In how many ways may possession be indicated in regard to a noun? 16. Which prepositions begin with *a, b, c, d, e, f, i, o, p, r, s, t, u, w*? 17. What other part of speech is a connective?

CI.—OFFICE OF PREPOSITIONAL PHRASES.

363. The word *prepositional* refers only to the *form* of a phrase; the **office** of a *prepositional phrase* is either **adverbial** or **adjective**.

364. A *prepositional phrase*, when it is *adverbial*, is not always placed next to the word that it modifies. It is sometimes placed after, and sometimes before it, and often it is considerably removed from it. A *prepositional phrase* performing an *adjective* office *stands next to its noun*.

Direction.—Determine whether the phrases in the following sentences are *adjective* or *adverbial* in office; then analyze each sentence according to the model given below:

1. The breath of autumn fell upon the woods.
2. The farmer should have hitched his horse to the stone post.
3. We have seen some beautiful flowers in this meadow.
4. The two boys carried the basket of apples between them.
5. In the spring the flowers will bloom.
6. John has caught a very large crab with a spear.
7. We took our light baggage with us.
8. James and John walked rapidly through the park.
9. We passed through Newark and Elizabeth.*
10. I took the book off the table.
11. The dingy walls of the rude sea-front gradually faded from our sight.

---

* A preposition may, like a verb, have a compound object.

Model for Analysis.

1. "A long train of cars passed slowly over a very high bridge."

365. This is a simple declarative sentence. The entire subject is "A long train of cars." The entire predicate is "passed slowly over a very high bridge." The simple subject *train* is modified by the adjectives *a* and *long*, and also by the prepositional phrase "of cars." The predicate-verb *passed* is modified by the adverb *slowly*, and also by the prepositional phrase "over a very high bridge." In the phrase "of cars" the principal word is the object *cars*. In the phrase "over a very high bridge," the principal word is the object *bridge*, which is modified by the adjectives *a* and *high*, and *high* is, itself, modified by the adverb *very*.

Questions.—1. Why are prepositional phrases used? 2. What two offices do they perform? 3. What is their position in a sentence? 4. What two offices does a preposition perform? 5. Name the two terms of relation connected by a preposition. 6. When is a phrase *adjective* in office? 7. When *adverbial*? 8. What is a prepositional phrase? 9. What is a preposition? 10. In what respect is a phrase *prepositional*? 11. In what respect is a phrase *adverbial*? 12. In what respect is it *adjective*? 13. Of what is a prepositional phrase composed? 14. What is analysis in grammar?

CII.—COMPOSITION LESSON.—SYNTHESIS.

366. Direction.—Combine the following statements into a simple sentence containing one subject, one verb, one object complement, and prepositional phrases:

>The captain stranded his vessel.
>He did so by his own carelessness.
>He stranded her on a sand-bar.
>It was in broad daylight.
>It was in sight of the harbor.

COMBINED.

The captain, by his own carelessness, stranded his vessel on a sand-bar, in broad daylight, in sight of the harbor.

Direction.—Combine the following statements into a simple sentence containing one subject, one verb, one object complement, and prepositional phrases:

ANALYSIS.—DIAGRAMMING. 121

The Rev. A. G. Spinner addressed a large audience.
He did so yesterday. He is a resident of this city.
He addressed the audience at Ocean Grove.
The address was on the moral phase of the temperance question.
Also on the religious and social phases of the question.

Direction.—Combine the following statements into a compound sentence, the first member containing five subjects and one verb, and the second containing one subject, one verb with an object, avoiding repetition.

The green ferns bloomed.
The green grasses bloomed.
The golden buttercup bloomed.
Tiny pearl-flowers bloomed.
Blue violets bloomed.
They bloomed beside the little stream.
The glad sunshine threw its mantle of blessing over one and all.

Direction.—Combine these statements into a simple sentence containing one subject, two verbs, each having one object, and arrange the phrases properly:

An unknown man fired a revolver.
He fired it at a telegraph operator.
This was done yesterday.
It happened in Atlanta.
Atlanta is in Georgia.
He slightly wounded the operator.

CIII.—MODELS FOR WRITTEN ANALYSIS.

367. 1. The flowers in the garden scatter their fragrance on the balmy air.

Class..................	Simple declarative.
Modified subject........	The flowers in the garden.
Predicate...............	Scatter their fragrance on the balmy air.
Simple subject..........	*Flowers*, mod. by adj. *the*, and the adj. phrase *in the garden*.
Predicate-verb..........	*Scatter*, modified by the adverbial phrase *on the balmy air*.
Object..................	*Fragrance*, modified by the poss. pronoun *their*.

9

ANALYSIS.—DIAGRAMMING.

2. The lucky fisherman caught a very fine lot of bass in the morning, but in the afternoon he did not get a single bite.

Class..................	Compound declarative.
First member...........	The lucky fisherman caught a very fine lot of bass in the morning.
Second member.........	In the afternoon he did not get a single bite.
Connective.............	**But.**
Simple sub., first mem...	*Fisherman*, mod. by the adj. *the* and *lucky*.
Predicate-verb..........	*Caught*, unmodified.
Object.................	*Lot*, mod. by adj. phrase *of bass*, and the adj. *fine*, which is, itself, mod. by adv. *very*.
Simple sub., second mem.	*He*, not modified.
Predicate-verb..........	*Did get*, mod. by adv. *not*, and adv. phrase *in the afternoon*.
Object.................	*Bite*, mod. by adj. *a* and *single*.

DIAGRAMS.

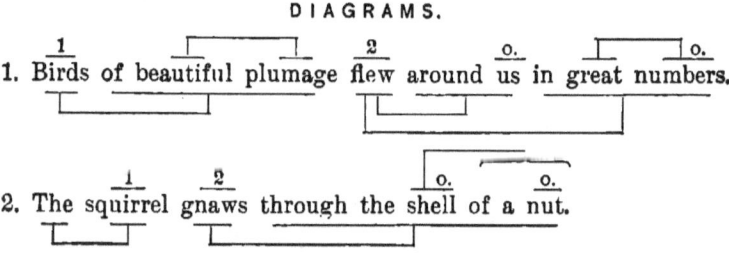

1. Birds of beautiful plumage flew around us in great numbers.

2. The squirrel gnaws through the shell of a nut.

Direction.—Use the following sentences as oral, and also as written, exercises in analysis; then use them for a lesson in diagramming:

1. The cork oak grows in large quantities in the Spanish peninsula.
2. The golden flowers of the dandelion shut up at night, and open again in the morning.
3. Squirrels and rabbits leaped along through the tall grass.
4. In my hurry, my foot slipped, and I fell to the ground.
5. This calm, cool, resolute man presented a noble example of courage to his comrades.

CIV.—ARRANGEMENT OF PHRASES.

368. Two or more adverbial phrases modifying the same word often occur in a sentence. When *more* than two such phrases occur in succession,* they are often separated from one another by the comma, to make the sense plain.

1. The party started for home in a terrible storm.
2. The ship stranded on the rocks, at daybreak, in a heavy fog.
3. A man of rank sat, on one cold night, in a small room, before a cheerful fire.

369. Comma Rule.—When more than two adverbial phrases occur in succession, they are generally separated from each other by a comma.

370. As a general rule, when more than two adverbial phrases occur in the same sentence, they should not all be strung together at the end, but they should be so distributed as to satisfy the ear and make the sense plain. Even when only two phrases occur, they are often distributed, as in 2, of the following sentences:

1. We shall start for California in the morning.
2. In the morning, we shall start for California.
3. On a clear day, the sun's rays shone through the window into the room.
4. We went from New York to Philadelphia in three hours.
5. With merry hearts, we wandered through the beautiful meadows.
6. Birds of beautiful plumage flew around us in great numbers.

Direction.—Select the prepositional phrases in the preceding sentences, and mention the word that each phrase modifies.

371. An adverbial phrase is out of its natural order, when it begins a sentence; when it stands between a verb and its subject; or between a verb and its object. [A *phrase* frequently stands between a verb and its object.]

372. Comma Rule.†—When a phrase is out of its natural order, it should be set off from the rest of the sentence by commas.

Direction.—Dictate the preceding, and also the following sentences as a lesson in punctuation. Analyze.

---

* Adverbial phrases occur simply in *succession* when one directly follows another, each modifying the same word.

† The tendency in modern usage seems to be to disregard this rule, except when it is necessary to prevent ambiguity or obscurity, or when the phrase is emphatic.

ARRANGEMENT OF PHRASES.

1. With weary feet, we began our homeward march.
2. We shall, in all probability, finish the work to-morrow.
3. Heaven, from all creatures, hides the book of fate.
4. In this life, we see many changes of fortune.

Questions.—1. Why is no comma used in 1, 4, and 6, of the first set of sentences [370]? 2. In which of the second set does a phrase stand between a subject and its verb? 3. Between a verb and its object? 4. In which sentences, in this lesson, do phrases occur in succession? 5. In which are they distributed? 6. In which does the phrase introduce the sentence?

CV.—ARRANGEMENT CONTINUED.

373. It is very important that phrases should be so arranged as to express most clearly and elegantly the sense intended to be conveyed. Sometimes a very ridiculous effect is produced by an improper arrangement.

Phrases improperly arranged.

1. A tailor made a coat for a boy of thick material.
2. An old man dug a deep well with a Roman nose.
3. A beautiful lady played on a piano with auburn hair.
4. A young man drove a flock of sheep on horseback yesterday.

Direction.—Arrange the preceding, and also the following, sentences so that the language will be smooth and the sense clear. Punctuate after arranging:

1. The youth strolled along the river in the evening at a very gentle pace in a pensive mood. 2. The Mayflower arrived on a stormy night with a hundred Pilgrims in the harbor. 3. Washington started through a trackless forest in mid-winter on his perilous journey. 4. General Proctor marched in May with two thousand men against the Americans. 5. The party started in a terrible storm on the next morning for home at daybreak.

374. The phrases in a sentence may sometimes be arranged in two or more ways. Sentence 5 may be arranged as follows:

1. On the next morning at daybreak, the party started for home in a terrible storm.

2. The party started for home on the next morning at daybreak, in a terrible storm.

Note.—The former of these two arrangements is preferable, as it avoids stringing the phrases all together at the end of the sentence.

Model for parsing Prepositions.

"The farmer built a fence around his field."

375. *Around* is a preposition connecting its object *field* with the verb *built*, and showing the relation between them.

Remark.—This form is chosen as it best satisfies both oral and written parsing. The following are used by other authors: 1. "Around is a preposition, and with its object *field* forms a phrase modifying the verb *built*." 2. "Around is a preposition introducing the phrase *around his field*, and connecting it with the verb *built*."

CVI.—PREPOSITIONS OMITTED.—ADVERBIAL OBJECTIVE. —INDIRECT OBJECT.

1. The party started for home *the next morning.*

Explanation.—In this sentence, *on* is omitted before the words in italics; the complete phrase is, "*on* the next morning." Such an omission is called an *ellipsis*, and the remaining part in italics is called an **elliptical phrase.**

376. An ellipsis of a preposition often occurs when the object of the phrase signifies *time, measure, distance, quantity, weight,* or *value*; as,

1. They went *home* on the morning train [*to* their home].
2. We staid a *week* at Saratoga [*for* a week].
3. We rode three *hours* through a beautiful valley [*for* three hours].
4. We walked two *miles* before breakfast [*over* the distance *of* two miles].
5. John jumped over a fence three *feet* high * [high *to* three feet].
6. I walked the *floor* all *night* [*over* the floor *during* all night].
7. We will start for California *to-morrow* [*on* to-morrow].
8. We saw him ten *times* that day.

---

* High is an adjective modifying *fence*, and *feet* is an adverbial objective modifying the adjective *high* [377].

377. The Adverbial Objective.—Each elliptical phrase in these eight sentences (as *home, a week, three hours*), performs the same *adverbial* office as the complete phrase; therefore the object in such a phrase (used either with or without a modifier), being a remnant of an *adverbial element*, is called the **adverbial objective**. This use of the elliptical form of a phrase is idiomatic, and (as in sentence 8) it is sometimes impossible to determine what preposition has been omitted; it is better, therefore, to consider the objects in these elliptical phrases as *adverbial objectives* modifying the verbs or adjectives with which they are used.

Note.—*To-morrow*, nearly always used without a preposition, is called simply an *adverb*, and the ellipsis need not be supplied in analysis and parsing. *To-day, to-night,* and *yesterday* are used in the same way.

378. The Indirect Object.—The verbs *give, show, make, bring, offer, forgive, promise, pay, ask, teach,* etc., often take two objects—one *direct*, and the other *indirect*. The *indirect* object is generally equivalent to a phrase, *to* or *for* being understood; as,

    1. The grocer gave *me** a ripe peach [gave *to* me].
    2. The tailor made *him* a coat [made *for* him].

Note.—This is another example of the adverbial objective, and it may be so considered; or the preposition may be supplied in analysis and parsing.

Direction.—Mention the *adverbial objective* in each of the following sentences; supply the ellipsis where it is possible; tell which adverbial objectives are indirect objects; determine what word each elliptical phrase modifies; analyze and parse.

    1. The postman brought me a letter. 2. We showed him the pictures. 3. We gave the horse oats, but he would not eat them. 4. The unfortunate man lived three days in great agony. 5. I paid him his wages. 6. Forgive your friends their faults. 7. The exhibition will close next Friday. 8. He had vast estates, north, south, east, and west. 9. They came home from the picnic in high glee.

---

    * A noun or a pronoun, used in this way, is sometimes called the *dative object*.

ELLIPTICAL PHRASES. 127

Questions.—1. Before what kind of objects are prepositions *not* expressed? 2. To what is the indirect object of a verb generally equivalent? 3. Why are *to-day, to-morrow,* and *yesterday* considered simply as adverbs? 4. Which is the indirect object in "They offered him a good position"? 5. What relation does *him*-hold in this sentence? 6. Give a sentence containing an *adverbial objective*, and tell why it is so called. 7. Give an example of an *indirect*, or *dative* object.

CVII.—LIKE, UNLIKE, NEAR, NIGH, AND OPPOSITE.

379. The preposition *to* or *unto* is generally omitted after the words *like, unlike, near, nigh,* and *opposite,* when they are adjectives or adverbs. *To* is generally omitted, also, before *home.*

380. Like and **unlike** are *adjectives* when used in a comparison of *things*; they are *adverbs* when used in a comparison of *acts.*

    1. We saw a bird somewhat *like* [to] the American eagle. [Things compared.]
    2. The great man wept *like* [unto] a child. [Acts compared.]

381. Near, nigh, and **opposite** are adjectives when position or place is merely *assumed*; they are adverbs when place is *asserted.*

    1. A house *near* the road afforded us shelter. [Position assumed.]
    2. We lived *near* the church. [Place asserted.]
    3. The old house *opposite* the church fell to the ground. [Position assumed.]
    4. They stood *opposite* the post-office. [Place asserted.]
    5. This man drives like Jehu.
    6. His house stands near the road.
    7. Do not come nigh me.
    8. She sings like a nightingale.
    9. My uncle lives near Lake George.

Note.—Some authors consider *near* and *nigh* to be *prepositions* directly followed by nouns and pronouns as objects.

Direction.—Select the prepositional phrases in the preceding sentences, supplying the omitted prepositions.

128 ELLIPTICAL PHRASES.

Questions.—1. After what adjectives or adverbs is *to* or *unto* omitted? 2. When are *like* and *unlike* adjectives? Adverbs? 3. When are *near* and *nigh* and *opposite* adjectives? 4. When are they adverbs? 5. What form of pronoun must follow a preposition? 6. What is omitted in the sentence, "We will go home to-morrow"?

CVIII.—OBJECTS OMITTED.

382. The *object* of a phrase is often omitted, only the preposition being retained. In such cases, the *preposition* is considered simply an *adverb* or an *adjective*—an *adverb* when the preposition is the remnant of an adverbial phrase—an *adjective* when it is the remnant of an adjective phrase. The ellipsis need not be supplied in analysis and parsing.

1. The carriage went *up* slowly [up *the hill*].
2. The wind scattered the leaves *around* [around *the lawn*].
3. We left the party *behind* [behind *us*].
4. They went *down* into the mine [down *the shaft*].
5. The stars *above* shone with unwonted splendor [above *us*].
6. The valley *below* rejoiced in sunshine and shower [below *us*].

Note.—*Above* and *below,* as here used, are generally called adjectives, without supplying the ellipsis.

Direction.—Detect the elliptical phrase in each of the following sentences; supply the ellipsis when a preposition is omitted; use the sentences for analysis and parsing:

1. Yesterday our shipmates again stopped for refreshments.
2. The dark and wondrous night came quickly on.
3. The poor old man leaned on his staff and tottered slowly along.
4. All day the rain poured in torrents.
5. We will attend the meeting to-morrow.
6. That eminent judge sat many years upon the bench.
7. A bad reputation stuck to him all his life.
8. His bad temper gave him much trouble.
9. The path near the river leads to the mill.
10. He might have come a shorter way.
11. He walks like his father.
12. He looks like his mother.
13. The house opposite the falls stands on solid rock.

COMPOUND PHRASES. 129

Review Questions.—1. What is an elliptical prepositional phrase? 2. What kind of nouns are often used as objects of omitted prepositions? 3. What verbs often take elliptical phrases after them? 4. When are *up, down,* and other prepositions called adverbs? 5. What are the rules for punctuating prepositional phrases? 6. How should more than two adverbial phrases occurring in a sentence be arranged? 7. What two offices do prepositional phrases perform? 8. In what sense is a phrase *prepositional? Adverbial? Adjective?* 9. What two terms of relation does a preposition have? 10. What ellipses need not be supplied in parsing and analysis?

CIX.—COMPOUND PHRASE.

1. Chestnut-trees grow *in these woods* and they grow *on yonder hill.*
2. Chestnut-trees grow *in these woods* and *on yonder hill.* [Condensed.]

Explanation.—In sentence 1, *and* connects two members of a compound sentence; but there is an unnecessary repetition of subject and verb, which is avoided in 2, by omitting this repetition, thus leaving *and* to connect the two phrases. *In these woods and on yonder hill,* taken as a whole, is a **compound phrase** which modifies the verb *grow.*

Questions.—1. What kind of sentence is 1? 2. What does *and* connect in 1? 3. What does *and* connect in 2? 4. What kind of phrase is found in 2?

383. Definition.—A **compound** phrase is one composed of two or more phrases connected by a conjunction.

Direction.—Select the phrases in the following sentences; tell whether they are simple or compound; and also tell what word each phrase modifies. Analyze each sentence and parse such words as may be deemed desirable:

1. The valleys rejoiced *in sunshine and in shower.* [Comp'd phrase.]
2. The valleys rejoiced *in sunshine* and *shower.* [Simple phrase, with compound object.]
3. Men of thought and men of action clear the way.
4. Men of experience and of practical wisdom generally succeed.
5. Very large trees fall to the ground with a great crash.
6. They hunted in the wood-shed and in the barn for eggs.

7. They fought with stone arrows and spears.
8. One day we suddenly came upon a fawn asleep.
9. The wild man of the woods ran like a deer.
10. The whole scene seemed like fairy-land.
11. A flock of wild geese flew directly* over our heads.
12. Undoubtedly,† the earth moves around the sun.

Model for Analysis.

384. The compound phrase in sentence 1 may be analyzed thus: *In sunshine and in shower* is a compound prepositional phrase consisting of two simple phrases connected by *and*. The principal word in the first phrase is *sunshine*; and in the second, *shower*.

Questions.—1. What is a compound phrase? 2. The phrase in 2, is simple with a compound object; what was omitted from 1, to make the phrase in 2, simple?

CX.—REVIEW.

In the preceding lessons we have learned the following facts:

385. A noun or a pronoun may be used as—

1. Subject of a verb: The *visitors* came, but *they* did not stay.
2. Object of a verb: We caught some *fish*, but we gave *them* away.
3. Object of a preposition: We waited for *them* in the *library*.
4. Modifier of a noun: *My* father found *Mary's* pet in the garden.

386. An adjective is used as—

1. Modifier of a noun: *Cold* air condenses vapor.
2. Modifier of a pronoun: Exercise made him *weary*.

387. A verb is used as—

1. The entire predicate of a sentence: The parrot *died*.
2. Principal part of the predicate: He *may have seen* him.

---

* The adverb *directly* modifies the adverbial phrase *over our heads*. The sense is not *flew directly*, but *directly over our heads*.

† In this sentence, *undoubtedly* is used rather to confirm the truth of the *whole statement* that follows it, than to refer simply to the act expressed by the word *moves*. [An adverb used in this way is called a *modal* adverb.]

388. An adverb may be used as—
1. Modifier of a verb: The wind blew *steadily*.
2. Modifier of an adjective: The angler caught a *very* fine trout.
3. Modifier of an adverb: We walked *too* rapidly.
4. Modifier of a phrase: We walked *almost* to the river.
5. Modifier of a sentence: *Certainly*, I shall go to-morrow.

389. A conjunction is used—
To connect words: The *thunder* **and** *lightning* frightened us.
To connect phrases: The valleys rejoiced *in sunshine* **and** *in shower*.
To connect sentences: *The thunder roared* **and** *the lightning flashed*.

390. A preposition is used—
1. To connect its object with another word: Fishes *live* in the *water*.

Remark.—We have learned, then, something about *seven* of the *eight parts of speech* into which the words of the language are assorted. There is one more class, called *interjections*, about which we shall learn as we progress.

Questions.—1. In how many ways may a noun or a pronoun be used in a sentence? 2. How many parts of speech may an adjective modify? 3. Name the five ways in which an adverb may be used. 4. In how many ways may a conjunction be used in a sentence?

CXI.—COMPLEX PHRASE.

391. Often two or more phrases occur in connection * without a conjunction, one growing out of or depending on another.
1. The merchant offered the position to an *industrious* man.
2. The merchant offered the position to a man *of industry*.

Explanation.—In sentence 2, the phrase "of industry" performs the same office as the adjective *industrious* in 1. "An *industrious* man" = "a man of *industry*"; therefore the adjective phrase "of industry" may be said to grow out of the adjective *industrious*.

---

* Simple phrases often occur in succession, each modifying some *word* in the sentence, not found in another phrase; as, "They passed through the gate into the garden." In this sentence each phrase modifies the verb passed. But one phrase often follows another, each succeeding phrase being *connected* with the object of the one preceding; as, "The bird fastened its nest to the branch of a tree." In this sentence the phrase *of a tree* modifies branch, and is connected with it by the preposition *of*.

COMPLEX PHRASES.

392. The phrase "to a man of industry" is composed of two phrases connected together by the preposition *of*, the second phrase modifying the object of the first phrase. These two phrases taken as a *whole* form a **complex phrase.** In this phrase "to a man of industry," the principal phrase is *to a man*, and *of industry* is the dependent phrase—*dependent* because it depends on, or modifies, the object of the principal phrase, in the sense of an adjective.

393. Definition.—A **complex prepositional phrase** is one composed of two or more phrases, each succeeding phrase modifying the object of the one preceding.

Direction.—Find in the following sentences *three* complex phrases; select the simple phrases and tell whether they are adjective or adverbial in use; mention the phrases that occur simply in succession. Analyze each sentence:

1. He dived to the bottom of the river for pebbles.
2. We waited in great anxiety for the morning.
3. He was sent to school at the age of eight years.
4. We rowed for the land with all speed.
5. The kite lodged among the branches of a large tree.
6. Ears of Indian corn hung in gay festoons along the wall.

Model for Analysis.

1. This shady path will lead us to the bend in the river.

394. This is a simple declarative sentence. The simple subject *path* is modified by the adjectives *this* and *shady*. The predicate-verb *will lead* is completed by the object complement *us*, and modified by the complex adverbial phrase *to the bend in the river*. The object *bend* in the *principal* phrase, is modified by the *dependent* adjective phrase *in the river*. [It is not necessary *always* to analyze the separate phrases.]

395. More than two phrases may occur in connection to form a complex phrase.

1. We passed through the grounds of a man of great wealth.
2. We staid for a week.at the house of our friend.
3. The lonely old man sat once more on the steps of the home of his childhood.
4. The captain loaded his vessel with a large cargo of oranges from the peninsula of Florida.

COMPOSITION. 133

Questions.—1. When do phrases occur in connection? 2. What is a compound phrase? 3. What is a complex phrase? 4. What is a dependent phrase? 5. What connects a dependent phrase with a principal phrase? 6. What connects the parts of a compound phrase? 7. Mention the *two* phrases in the sentence, "He dived to the bottom of the river for pebbles." 8. Which of the two phrases is complex? 9. Which is simple? 10. What word does it modify? 11. In the complex phrase, which of the phrases is dependent?

CXII.—SYNTHESIS.

(These exercises should not all be taken in one lesson.)

396. Direction.—Combine into a simple sentence containing one subject, one verb, and phrases properly arranged and punctuated:

The old clock stopped.
It stopped suddenly.
It was in the kitchen.
It stopped early in the morning.
It stopped without any cause of complaint.

Direction.—Combine into a simple sentence and arrange the phrases properly and punctuate:

The two brothers walked together.
They walked arm in arm.
It was in the cool of the evening.
They walked toward the landing.
The landing was at the foot of the hill.

Direction.—Combine into a simple sentence containing one subject, one verb, one object, with phrases properly arranged:

Mr. Cammeyer entertained the guests.
They were guests of a hotel.
It was the Argyll hotel.
It is situated at Babylon.
Babylon is on Long Island.
It was done on Tuesday.
He entertained them with artistic performances.
The performances were on the banjo.

Direction.—Combine the following statements into a simple sentence containing one subject, three verbs, *rushed*, *burst*, and *appeared*, and phrases properly set off by commas:

The fireman rushed up the stairs.
The stairs were burning.
He was cool.
He was fearless.
He burst into a room.
It was the room of the frantic woman.
He appeared on the roof.
He appeared in less than a minute.
He appeared with a child in his arms.

CXIII.—IDIOMS.—IDIOMATIC PHRASES.

397. Idioms.—An idiom is an expression peculiar to a language, not admitting of analysis in the usual way; as,

1. I had *rather* stay at home. [Rather = preferably, or in preference.]
2. He had *better* stay at home. [Better = more advantageously.]

These idiomatic expressions do not admit of satisfactory analysis. In a regularly constructed sentence an adverb may be omitted or transposed without *destroying* the sense; but if we omit the adverb *rather*, there will remain "I had stay at home," which is nonsense. Transposing *rather*, or its equivalent "in preference," we have "I had stay at home *in preference*,"* which is almost meaningless. Yet such expressions, as 1 and 2, are used by many of the best writers, and are defended by some grammarians.

398. Idiomatic Phrases.—The *phrases* in the following sentences, though apparently prepositional in form, are *idiomatic*. A few only are elliptical prepositional phrases; as, *at last*, which *may* be taken to mean *at the last moment*; but *in vain* does not mean *in a vain manner*, nor does *at once* mean *at one time*. All such *phrases*, therefore, are classed as **idiomatic phrases**, each being used as *one whole*, and equivalent to an *adjective* or an *adverb*; as,

1. They arrived *at last* [finally]. 2. He obeyed *at once* [promptly]. 3. He struggled manfully, but *in vain* [unsuccessfully]. 4. *Side by side* we walked along [together]. 5. They fought *hand to hand* [closely]. 6. They engaged in a *hand-to-hand* conflict [close—*adjective*]. 7. How we sang together in the good days *of old*! [ancient—*adjective*]. 8. He did not come *at all* [ever]. 9. The merry little minnows darted *to and fro* in the shallow pool.

399. Definition.—An idiomatic phrase is one that does not admit of analysis in the usual way, but is used (as *a whole*) as a modifying element.

---

* These expressions (sentences 1 and 2) are difficult (if not impossible) to analyze. Considering *stay* as an *infinitive* does not relieve the awkwardness nor restore the sense lost by the transposition of the adverbial modifier. Besides, "I had *to stay* at home in preference" does not at all express the sense of sentence 1. In all such expressions, *would* should take the place of *had*. "I *would* rather stay at home," "He *would* better stay at home."

Direction.—Analyze the nine preceding sentences, calling "at last," etc., *idiomatic phrases*.

400. Other Idiomatic Phrases.—At least; at first; at present; as yet; by and by; by the by; by the way; long ago; little by little; out and out; step by step; through and through; at random; at all; by far.

CXIV.—OTHER PREPOSITIONS.

401. A, meaning *at*, *on*, or *in*, is rarely used as a preposition, except before a participle and in business accounts; as,
  1. Toward evening we went *a*-fishing [at fishing].
  2. Bought 12 lbs. of sugar @ 6 cents [at 6 cents].

Note.—Such expressions as "went *a-fishing*" and "went *a-hunting*" are not now used by good writers.

402. *Excepting, concerning, respecting*, and *touching* are, by most authors, placed in the list of prepositions.

403. Phrase-Prepositions.—Two prepositions, taken together as one, may be called a *phrase-preposition*; as,
  1. The dog came *from under* the table.

These two words *may* be separately considered, and *from* be called a preposition having for its object the phrase "under the table"; as,
  2. The dog came **from** *under the table*.

An ellipsis *may* be supplied, thus giving each preposition a *word object*, and forming a complex phrase; as,
  3. The dog came from [a place] under the table.

404. Other Phrase-Prepositions.—According to; contrary to; as to; from beyond; from out; from over; from between; out of; over against; instead of; round about, etc.

Direction.—Supply a *phrase-preposition* for each blank space:
  1. They drew water —— this well.
  2. I have nothing to say —— his character.
  3. They proceeded —— my directions.
  4. They came —— Jordan.
  5. They came —— Judea.
  6. God had set one —— the other.

CXV.—PROPER USE OF PREPOSITIONS.

405. Beside, besides.—*Beside* means *by the side of.* "We sat *beside* the river." *Besides* means *in addition to.* "We found many beautiful specimens *besides* these." [*Besides*, in the sense of moreover, or beyond, is a conjunctive adverb (660). "We did not go, for want of time; *besides*, it rained."]

406. By, with.—*By* is used when a conscious *agent* is implied in the act. *With* is used when an *instrument* is implied; as,

1. The field was dug up *by* the *laborer* [agent] *with* a spade [instrument].
2. He was struck *by* a thunderbolt [agent].
3. Jupiter struck him *with* a thunderbolt [instrument].
4. We were attended [or accompanied] *by* friends [living beings].
5. The act was attended *with* disastrous results [things without life].

407. In, at.—*In* is larger in meaning than *at*; consequently, *in* is used before names of countries, cities, and large towns. *At* should be used before the names of villages, single houses, and foreign cities far distant; as,

1. He was educated *at* Yale college.
2. He lived *in* Brooklyn, but he died *at* Canton.
3. He spent his vacation *in* New Hampshire, *at* the village of Conway.

408. To, at.—*To* denotes motion or direction toward an object. *At* denotes nearness or presence in connection with mere locality; as,

1. He went to Boston.
2. They sailed to Charleston.
3. He staid at home.
4. We bought the goods at Stewart's.

409. In, into.—*Into* implies entrance, or motion, which *begins outside* of a place or thing, and *ends inside*. *In* implies *place where*, after entrance is made, or motion that *begins* and *ends* inside; as,

1. Mary went *into* the house.
2. She remained *in* the house during the afternoon.
3. He put the knife *into* his pocket.
4. The knife is in his pocket yet.
5. We went into the park.
6. We walked in the park a long time.
7. We went into the next room.
8. We remained in the room an hour.

Direction.—Dictate the eight preceding sentences, leaving out the prepositions, and require pupils to supply them.

USE OF PREPOSITIONS. 137

410. Of, for.—A taste *of* a thing implies actual enjoyment. A taste *for* a thing implies a capacity for enjoyment.

411. Of, in.—We are disappointed *of* a thing when we fail to get it. We are disappointed *in* a thing when we have it and it does not satisfy our expectation.

412. From, to, with.—We say, "different *from*," not "different *to* or *than*." We say, "I differ *with* you in opinion." One *thing* differs *from* another in appearance.

413. To, for.—A person or thing is adapted *to* any purpose or use, not adapted *for*. Adequate *to*, or equal *to*, a task—not *for*.

414. With, to.—We compare one thing *with* another in regard to quality or quantity. We compare one thing *to* another for the sake of illustration. We accord a privilege *to*, and are in accord *with*, a person. A man's actions correspond [are consistent] *with* his professions; but a man may use a word that does not correspond *to* his idea [not suitable]. A man may say a word suited *to* the occasion; and may be well suited *with* his circumstances.

415. Between, among.—We divide anything *between* two persons —*among* three or more.

416. In, to.—We confide *in* a person with reference to his general character. We confide a matter *to* a person for safe-keeping.

417. Of, with.—We accuse a person *of* a crime, not *with* a crime. We charge a person *with* an act, not *of* an act.

418. But, for, since.—These and a few other prepositions are also used as conjunctions; as,

1. I have not seen him *since* last Christmas. [Preposition.]
2. I will not attempt it, *since* I can not do it well. [Conjunction.]
3. They made a collection *for* the poor. [Preposition.]
4. I must go, *for* it is late. [Conjunction.]
5. All *but* him had finished. [Preposition.]
6. We tried, *but* we did not succeed. [Conjunction.]

Direction.—Fill the blank spaces in the following sentences with the proper prepositions:

1. He poured ink —— the inkstand. 2. We went —— the country. 3. The Delaware River empties —— the Delaware Bay. 4. The wheat was cut —— a machine. 5. The field was won —— hard fighting. 6. We saw you —— the concert. 7. We stopped —— Ovington's. 8. He accused me —— stealing his knife. 9. My book is different —— yours.

10

CXVI.—USE OF PREPOSITIONS, ETC.

419. Direction.—Supply the proper prepositions in the blank spaces in the following sentences:
1. We walked out —— a slippery morning. 2. They live —— Philadelphia —— a hotel. 3. Very little grows on this soil —— the cactus. 4. The careless boy left his book —— home. 5. They accused him —— neglecting his duty. 6. Received, New York, Jan. 1, 1886, —— Mr. James, $25. 7. The soil is adapted —— cotton and rice. 8. You may rely —— what I say, and confide —— his honesty. 9. I am tall in comparison —— you. 10. He put the knife —— his pocket. 11. They have nice goods —— the new store. 12. The boy fell —— the river from a narrow bridge. 13. My family will spend the summer —— the Catskills, —— the village of Windham. 14. The man, living on yonder hill, abounds —— wealth. 15. This mountain lake abounds —— fish. 16. He was injured —— an explosion of gunpowder. 17. The unfortunate man died —— small-pox. 18. The excessive heat of the afternoon was followed —— a thunder-shower. 19. This circumstance has no resemblance —— the other. 20. This is a very different machine —— the one we saw yesterday. 21. We remained —— the south —— a little village. 22. There is no need —— so much preparation.

Unnecessary Use of Prepositions and Adverbs.

420. 1. Give me both *of* those books. 2. He got on *to* the stage. 3. They ascended *up* the hill. 4. They returned *back* from the concert. 5. They advanced *forward*. 6. I cut this silk off *of* the large piece. 7. He knows more than you think *for*. 8. The spring is near *to* the house. 9. What went ye out *for* to see?

Improper Omission of Prepositions.

421. 1. I put some apples into the basket and [ ] my hat. 2. The statement is worthy [ ] your notice. 3. Such a man is unworthy [ ] respect. 4. The rod is [ ] seven to nine feet long. 5. There is no use [ ] arguing about it. 6. There is nothing to prevent him [ ] going.

422. Prepositions used as Adjectives.—1. We will take the *down* train. 2. His name will live in *after* ages. 3. The *above* illustration is sufficient. 4. Men generally sympathize with the *under* dog.

Unthought-of; unsought-for; uncared-for; unheard-of, are compound adjectives having prepositions as suffixes.

CXVII.—WORDS FREQUENTLY MISUSED.

423. A few words in common use are frequently misused, especially in conversation.

424. Like, love.—*Like* means, *to be pleased with to a moderate degree.* *Love* means, *to be delighted with*; to have an affection for, or an attachment to, some person or object.

We *like* good food; fun; the country; flowers; pictures; any pleasure or recreation; or people who *simply please* us.

We *love* our parents or companions; our home or country; truth and honor.

Direction.—Fill the blank spaces properly in the following sentences:
1. Some children —— to go to school.
2. The true soldier —— his country.
3. I —— the lady to whom you introduced me yesterday.
4. Some pupils —— to study arithmetic.
5. Some people —— to dance.

425. Get.—*Get* means *to obtain by one's own effort.*

A person may *get property*; may *get into difficulty*; may *get a lesson*; may *get to Boston*; may *get to bed*; may *get up*; may *get over*; may *get off*.

Get may be used in the sense of *become* without losing the idea of effort. A person may *get angry*; may *get wet* or *get sick* [by exposure]; may *get well*; may *get strong*.

Get should *not* be used to express what comes to a person unavoidably; nor to express *necessity, obligation*, or *mere possession.* We should not say, "He has *got* the measles"; "The mouse *got* caught in a trap"; "I have *got* to go to Chicago"; "I have *got* to do my duty"; "I have *got* to get another coat"; "I have *got* a fine piano"; "He hasn't *got* any money." Say, "He *has* the measles"; *mouse was caught*; *must go* to Chicago; *should do* my duty; *have* a piano, etc.

426. Stop, stay.—To *stop* means to cease moving. To *stay* means *to remain* an indefinite length of time after *stopping* at a place; as,

1. On our way to New York we *stopped* at Chicago, where we *staid* a week.

Direction.—Supply the proper form of *stop* or *stay* in each of the following sentences:

1. We are now —— at the Delavan House.
2. They —— overnight at Cincinnati.
3. How long will the train —— for refreshments?
4. We bought a —— ticket.

Direction.—Supply a verb and a preposition for each of the following sentences:

1. With whom did you —— —— Baltimore?
2. At what station did you —— —— refreshments?
3. At what hotel did you —— —— New Orleans?
4. Why did you not —— overnight —— Boston?
5. Why did you not —— longer —— San Francisco?

427. Like, unlike, etc.—Some consider *like* and *unlike*, etc., to have the value of prepositions in such sentences as, "He walks *like* his father"; "This boy, *unlike* his brother, often gets into trouble." Most authors, however, prefer to call them adjectives or adverbs, and supply *to* or *unto* as the governing word.

Like must not be followed by a noun or pronoun in the nominative case; as, "He does not walk *like* I do." [Say, "walk *as*," etc.]

CXVIII.—ANALYSIS AND PARSING.

428. Direction.—Examine carefully the following sentences, determine where commas should be placed, and give reasons. Write from dictation and punctuate. Analyze and parse.

Sentences for Punctuation, Analysis, and Parsing.

1. The beautiful fern lies in rusty patches on the open hill-side
2. Fishes swim in the sea and birds fly in the air
3. Do you know the way to the top of the mountain
4. The lawn in front extends to the river
5. The thief crept into the house through a very small window and stole a valuable set of jewelry
6. Suddenly out sprang a beautiful fawn
7. Mark Haley's breast the storm defies
8. "Night drew her sable curtain down
    And pinned it with a star"

9. The geraniums of California grow to a very large size and they sometimes form hedges for gardens
10. A flock of blackbirds flew directly over our heads
11. I urged him strongly but he declined my invitation with thanks
12. We sigh for change and spend our time for naught
13. In the evening we rode home through darkness and storm
14. Which path will lead us to the bend in the river
15. Misfortune makes some people very gloomy
16. That venturesome sailor swam a mile out to sea
17. "In silence majestic they twinkle on high
    And draw admiration from every eye"
18. The wind blew all day with violence from the north
19. Fruit in air-tight jars will keep several years in good order
20. That industrious young man succeeded beyond his expectations
21. With haughty steps the boisterous actor strode across the stage
22. "On prey intent the wily foe
    Approached with cautious steps and slow"
23. A few well-directed efforts frequently produce great changes in the events of a man's life
24. They rowed the boat across the pond and up the stream
25. Often two or three wild deer came with the tame fawn, almost to the edge of the wood but they never ventured fairly out of the forest

CXIX.—AGREEMENT OF VERB WITH SUBJECT.

429. Care should be taken not to let the ear be deceived into allowing the verb to agree in number with the object of a preposition; as,

1. This book of poems *affords* me much pleasure. [Not *afford.*]

Direction.—Determine which of the two words in the brackets is the correct one, in each of the following sentences, and give the reason for your decision:

1. A variety of pleasing objects [charms or charm] the eye.
2. Fifty pounds of wheat [contains or contain] forty pounds of flour.
3. Not one of my neighbor's sons [has or have] succeeded in business.
4. A cargo of fine oranges [have or has] just arrived from Florida.
5. There [goes or go] my neighbor and her daughter.
6. Large quantities of rice [comes or come] from South Carolina.
7. Time and tide [waits or wait] for no man.

8. [Has or have] the goods arrived in good condition?
9. There [comes or come] father and mother.
10. The regiment [consists or consist] of a thousand men.
11. A great variety of flowers [make or makes] a garden beautiful.
12. This great orator and statesman [deserve or deserves] great honor.
13. A bushel of handsome pears [were or was] taken from one tree.
14. The number of inhabitants [do or does] not exceed two thousand.

430. The word *number*, followed by *of* having a plural object, requires a plural verb; as, A *number* of persons *have* arrived. But *number* preceded by *the* takes a singular verb [see sentence 14, above]. The words *variety, abundance,* and *plenty* follow the same rule [see sentences 1 and 11].

CXX.—INTERMEDIATE EXPRESSIONS.—PUNCTUATION.

1. The rest of the family, *however*, came in the afternoon.
2. I did not tell you, *by the way*, of our dangerous adventure.
3. His conduct, *according to his own account*, was inexcusable.

Explanation.—In sentence 1, *however* is thrown in between the subject and its verb, thus making a slight break in the sentence; it is, therefore, set off by commas. Sentences 2 and 3 are broken into in the same way.

431. Such expressions as *however, therefore, indeed, in truth, by the way,* etc., are frequently *thrown in between* the parts of a sentence, and they are, therefore, called **intermediate expressions**. Having little or no modifying force, they may properly be called *independent*.

432. Comma Rule.—All intermediate expressions should be set off by commas.

Direction.—Select the intermediate expressions in the following sentences, and tell where commas should be placed:

1. All our duties indeed required much thought.
2. Our baggage therefore came on the next train.
3. This by the way we could not easily accomplish.
4. The boys perhaps are better prepared.
5. He did not know however that we were coming.
6. The whole town in fact took part in the celebration.

ABBREVIATED SENTENCES. 143

433. Direction.—Complete the following sentences by inserting a single word [verb] in its correct form in 1 to 6 inclusive, an adjective in 7, and the correct form of the relative *who* in the last:

1. Great pains —— taken with his education.
2. He or his brother —— the book.
3. Neither he nor his brother —— wealthy.
4. The committee —— unanimous in their opinion.
5. Neither he nor I —— frightened.
6. The weight of the boxes —— so great that it excited suspicion.
7. That house is the —— of the three.
8. They were not the men —— we saw yesterday.

Note.—In sentence 8, the word to be supplied is the complement of the verb *saw*. The sentences in this lesson should not be used for analysis and parsing.

CXXI.—ABBREVIATED COMPOUNDS.—PUNCTUATION.

434. Language is made elliptical by condensation; therefore a proper understanding of the construction of sentences as we find them, depends on the ability to detect ellipses and to supply them.

435. It is shown [147-151] that disagreeable repetition is avoided by condensation; as,

1. *Oxen* and *horses* eat hay.
2. The sun *rises* and *sets*.
3. The farmer raises *rye* and *wheat*.
4. The girls wrote slowly and neatly.
5. Idle and extravagant people do not prosper.

436. We have also learned that prepositional phrases may be connected by conjunctions; as,

1. We walked *up the street* and *over the bridge*.
2. She dresses *richly* and *in good taste*.

Note.—In sentence 2, *and* connects two *adverbial elements*—an adverbial word *richly* to an adverbial phrase *in good taste*.

437. A conjunction is used to connect similar parts, or elements, in a sentence; i. e., two nouns or pronouns; two adjectives; two verbs; two adverbs; two phrases; a word and a phrase performing the same office [sentence 2, 436].

438. When more than two words of the same part of speech are connected there is still an unpleasant repetition; as,

1. Oxen *and* sheep *and* horses eat hay.
2. The boat tilted *and* filled *and* sank.
3. A little girl bought a large *and* ripe *and* juicy peach.

This repetition is avoided by omitting all the conjunctions, or all but the last, and using a comma for each omission; as,

1. Oxen, sheep, and horses eat hay.
2. The boat tilted, filled, and sank.
3. A little girl bought a large, ripe, juicy peach.

CXXII.—SERIES OF WORDS.—PUNCTUATION.

439. A succession of three or more words of the same part of speech, or a succession of similar phrases, is called a *series*; as,

1. Empires rise and flourish and decay.
2. Empires rise, flourish, and decay.
3. The farmer raises wheat, oats, and corn.
4. A wide, smooth, shady path led to the river.
5. Our soldiers fought long, bravely, and successfully.
6. John, William, Henry, and Joseph formed the party.
7. Through spring, summer, and autumn, we have a constant succession of flowers.
8. He had a good mind, a sound judgment, and a vivid imagination.
9. Cotton grows in Brazil, in Egypt, in India, and in the United States.
10. Our army went into winter quarters, the enemy crossed the river, and hostilities ceased for a time.

Explanation.—Sentence 9 contains a series of phrases; sentence 10, a succession of members that should be separated by commas. In 1, no conjunction is omitted, therefore no comma is required. In 4, the conjunctions are all omitted, and a comma properly supplies the place of each omission. In the other sentences, the conjunction is retained between the last two of each series, and a comma is inserted before the conjunction.

440. Comma Rule.—When the conjunction is omitted from a series of words or phrases, a comma must be used to denote each omission:

SERIES OF WORDS.—PUNCTUATION. 145

(1) When the conjunction is retained between the last two words of the series, a comma is also inserted before the conjunction [439, 2, 3, 5].

(2) A comma is used between *two* words of the same part of speech when the conjunction is omitted, and sometimes between two sentences; as,

1. The stern and rigid Puritans worshiped here.
2. The stern, rigid Puritans worshiped here.
3. Crack went the whip, round went the wheels.

(3) When no conjunction joins the last two words of a series forming a compound subject or a compound predicate, a comma should *follow* the *last word* also; as,

1. The sun, the moon, the stars, revolve.
2. Charity beareth, believeth, hopeth, all things.

Direction.—Dictate the sentences to be written as a lesson in punctuation. Use them for analysis and parsing.

(4) When no conjunction connects the last two of a series of adjectives standing *before a noun*, a comma should not separate the last adjective from its noun; but when the series directly follows the noun, a comma is used to separate the noun from the nearest adjective; as,

1. This brave, loyal, patriotic man died in his country's defense.
2. We bought some Florida oranges, large, ripe, and sweet.

(5) When a series is composed of adjectives, and each preceding adjective modifies the others in combination with the noun, as *one whole*, no comma is required; as,

1. That wealthy man drives a beautiful white horse.
2. That unfortunate old blind man fell into the river.
3. An industrious young mechanic planned and built the house.

Explanation.—In sentence 1, no comma should separate *beautiful* and *white*. The idea expressed by *beautiful* does not reside in the horse *apart* from his color, but in connection with it; beautiful, therefore, modifies *white horse*, as though written *white-horse*. In 2, *that* modifies "unfortunate old blind man," *unfortunate* modifies "old blind man," and *old* modifies "blind man," and no commas are required to separate the adjectives.

(6) Sometimes, to make the sense more emphatic, the conjunction is not omitted in a series; no commas are then required unless the series is composed of adjectives each of which is emphatic; as,

1. All beauty and wisdom and power reside in the Creator.
2. They were poor, and hungry, and cold, and friendless.

441. Comma Rule.—When a series consists of pairs of words or of phrases, a comma should be used after each pair; as,

1. Anarchy and confusion, poverty and distress, desolation and ruin, follow a civil war.
2. Cotton grows in Egypt and in India, in Brazil and in the United States.

Questions.—1. Why are sentences abbreviated, or condensed? 2. What parts of a simple sentence does a conjunction connect? 3. Can a conjunction connect a word and a phrase? 4. What is a *series* of words or phrases, and from what does it arise? 5. Should a comma be used in a series when the conjunction is not omitted? 6. When should a comma be used between *two* words of the same part of speech? 7. What rules are given for the punctuation of a series of words or phrases? 8. When should a comma be placed *after* the last word of a series? 9. What is the rule for using the comma in case of pairs of words or of phrases? 10. When should no comma be used in a series of adjectives having no connective?

CXXIII.—OTHER RULES FOR THE COMMA.

442. Comma Rule.—The omission of a verb in a member of a compound sentence should be denoted by a comma; as,

1. Labor brings pleasure, but idleness brings pain.
2. Labor brings pleasure; idleness, pain.

443. Comma Rule.—When a number of phrases are arranged out of their natural order, they should be set off by commas; as,

1. Upon the stairs, a tall, grim clock, with long hands and hungry face, ticked in cautious measure.

444. Comma Rule.—A comma is placed after a *surname* when written before the *given name*; as, Garfield, James A.

445. Comma Rule.—Words repeated should be separated from each other, and from the rest of the sentence, by the comma; as,

1. Treason, treason, treason, re-echoed from every part of the house.

446. Comma Rule.—A comma should be used whenever the sense would not be clear without it; as,

1. He has four yoke of oxen, and horses.
2. They landed, and killed a hundred Indians.

Note.—In sentence 1, if the comma be omitted, the sense would seem to be, " He has two yoke of oxen and two yoke of horses." But the term *yoke* does not apply to *horses*; we speak of a *span* of horses, and a *yoke* of oxen. In 2, without the comma the sense might seem to be, that they landed the Indians and then killed them.

447. Direction.—Punctuate the following sentences by using commas where they properly belong, giving reasons in each case; then use the sentences for a lesson in analysis and parsing.

Sentences for Punctuation and Analysis.

1. We should seek truth steadily patiently and perseveringly. 2. The little minstrel sang a song played a tune and danced a jig. 3. The contractor graded leveled and paved the street 4. Hope and fear pleasure and pain diversify our lives 5. No no no you can not go. 6. A youth a boy or a mere child could answer that question. 7. He left his wife his children his mansion and his titles. 8. Every afternoon the clouds rolled up and the sky grew black. 9. Indolence produces poverty; and poverty misery. 10. Sink or swim live or die I give my heart and hand to this vote. 11. The horse reared and threw his rider. 12. I have a house with twelve rooms and out-buildings. 13. Séramis built Babylon; Dido Carthage; and Romulus Rome. 14. The troops landed and killed a hundred Indians. 15. By industry and perseverance we obtain the knowledge necessary for a useful life. 16. We may find tongues in trees books in the running brooks sermons in stones and good in everything. 17. Just before us on the side of the bank there nestled an old stone mill. 18. Three soft white mice lay in the old woolen hat. 19. Fine weather good sleighing and a fleet horse made the journey short. 20. The sick child called for water water water continually. 21. He will come to-day tomorrow or next week to remain two months. 22. For eighteen months without intermission this destruction raged from the gates of Madras to the gates of Tanjore. 23. Far above us towered an iron-bound coast dark desolate barren and precipitous. 24. There mountains rise and circling oceans flow. 25. The sweet soft voice the light step the delicate hand the quiet noiseless discharge of those thousand little offices of kindness add greatly to the comfort of the sick. 26. A deep calm broad river rolled through the meadow-land and past forest field and hill and happy human homes.

CXXIV.—USES OF ARTICLES.—CONNECTED ADJECTIVES.

448. When two adjectives are connected by a conjunction, care should be taken that they both properly describe the following noun, or that some word shall precede them to indicate that the former adjective belongs to some noun understood.

449. Two connected adjectives, neither of which is preceded by an article or by the adjective *both*, should relate to the same noun; as,

    1. I bought some black and white ribbon [checkered].
    2. The farmer planted early and late potatoes [incorrect].

Explanation.—The potatoes mentioned in sentence 2 could not be both early and late; there were *two* kinds. The sentence should be, "The farmer planted early potatoes and late potatoes"; or, better, "The farmer planted both early and late potatoes."

450. When two or more adjectives are used in connection, each modifying the name of the same thing, an article should be used before the first adjective only; as,

    1. I have a black and white dog [one dog, spotted].
    2. I have a red, white, and blue flag [one flag].

451. But when two or more adjectives are used in connection, each modifying the name of a *different* thing, the article is repeated with each adjective; as,

    1. I have an old and a new hat [two hats].
    2. I have a red, a white, and a blue flag [three flags].

Explanation.—In sentence 1, *hat* is understood after *old*; and, in 2, *flag* is understood after each of the adjectives *red* and *white*.

Questions.—1. When is it correct to say, "I have a blue and white scarf"? 2. Is it correct to say, "He carried a long and short rod"? "We have some sweet and sour oranges"? 3. When must an article be used before only the first of two or more connected adjectives? 4. When, before each of two or more connected adjectives? 5. Why is "I met a tall and short lady" incorrect?

Direction.—As a review, dictate all the sentences in this lesson as an exercise in punctuation, and in the use of articles.

CXXV.—USES OF ARTICLES.—CONNECTED NOUNS.

452. The is used to refer to some *particular* thing or things; as, "*The sun* rises in *the east*"; "*The stars* sometimes shine brightly"; "*The house* on *the hill* faces *the south*." *The* is used before a singular common noun to distinguish the *class* without referring to any particular one; as, "*The oak* comes from *the acorn*"; "*The horse* has great strength." *The* is used before an adjective of the comparative degree to intensify its meaning; as, "*The higher* we climb, *the farther* we can see." Used in this way, *the* is an *adverb*.

453. Article repeated.—The article should be repeated before two nouns connected by *or* or *nor*; as,
1. Either *the* owner or *the* tenant must pay the water-tax.
2. He paid neither *the* principal nor *the* interest.
3. Neither the judge nor the jury could refrain from laughter.
4. *Which* may represent an animal or a thing.

454. The article should be repeated before each of the particulars included in a class; as, "Nouns have three cases—*the* nominative, *the* possessive, and *the* objective."

455. When the first of several connected nouns takes an article, it should generally be repeated with each of the others, and it *must* be repeated when the same form of the article is not applicable to all; as,
1. *A* man, *a* boy, and *a* horse received severe injuries.
2. *The* oak, *the* pine, and *the* ash abound in this forest.
3. *An* oak, *a* pine, and *an* ash shade the lawn.
4. *A* horse, *an* ox, and *a* calf graze in the same field.
5. I have just sold a house and a lot [separate property].
6. I have just sold a house and lot [taken together].
7. A man, woman, and child stood by the river [allowable].
8. The men, women, and children suffered alike [allowable].

Note.—In sentence 1, it is presumable that the individuals mentioned were taken separately; i. e., they were not of the same party. The article is repeated to make the sense clear. In 7 and 8, it is presumable that the individuals mentioned were considered as belonging to *one party*. In such cases, for the sake of brevity, the custom is to omit the article before all but the first when the sense will be clear without it.

456. Article omitted.—The article is omitted before *proper* nouns, *abstract* nouns, and the *names* of the *arts* and *sciences*, and *other nouns* when used in such general or unlimited sense as not to require it; as,

1. *Virtue* seeks no reward.
2. *Botany* treats of plants.
3. *Anger* resteth in the bosom of fools.
4. *Gold* abounds in Colorado.
5. *Orthography* treats of the forms of *letters* and *words*.
6. Use essence of peppermint [not *the* essence].
7. He has rheumatism [not *the* rheumatism].
8. He died of cholera [not *the* cholera].
9. I never saw that kind of bird before [not kind of *a* bird].
10. What kind of element is an adverb [not kind of *an* element]?
11. We saw a strange kind of insect [not kind of *an* insect].
12. He made some sort of promise [not sort of *a* promise].

Note.—*The* is used before *plural* proper nouns. *The* is also used before singular proper nouns for the sake of emphasis or discrimination, and when it precedes an adjective denoting eminence; as, "You have read of the twelve Cæsars"; "The Browns called last evening"; "The Ohio empties into the Mississippi"; "The immortal Washington lives in the hearts of his countrymen."

Direction.—Insert *the, an, a,* or *both* in the following sentences where it is necessary to make the sense clear, and give the reason for each insertion:

1. He carried large and small basket. 2. I like sweet and sour cherries. 3. This scholar has active and energetic mind. 4. *Congeal* contains long and short vowel sound. 5. We have now learned present, past, and future tenses. 6. I have black and white dog. 7. The farmer sold his large and small potatoes. 8. Where did you get that kind of melon? 9. We have learned about definite and indefinite article. 10. We have learned about definite and indefinite articles. 11. We found hot and cold spring about twenty feet apart. 12. We found a new kind of flower in the woods.

Questions.—1. What is the use of *the* in "The more he ate the fatter he grew"? 2. For what is *the* used in "The apple is a wholesome fruit"? 3. Give the two instances when the article should be repeated before connected nouns. 4. When should an article be omitted before a noun? 5. Why may we not say, "A short and tall gentleman sat in the seat beside us"?

CXXVI.—ARRANGEMENT OF ADJECTIVES.

457. In arranging two or more adjectives in a series, regard must be had to the sound. They should generally be placed in order of length—the shortest farthest from the noun if they precede it, but nearest, if they follow it; as,

1. This proud, ambitious man gave a costly entertainment.
2. That strong, manly, courageous youth won an honorable name.
3. A tall, handsome, attractive lady gracefully entered the room.
4. The whole party, weary and disheartened, returned home.

458. When one adjective of a series unites with the noun more closely in sense than the others, it should stand next to the noun without regard to the length—a descriptive nearer than a limiting adjective; as,

1. That wealthy merchant drives a beautiful *white* horse.
2. An ugly pet dog bit that unfortunate old *blind* man.
3. Many thoughtless, inconsiderate *young* men spend money foolishly.
4. The company erected an expensive *wooden* building.

459. The adjectives that most frequently unite closely in sense with their nouns are those indicating *age, color, use, infirmity,* and the *materials* of which things are made, these ranking in closeness of relation in the order here given—the last bearing the closest relation. These adjectives denote qualities that are inseparable from the things they describe, and when used with their nouns they often suggest a compound term. We say, "Please to pass the *bread basket* [bread-basket]. Also, the idea of color can not be separated from the thing possessing the color. In the sentence—

He drove a beautiful *white horse,*

the words *white horse* suggest an *animal* in the same way that the words *black man* suggest a *negro*. It is plain, therefore, that *beautiful* does not modify the noun *horse* only, but the whole idea contained in the term *white horse.* In the sentence—

An ugly pet dog bit that unfortunate old blind man,

the adjective *ugly* modifies *pet dog,* and *pet* modifies *dog; that* modifies *unfortunate old blind man; unfortunate* modifies *old blind man; old* modifies *blind man; blind* modifies *man.* In a succession of adjectives like this, each of which modifies the following adjectives taken with the noun, as *one whole,* commas are not required, no conjunction being omitted.

ARRANGEMENT OF ADJECTIVES.

These adjectives do not indicate *distinct* qualities, as do adjectives that are connected by a conjunction [440, 5].

Direction.—Examine each of the following sentences, and determine which adjectives indicate *age, color, use, infirmity,* or *materials*. Give reasons for the arrangement of the adjectives, and also for the *use* of commas, or for their *omission* when two or more adjectives are used in succession:

1. A careless expressman broke that beautiful marble statue.
2. That poor, industrious old blind man makes good baskets.
3. Fragrant red roses scented the room.
4. That brave, noble, patriotic man bears an excellent reputation.
5. Large feathery snow-flakes filled the air.
6. Large yellow pumpkins covered the ground.

Direction.—Re-write the following sentences, arrange the adjectives properly, and punctuate; give reasons for arrangement and punctuation:

1. We like little pretty flowers.
2. The cartman sold a black blind old horse.
3. Red beautiful apples covered the ground.
4. The society erected a marble costly new fountain.
5. The wooden old yellow building tumbled down.
6. Mary found a silk lady's black glove.

Direction.—Form sentences, using the following adjectives properly arranged before the nouns with which they are connected. Give reasons for the arrangement and punctuation:

1. { Swiss, ten / gold, small } watches.   3. { Round, ten / wooden, small } tables.
2. { Red, sweet / small, some } apples.   4. { Wooden, new / white, handsome } cottage.

Sentences for Punctuation and Analysis.

460. 1. The rain waters the fields and farms, fills the streams, rivers, and lakes, and furnishes drink for men and cattle, and all creatures on the earth. 2. The earth moves around the sun and the moon moves around the earth. 3. On this march, we traversed almost the whole circuit of the hills around Jerusalem. 4. The largest and the most delicious fruits grow on the most thrifty trees. 5. The poor and the rich, the weak and the strong, the young and the old, have one common Father.

CXXVII.—REGULAR AND IRREGULAR VERBS.

461. Besides the present and past *tense-forms*, there belong to a verb *two other forms* that are *not real verbs* because neither of them alone can be used with a subject to make an assertion. These forms are called *participles*.

Regular Verbs.

PRESENT TENSE.	PAST TENSE.	PRESENT PARTICIPLE.	PAST PARTICIPLE.
Wish,	wished,	wishing,	wished.
Peel,	peeled,	peeling,	peeled.
Reap,	reaped,	reaping,	reaped.
Slip,	slipped,	slipping,	slipped.

Irregular Verbs.

PRESENT TENSE.	PAST TENSE.	PRESENT PARTICIPLE.	PAST PARTICIPLE.
Arise,*	arose,	arising,	arisen.
Break,	broke,	breaking,	broken.
Begin,	began,	beginning,	begun.
Be, or am,	was,	being,	been.
Choose,	chose,	choosing,	chosen.
Come,	came,	coming,	come.
Do,	did,	doing,	done.
Eat,	ate,	eating,	eaten.
Give,	gave,	giving,	given.
Have,	had,	having,	had.
Know,	knew,	knowing,	known.
See,	saw,	seeing,	seen.

462. The present participle is so called because it represents an act as *going on* at the time referred to by the predicate-verb in the sentence. It is **always** formed by adding **ing** to the *verb-root*.

463. The past participle is so called because it represents an act as *finished* at the time referred to. This participle (as well as the past tense) is variously formed; as, arisen, eaten, chosen, done, by adding **n**, **en**, or **ne** either with or without change of vowels; or it is formed by simply changing a vowel in the *verb-root*; as, begun, from begin.

---

* For complete list of irregular verbs, see [764].

154 VERBS—REGULAR AND IRREGULAR.

The verbs in the first list are called **regular verbs**, because they form their *past tense* and *past participle* in a *regular way*—by always adding **ed** to the verb-root. The verbs in the second list are called **irregular verbs**, because they do not form their past tense and past participle in any regular way.

464. Definition.—A **regular verb** is a verb that forms its past tense and past participle by adding **ed** to the verb-root.

465. Definition.—An **irregular verb** is a verb that does *not* form its past tense and past participle by adding *ed* to the verb-root.

466. From the *verb-root*, there are derived (as we see) three other forms, the *past tense*, the *present participle*, and the *past participle*. These four forms are called the four *principal parts* of the verb because, from these, other forms of a verb are derived by means of auxiliaries.

Questions.—1. How many principal parts has a verb? 2. What is a regular verb? 3. An irregular verb? 4. How is the present participle of a verb always formed? 5. How are the past tense and past participle always formed? 6. Is there any regular way of forming the past tense and past participle of an irregular verb? 7. How are the past tense and past participle of *choose* formed? 8. Of *begin*? 9. Of *come*? 10. Of *eat*? 11. *Give*? 12. *Know*?

Remark.—Most of the verbs in our language are regular in form; therefore no list of them need be given.

CXXVIII.—THE USE OF AUXILIARIES.

467. Although the present and past participles *imply* action, neither of them can be used as a verb to make an *assertion* unless accompanied by an auxiliary.

It would *not* make sense to say—

1. James *writing* his composition.
2. The boys *broken* the oars.
3. Mary *chosen* Longfellow's poems.
4. They *eaten* dinner before our arrival.

THE USE OF AUXILIARIES. 155

It *is* correct to say—
1. James *is writing* his composition.
2. The boys *have broken* the oars.
3. Mary *has chosen* Longfellow's poems.
4. They *had eaten* dinner before our arrival.

Explanation.—In sentence 1, the auxiliary *is* is correctly used with the participle *writing*, thus making the *progressive* form, *is writing*. In 2, 3, and 4, *have*, *has* and *had* are correctly used with the past participles *broken*, *chosen*, and *eaten*, respectively, thus making the *compound form* of the verb. In *have broken*, *broken* is the principal part of the verb.

468. Any form of the verb *be* (*am, is, are, was, were, been*) used with the present participle, as in 1, makes a verb of the **progressive form.**

Direction.—Parse only such verbs as are in the *present, past,* and *future tenses.*

469. When *have, has,* or *had* is used as an auxiliary, only the *past participle* can be used as the principal part of the verb.

Explanation.—"We have saw the falls" is incorrect, because the past tense *saw* is used with an auxiliary, to form a verb.

Direction.—Complete the verb in each of the following sentences by using in the blank space the correct form of the verb in brackets at the end:
1. I have not —— him to-day. [see.]
2. I have —— the work already. [do.]
3. He has —— home. [go]
4. The tree has —— across the street. [fall.]
5. He has —— for the books. [come.]
6. I have —— him a long time. [know.]

Caution.—The *past participle* must *not* be used for the *past tense* of the verb, nor must it ever be used alone as a verb.

Direction.—Correct the following, and give reasons:
1. I done that work in an hour.
2. I seen him yesterday in the park.

Caution.—The present tense should not be used to denote a past act.

Direction.—Correct the following, and give reasons:
1. I see him yesterday at the fair.
2. He come home last week.
3. That move give you the advantage.

THE USE OF AUXILIARIES.

470. Other auxiliaries may be used with *have* or *had* to form *one verb*:

Note.—Do not require pupils to give the tense of the verbs in these sentences:

1. You *should have gone* before.
2. He *might have come* earlier.
3. I *may have seen* him once before.
4. He *must have known* better.
5. How *could* we *have done* it sooner?
6. They *will have eaten* dinner before the arrival of the train.

471. *Have, has,* and *had,* as *auxiliaries,* are used only with the past participle, and this participle is never used as a verb unless joined with these auxiliaries, or with some form of the verb *be.*

472. When *thou* is used as a subject, the verbs take such forms as: *goest, hast* gone; *keepeth, hadst* kept; *shalt* keep; *shouldst* keep, etc.; as, "Thou *hast* kept the best wine until the end of the feast."

Questions.—1. What is the verb in 1, of the last six? 2. What is its principal part? 3. Considered by itself, what part of speech is this principal part? 4. With what auxiliaries must the past participle be used to become the principal part of a verb? 5. How many auxiliaries belong to the verb in 1? 6. Of how many words is the whole verb composed? 7. Which are the principal parts of the verbs in 2, 3, 4, 5, and 6? 8. What errors are made in the sentences under [469]? 9. Of what is the progressive form of the verb composed?

CXXIX.—APPOSITION.

473. It has been seen that nouns and pronouns in the possessive case are used to modify other nouns; as,

Washington's forces crossed the Delaware.

474. A noun is also used in an adjective sense when, for the sake of explanation, it is a repetition of a subject, an object, or of a noun or pronoun denoting possession; as,

1. Webster, the *statesman,* lived in Massachusetts.
2. Webster, the *lexicographer,* once taught a school.

APPOSITION.

    8. The tyrant *Nero* committed many cruel acts.
    4. The Romans hated the tyrant *Nero*.
    5. They assailed his, my *father's*, honor.
    6. Paul, the apostle, lived in Nero's reign.

Explanation.—*Statesman* (in 1) is used in an adjective sense because it explains the noun Webster by showing which man by that name is meant. *Nero* (in 3) is a repetition of tyrant for the purpose of explanation. In 4, *Nero* explains the object *tyrant*. In 5, *father's* explains *his* by showing *whose* honor.

475. Nouns used, like *statesman*, *lexicographer*, *Nero*, and *father's*, in the preceding sentences, to explain other nouns or pronouns, are *modifying* words. They are called *explanatory* nouns; also *appositive* nouns, or nouns in apposition. *Apposition* means placed near to, and these nouns are placed near the words they explain; i. e., in *close* connection—not *joined* by any connective word.

Questions.—1. What kind of noun is *statesman* on account of its use in sentence 1? 2. *Lexicographer* in 2? 3. *Nero* in 3 and 4? 4. Does *Nero* explain a *subject*, or an *object*, in each of 3 and 4? 5. By what is *Webster* modified in 1 and in 2? 6. By what is *tyrant* modified in 3 and 4? 7. By what is *his* modified in sentence 5?

Direction.—Mention the explanatory nouns in the following sentences, and also the words modified by them:

    1. I Paul saw these things.
    2. Franklin, the eminent philosopher, learned the printer's trade.
    3. We, the people of the United States, do ordain this Constitution.
    4. David, the son of Jesse, slew Goliath, the Philistine.

Explanation.—In 1, the explanatory noun Paul is unaccompanied by modifiers, and is therefore *not* set off by commas. In 2, *son* is modified by *the* and *of Jesse*, and is set off by commas.

476. Definition.—An explanatory (or appositive) phrase is one composed of an explanatory noun taken with all its modifiers; as, "the son of Jesse."

Remark.—When the appositive noun has one or more modifiers, the whole *phrase* is the modifying element. The explanatory noun is the *principal* word in the phrase.

477. Punctuation Rule.—An explanatory (or appositive) phrase must be set off from the rest of the sentence by commas;

but when the explanatory term is unaccompanied by a modifier, no comma is required.

Direction.—Select the explanatory phrases in the preceding sentences and give the reasons for the use of commas. Also mention the word modified by each phrase.

Questions.—1. What noun is in apposition with *I* in 1? 2. With David in 2? 3. With Goliath? 4. With Franklin? 5. With *we*? 6. What is an appositive phrase? 7. What is its office? 8. What is the rule for punctuating an appositive phrase? 9. What other kind of phrase is used like an adjective? 10. What is an explanatory noun? 11. What is its office?

CXXX.—MODELS FOR ANALYSIS.

1. The Romans hated the tyrant Nero.

478. This is a simple declarative sentence. The entire subject is "The Romans," and the predicate, "hated the tyrant *Nero.*" The simple subject *Romans* is modified by the adjective *the*. The predicate-verb *hated* is completed by the object complement *tyrant*, which is modified by the adjective *the* and the appositive noun *Nero*.

2. The Franks, a warlike people of Germany, gave their name to France.

This is a simple declarative sentence. The entire subject is, "The Franks, a warlike people of Germany," and the predicate, "gave their name to France." The simple subject *Franks* is modified by the adjective *the* and the appositive phrase *a warlike people of Germany*, in which phrase the principal word is *people*, modified by the adjectives *a* and *warlike*, and also by the phrase *of Germany*. The predicate-verb *gave* is modified by the phrase *to France*. The object *name* is modified by the possessive pronoun *their*.

Sentences for Punctuation and Analysis.

1. My friend the old professor has resigned his position.
2. Experience the great teacher makes no allowance for stupidity.
3. I Darius King of Persia have decreed it.
4. Washington the great hero and statesman enjoyed the confidence of the people.
5. Peter the hermit resembled Peter the apostle.
6. The steamer Oregon sank near the shore of Long Island.

APPOSITION. 159

CXXXI.—CASE OF NOUNS IN APPOSITION.

479. An appositive noun or pronoun depends *for its case* on the word which it explains; but it frequently *differs* from such word in *gender, person,* and *number*; as,
1. The lecturer referred to Sydney Smith, *him* of witty memory.
2. We stopped at my brother *John's*.
3. I bought the paper at Smith's, the *book-seller*.
4. I, your best friend, will not desert you.

Explanation.—In sentence 1, Sydney Smith being the *object* of the preposition *to*, the appositive pronoun must be in the *objective* form *him* —not in the nominative form *he*. In 2, if *John* be omitted, *brother* would take the possessive sign [brother's *house*]. *John* is introduced to explain, by showing *which* brother, thus becoming an appositive noun; but if both possessives were fully written [we stopped at my brother's John's house] there would be an unpleasant repetition of the *s*-sound. For the sake of *euphony*, therefore, the possessive sign is omitted from *brother*. *Brother* is in the possessive case, and *John's* is in apposition with *brother*. In 3, *store* is understood after *Smith's* and *book-seller*. Omit *Smith's*, and book-seller will take the possessive sign [book-seller's store]. In 4, by using the name *friend*, the person speaks *of* himself. Therefore, *friend* is in the *third* person, while *I* is in the first person.

480. Rule for Construction.—An appositive noun or pronoun must be in the same case as the word which it explains.

Direction.—Analyze the preceding and the following sentences, and parse the appositive nouns in this and the preceding lessons according to the models here given:
1. He visited his brother John.
2. My friend, the lawyer, lost his case.
3. William found his brother John's book.
4. They called him a hero.
5. They elected him President.

481. Models for Parsing.—*John* is a proper noun, mas., third, sing., and is in apposition with *brother* in the objective case.

Lawyer is a common noun, mas., third, sing., and is in apposition with *friend* in the nom. case.

John's is in apposition with *brother* in the poss. case.

Hero is in apposition with *him* in the obj. case.

APPOSITION.—EMPHATIC PRONOUNS.

Note.—The verbs *elect*, *make*, *name*, *call*, seem to take two objects, the second of which, like *President* (in 5) is called, by some authors, the *factitive* object, because it denotes that which the person is *made* to be. *Factitive* comes from the Latin *facere*, to *make*.

CXXXII.—EMPHATIC PRONOUNS.

482. Sometimes a compound personal pronoun is placed in apposition with a noun or pronoun for the sake of emphasis. Such a pronoun may be properly called an *emphatic pronoun*; as,

    1. The king *himself* has decreed it.
    2. She selected the goods *herself*.

483. Nouns repeated for the sake of force or emphasis are said to be in apposition; as,

    1. I met a fool, a crazy *fool*.
    2. "Treason, *treason!*" shouted the multitude.

484. Sometimes a noun is joined with another in a sort of apposition by the conjunction *as*, and also by *or*; as,

    1. He received a medal as a *reward*.
    2. The puma, or American *lion*, inhabits South America.

Note.—When *or*, as in 2, connects equivalent terms, it is called *explanatory or*, and, with the equivalent explanatory term, it should be set off by commas.

485. The appositive term, when only a *single word*, should be set off by commas when it becomes necessary to make the meaning clear; as,

    1. Elizabeth's favorite, Raleigh, was beheaded by James I.

Explanation.—Without the commas, the sentence may be taken to mean that, of several Raleighs, her *favorite* Raleigh was beheaded.

Direction.—Write the following sentences, underlining the appositive noun or pronoun, and punctuating properly:

1. Hope the star of life never sets. 2. We saw Dr. Edwards him of Union College. 3. They regard winter as the season of domestic enjoyment. 4. The tadpole or polliwog becomes a frog. 5. Homer wrote two great works the Iliad and the Odyssey. 6. Jones as my attorney sold the land. 7. We girls will start now. 8. The girls will not wait for us boys. 9. Out of this nettle danger we pluck the flower safety.

486. The explanatory term does not always follow the word explained; as,

    1. A prompt, decisive *man*, no breath our father wasted.
    2. As a *statesman*, he had great ability.

Direction.—In each of the following sentences, select the appositive word and give its case:

    1. We girls belong to the third class. 2. When shall we girls meet again? 3. This play-ground belongs to us boys. 4. Dom Pedro, the Brazilian emperor, once visited the United States. 5. My son William has entered college. 6. As a mathematician, he has no superior. 7. He himself did not know the answer.

The Possessive Case.

487. Special Rule 1.—When nouns denoting possession are in apposition, the noun which they limit being expressed, the last word takes the possessive sign; as,

    1. The Emperor Napoleon's army march to victory.
    2. We visited Webster the statesman's grave.

But when the limited word is understood, the possessive sign is added to the first noun.

    1. I bought the paper at Smith's the book-seller.

488. Special Rule 2.—To indicate common possession the sign is added to the last of two or more possessives modifying the same word; as,

    1. Reed and Kellogg's Grammar.
    2. Lord and Taylor's dry-goods' store.

But when common possession is not indicated, each word takes the possessive sign; as,

    1. Webster's and Worcester's Dictionaries.
    2. Mary's and Lucy's books.

489. Special Rule 3.—When two or more consecutive words are taken together to denote but one possessor, the last word takes the possessive sign; as,

    1. The heir-at-law's case.
    2. The Queen of England's crown.

SYNTHESIS.

Direction.—Change the following sentences so that possession in each case shall be expressed by using the possessive sign; and in the last two sentences in *two* ways—one expressing common possession, and the other separate possession:

1. The speech of the king was applauded. 2. America was discovered during the reign of Ferdinand and Isabella. 3. They were mentioning the victories of Grant and Sherman. 4. We passed the store of Lord and Taylor. 5. The death of the Duke of Manchester occurred in 1843. 6. The mother of the wife of Peter lay sick of a fever. 7. The reign of William and Mary was one of the most distinguished in English history. 8. They brought the head of John the Baptist on a charger. 9. Do this for the sake of David thy father. 10. The books belonging to Sarah and Fanny are new. 11. The baggage belonging to John and William was lost.

Remark.—The expressions, "some one else's books" and "somebody else's affairs," are considered good English; but they are awkward, and should be avoided. Say, "The books belong to some one else"; "He is always meddling with the affairs of somebody else."

CXXXIII.—SYNTHESIS.

490. Direction.—Combine the following statements into a simple sentence containing one subject, one verb, one object complement, an appositive phrase, and prepositional phrases, one of them being elliptical:

Capt. Webb lost his life.
He was a noted English swimmer.
He lost his life in the whirlpool.
It happened last week.
The whirlpool is in the Niagara River.
It is below the falls.

Direction.—Combine the following statements into a simple sentence containing one subject, one verb, a compound appositive phrase, a single noun in apposition, prepositional phrases. Abbreviate Maryland and New Hampshire properly:

Major Geo. H. Chandler is critically ill.
He is afflicted with neuralgia of the heart.
He is a lawyer.
He is the brother of Secretary Chandler.
He lives in Baltimore.
Baltimore is in Maryland.

He is at the home of his brother.
His brother's home is in Canterbury.
Canterbury is in New Hampshire.

Direction.—Combine the following statements into a simple sentence containing one subject, four verbs, and prepositional phrases. The second verb must have two object complements, and the third and fourth, one each:

A whirlwind passed through Onondaga.
It also passed through Leslie.
Onondaga and Leslie are in Ingham County.
Ingham County is in Michigan.
This happened on Monday.
It was about noon.
The whirlwind wrecked fifteen houses.
It also wrecked fifteen barns.
It killed three persons.
It fatally injured another.

CXXXIV.—HOW TO USE SIT, SET, LIE, AND LAY.

PRES. TENSE.	PAST TENSE.	PRES. PARTICIPLE.	PAST PARTICIPLE.
Sit,	sat,	sitting,	sat.
Set,	set,	setting,	set.
Lie,	lay,	lying,	lain.
Lay,	laid,	laying,	laid.

491. Lay and **set** are *transitive* verbs, and must be used in a transitive sense. When we *put anything down*, we *lay* or *set* it down.

Lie and **sit** are *intransitive* verbs, and must be used in an intransitive sense. When we rest, we *sit* or *lie* down.

Direction.—Fill the blanks in the following sentences, using one of these four verbs properly:

1. I sometimes —— down on the lounge in the afternoon. 2. Yesterday I —— down and slept an hour. 3. After I had —— down yesterday my friend called. 4. Mary —— the lamp on the table a few moments ago. 5. We —— on the bench by the brook yesterday. 6. We often —— there and read. 7. I —— the paper on the table only a moment ago. 8. —— down on the sofa and rest awhile. 9. —— on this chair; the other

is broken. 10. I have —— on this bed for two long weeks. 11. I —— the book on the table and there it —— yet.

Remark.—It is correct to say, "I laid the book on the table and there it *lies* yet," because, in the latter part of the sentence, the act is referred to the book. It is also correct to say, "The sleepy little child *laid* her head on my lap."

Direction.—Fill the blanks with any of the four verbs (or their participles) that will fill out the sense in the following composition:

On entering school this morning, I —— on the back seat and —— my books on the floor beside me. When I —— down a slate was —— on the desk, which the teacher took and —— on her table; she also took an inkstand and —— it on her desk. Mary Brown's baby sister became tired of —— still, so she —— down on the seat and —— her head on Mary's lap. When she awoke she —— up and rubbed her eyes. After school, on arriving home, I —— down on the lounge to read, but soon fell asleep. When I awoke, I found that I had —— an hour. I then —— my book on the table and —— by the window. I had —— there but a minute, when the bell rang for tea.

CXXXV.—ATTRIBUTE COMPLEMENT.

492. Most intransitive verbs are *complete verbs*; that is, they do not require a complement to fill out the meaning; as,

    1. He arose early.
    2. The swan swims gracefully.

Nouns and Pronouns as Attribute Complements.

493. Some intransitive verbs, however, are incomplete verbs, and require a noun, a pronoun, or an adjective to complete the predicate; as,

    1. Franklin *was* a *philosopher*.
    2. That industrious boy *became* a prosperous *man*.
    3. My friend *is* a *merchant*.
    4. These boys *are* good *students*.
    5. The Greeks *were* a warlike *people*.
    6. I *am he*.
    7. He *has been* a bad boy.

ATTRIBUTE COMPLEMENT.   165

Explanation.—In sentence 1, the noun *philosopher* completes the predicate, and *ascribes* or *attributes* a quality of mind to the person named by the subject. *Philosopher* is therefore called the **attribute complement** of *was*. In sentence 3, the noun *merchant* attributes condition [in life] to the subject *friend*, and is the *attribute* complement of *is*. In sentence 6, the pronoun *he* is the *attribute* complement of *am*, and refers to *I*. In 7, *boy* is the attribute complement, and refers to *he*.

494. There is a shade of resemblance between the *attributive* and the *appositive* use of a noun. The difference is, that in the *attributive* use the quality or condition denoted by the noun is *affirmed*; whereas, in the *appositive* use, the quality or condition is *assumed*; as,
1. John Milton was an eminent *poet*.
2. John Milton, the eminent *poet*, was also a philosopher.

The Adjective as Attribute Complement.

495. An **adjective**, as an **attribute complement**, ascribes quality to the subject; as,

1. The lion is *fearless*.
2. Snow is *white*.
3. Some apples are *sweet*.
4. The man became *insane*.

Explanation.—The adjective *fearless*, in 1, completes the predicate, and refers to the subject *lion*.

Note.—The adjective *sweet* expresses an *attribute* [quality] called *sweetness*. In the sentence, "I have a *sweet* apple," the attribute is implied, or assumed; but in "This apple is *sweet*," the attribute is *affirmed* of the subject, and the adjective *sweet*, being used in the predicate, is called the *predicate adjective* or *adjective attribute*. Although *fearless* (in sentence 1) *refers* to the subject, yet, not being in the same construction with it, this adjective really *modifies animal* understood—a noun in the same construction.

496. *Inverted*, or *rhetorical*, order is often produced by placing the predicate adjective before the verb; as,
1. *Wide* is the gate, and *narrow* is the way.
2. *Dim* grow its fancies, *forgotten* they lie.
3. *Sad* and *weary* was the march to Valley Forge.
4. *Fiercer* and *brighter* became the lightning.
5. *Faithful* was he to the last.
6. *Wise* are all his ways.

CXXXVI.—HOW TO DISTINGUISH THE ATTRIBUTE COMPLEMENT.

497. An *object complement* names a person or thing entirely different from the subject; as,

1. Brutus stabbed *Cæsar*.
2. Columbus discovered *America*.

498. An *attribute complement*, when a noun or pronoun, is only another name for the subject; as,

1. Brutus was an *assassin*.
2. Columbus was a *navigator*.

An *attribute complement*, whether a noun, a pronoun, or an adjective, always *points* to the *subject*.

Direction.—In each of the following sentences, name the complement, tell whether it is an attribute or an object, and state its part of speech:

1. The prize was a silver medal.
2. Byron was an English poet.
3. Robbers attacked the travelers.
4. The children were sick.
5. Grant was a great general.
6. The wind blew fiercely.
7. My father was a soldier.
8. You will be late.
9. We chose him as our leader.
10. He injured his hand.
11. The man is very wealthy.
12. The moth is an insect.
13. The general led his army to victory.
14. I am weary.
15. Camels carry heavy burdens.
16. It is she.
17. Camels are patient animals.
18. I am he.
19. 'Tis I, Hamlet, the Dane.
20. His remark was inappropriate.

499. A predicate noun or pronoun must be in the same case as the subject to which it refers; as, "I am *he*"; "It was *she*" [not *her*].

500. Definition.—An *attribute complement* is a *noun*, *pronoun*, or *adjective*, completing the predicate of a sentence, and relating to the subject.

501. Rule for Construction.—A noun or pronoun used as an attribute complement must be in the same case as the subject to which it refers.

502. The *attribute complement*, when a *noun* or a *pronoun*, is a sort of repetition of the subject, and is often called the *predicate nominative.** An adjective attribute is often called the *predicate adjective.*

Direction.—Fill the blank space in each of the following sentences, with the proper form of the personal pronoun indicated in the brackets, and give a reason for each choice. Do not use the sentences for analysis:

1. That can not be —— [sing. f.].
2. It was —— who saw you [s. m.].
3. It was —— I saw [p. f.].
4. It could not have been —— [s. m.].
5. If I were —— I would not do it [s. f.].
6. I know that was —— [s. f.].
7. I would go if I were —— [2d s.].
8. That is —— in the hall [s. f.].

Questions.—1. How does an *object* differ from an *attribute noun* or *pronoun*? 2. By what other name is the attribute complement sometimes known? 3. Which form of a personal pronoun must be used as an *attribute complement*? 4. Mention all the nominative forms of the personal pronouns. 5. Mention all the objective forms. 6. Which forms are used as complements of transitive verbs? 7. What kind of verbs may be followed by *predicate nouns*? 8. In how many relations may the pronoun *I* be used in a sentence? 9. Why is it necessary to distinguish *object* and *attribute* complements?

CXXXVII.—MODELS FOR ANALYSIS AND PARSING.

1. Columbus was a bold navigator.

503. Models for Analysis.—This is a simple declarative sentence. The simple subject *Columbus* is unmodified. The entire predicate is "was a bold navigator." The predicate-verb *was* is completed by the attribute complement *navigator*, which is modified by the adjectives *a* and *bold*.

2. These apples are very sour.

This is a simple declarative sentence. "These apples" is the entire subject, and the predicate is "are very sour." The simple subject *apples* is modified by the adjective *these*. The predicate-verb *are* is completed by the adjective complement *sour*,† which is itself modified by the adverb *very*.

---

* The attribute complement following an *infinitive verb* is sometimes a repetition of an *object*; as, "We knew *him* to be an *impostor.*" In such a use *impostor* could not be called a *predicate nominative* [712].

† In analysis, *sour* is spoken of in connection with the predicate, but in parsing it is spoken of as referring to the subject.

Sentences for Parsing.

1. I am *he*.
2. That industrious boy became a prosperous man.
3. The snow is white.*

504. Models for Parsing.—(1) In 1, *he* is a personal pronoun, masculine, third, singular, and is in the nominative case, being the attribute complement of the intransitive verb *am*. (2) In 2, *man* is a common noun, masculine, third, singular, and is in the nominative case, being the attribute complement of the intransitive verb *became*. (3) In 3, *white* is a predicate adjective, completing the predicate and referring to the subject. (4) In 1, *am* is an irregular intransitive verb in the present tense, and agrees with its subject *I* in the *first* person, and *singular* number.

Sentences for Analysis and Parsing.

1. Disappointment is the common fate of man.
2. "The way was long, the wind was cold,
   The minstrel was infirm and old."
3. A thing of beauty is a joy forever.
4. The poetry of earth is never dead.
5. The French emperor, Napoleon, was a great general.
6. There is no substitute in this world for thorough-going, ardent, and sincere earnestness.
7. Thomson, the author of "The Seasons," is a delightful poet.

CXXXVIII.—INCOMPLETE INTRANSITIVE VERBS.

505. The principal incomplete intransitive verbs are *be* (*am, is, was, are, were*), *appear, seem, become, feel, look, taste,* and *smell*.

506. Singular Forms.—*Am, is,* and *was* are singular forms, and must be used with singular subjects.

507. Plural Forms.—*Are* and *were* are plural forms, and must be used with plural subjects.

---

* In such sentences as "Snow is white," some authors call *is* the copula and *white* the predicate, because *whiteness* is *predicated* of *snow*. The verb is said to *connect* or *unite* the attribute to the subject. But this is an unnecessary extension of analysis and multiplication of terms.

INCOMPLETE INTRANSITIVE VERBS. 169

508. *Be* (generally used with an auxiliary) has no change of form in its use with a subject; as, "He *will be* late"; "They *will be* late"; "If he *be* absent."

509. Each of the verbs *appear, feel, look, smell, taste,* and *become,* has two meanings—one implying action on the part of the subject, and the other *not* implying action. When these verbs do not imply action, they require an *attribute complement.*

510. The verbs *feel, smell, taste,* and *become* are sometimes used in a transitive sense, and take *object complements.*

Direction.—In each of the following sentences determine whether the verb is used in a *transitive* or an *intransitive* sense, and give reasons:

    1. The bluebird appears suddenly in the spring.
       The child appears weary.
    2. We looked an hour for the lost ring.
       The flowers looked beautiful.
    3. We smelled the odor of the flowers.
       The flowers smelled sweet.
    4. We tasted sulphur in the water.
       The milk tasted sour.
    5. He felt the rebuke keenly.
       He felt very sick.
    6. The dress becomes her well.
       The boy became a prosperous man.

Questions.—1. Which are the principal incomplete verbs? 2. Which forms of the verb *be* are singular? 3. Which are plural? 4. Which form may be used with either a singular or a plural subject? 5. What is a transitive verb? 6. What is an intransitive verb? 7. What form of a pronoun is used as an attribute? 8. To what does a predicate adjective relate?

511. The Copula.—The verb *be* or *am* may be used as an *incomplete* verb:

(1) To predicate quality of the subject; as,
    1. I *am* feeble.   3. He *had been* sick.
    2. William *is* healthy.   4. They *were* happy.

(2) To predicate *identity*; as,
    1. John *is* a clerk.   3. Franklin *was* a philosopher.
    2. They *were* good friends.   4. William *is* an honest lad.

In these two uses the verb *be* or *am*, in its different forms, is called a **copula**, because it *couples* or links the complement to the subject. Each of the verbs *appear, become, continue, seem, feel, smell, stand, sit*, etc., is also sometimes used as a *copula*.

512. The verb *be* or *am* may be used as a *complete* verb to predicate existence; as,

1. Before Abraham *was*, I *am*.
2. And there was Mary Magdalene and the other Mary.
3. There *was* a certain rich man in Damascus.
4. God *is* eternally, and ever *shall be*.

Note.—In the use of the verb *be* as a copula, a word or a phrase completing the predicate refers to the subject. But a word or phrase used with *be*, when it denotes *mere existence*, modifies the verb.

CXXXIX.—ADJECTIVE OR ADVERB?

513. Care must be taken *not* to use adverbs instead of adjectives as the complements of incomplete verbs.

It is correct to say—

1. He looks *kind* [cast of countenance].
2. He looked *kindly* at the child [manner of looking].
3. He feels *anxious* about his business [state of mind].
4. He feels his loss *keenly* [manner of feeling].
5. The rose smells sweet [quality of odor—not manner of smelling].
6. His voice sounds *harsh* [quality of voice].
7. The man remained *silent* [state—no action].
8. The soldiers looked *gay* [appearance—not manner of looking].
9. We arrived *safe* [state—not manner of arriving].
10. They escaped all *safe* to the land [state].

Direction.—In each of the following sentences, determine which word in italics is the correct one, and tell what part of speech it is. Tell the part of speech of each italicized word in the preceding sentences:

1. He looks *mean* or *meanly*?
2. He looks *feebly* or *feeble*?
3. The lawn looks *beautiful* or *beautifully*?
4. He looks *bad* or *badly* [meaning ill]?
5. He feels *wretchedly* or *wretched*?
6. The music sounds *sweet* or *sweetly*?

ACTIVE AND PASSIVE VOICE. 171

    7. Magnesia feels *smooth* or *smoothly*?
    8. He sat *silently* or *silent* in his chair?
    9. He is *nicely*, I thank you [incorrect].

Remark.—This error in the use of *nicely* (in 9) is often made by educated people.

The *attribute complement* may be a *phrase*; as,

    1. His action was *in bad taste* [inappropriate].
    2. He is *without fear* [fearless].
    3. George was in fault.
    4. The slanderer is beneath contempt.
    5. The general is in fine health.
    6. The watchmen are on their guard.
    7. The patient is in distress.
    8. His character is above suspicion.
    9. The old lady is in excellent spirits.

Direction.—Select in each of the preceding sentences the attribute phrase.

CXL.—VERBS.—ACTIVE VOICE AND PASSIVE VOICE.

514. Verbs in general are separated into *two* classes, *transitive* and *intransitive* [107]. Intransitive verbs are of two kinds, *complete* and *incomplete* [107, f. n.].

515. A *transitive* verb has *two* forms—one representing its *subject as acting*, and the other representing its *subject as receiving the act*; as,

    1. The officer seized the thief.   3. We have picked the berries.
    2. The thief was seized by the officer.   4. The berries have been picked.

Explanation.—In 1, the subject *officer* is represented as *acting*. The object *thief* is the *receiver* of the act, and, when (to express the same sense in another way) *thief* becomes the subject of sentence 2, it still remains the receiver of the act. The *subject* (in sentence 1) appears in sentence 2 as the *object* of a *preposition*. The subject *we* (in 3) is entirely omitted in 4. The verb *seized* (in 1) is the past tense of *seize*; but **seized** (in 2) is the past participle used with the auxiliary *was*. *Seized* (in 1) represents the subject *officer* as *acting*, but *was seized* (a different form of the verb) represents its subject *thief* as receiving the act. This variation in the form and use of a transitive verb showing whether the subject *acts* or *is acted upon* is called **voice**. The form **seized** or **have picked** is the **active voice** of the verb. **Was seized** or **have been picked** is the **passive*** voice.

516. A verb in the **passive voice** is formed by using the **past participle** of a **transitive verb** with any form of the verb **be**, either with or without other auxiliaries.

517. Definition.—Voice is the variation in the use and form of a transitive verb that shows whether the subject acts or receives the act.

The **active voice** represents the subject as *performing* the act.
The **passive voice** represents the subject as *receiving* the act.

Questions.—1. How many kinds of intransitive verbs are there? 2. How many kinds of transitive verbs? 3. What is voice? 4. Active voice? 5. Passive voice? 6. How is the passive voice of a verb formed? 7. What kind of verbs may have the passive voice? 8. What part of the sentence containing a verb in the active voice becomes the subject of a verb in the passive voice?

CXLI.—THE PASSIVE VOICE.

518. The passive voice is a grammatical device for varying the language; for concealing the actor when we wish to direct special attention to the act and its recipient; for speaking of the act and its result when the actor is unknown.

519. A sentence containing a verb in the active voice is changed to a sentence containing a verb in the passive voice, by making the *direct object* of the verb in the former, the *subject* of the verb in the latter; as,

1. Columbus discovered *America*.
2. Whitney invented the *cotton-gin*.
3. The hunter shot an *eagle*.

1. *America* was discovered by Columbus.
2. The *cotton-gin* was invented by Whitney.
3. An *eagle* was shot by the hunter.

---

* *Passive* = suffering or enduring, and a verb in the passive voice represents its subject as *receiving* or *enduring* the act.

Note.—The subject of the active verb may be omitted entirely in the sentence containing the passive, when it will sound awkward to retain it, or when it would add nothing definite or necessary.

Parsing Model.

1. The fox *was caught* by the hound.

520. *Was caught* is an irregular, transitive verb, *passive voice*, past tense, and agrees with its subject fox in the third, singular. [Parse only such verbs as are in the *present, past,* or *future tenses.*]

Direction.—Determine whether the verb in each of the following sentences is in the active voice or in the passive voice; re-write each, changing the verbs in the active voice to the passive, and those in the passive voice to the active. Analyze; parse the verbs in the *present, past,* and *future tenses:*

1. A careless boy broke the window. 2. Pompey was conquered by Cæsar. 3. Will you return the book to me? 4. I bought this knife for a dollar. 5. The fox was caught by the hound. 6. Every day brings new duties. 7. The merchant has written a dispatch. 8. I have sent the messenger. 9. He has loaded his ship with iron. 10. Little minds are tamed and subdued by misfortune, but great minds rise above it. 11. The rewards were given to the best scholars. 12. These rocks have lain in their present position many years, and they may lie there many years longer. 13. The beautiful fleet soon carried him out of danger. 14. Young persons should select their companions with great care. 15. We should have arranged these matters before this time. 16. The work should have been finished by the contractor before December.

CXLII.—PASSIVE VERBS, COMPOUND, ETC.

521. Intransitive verbs have no passive voice, for the action expressed by such verbs being confined entirely to the subject, no object is acted upon.

522. Certain verbs in the active voice are sometimes used in a passive sense. But, used in this way, they denote the *capacity* to receive an act in a certain way, rather than the actual reception of it; as, This field *plows* well. Sycamore *splits* badly. These goods *sell* readily. Potatoes *are selling* high. This cloth *wears* well.

PASSIVE VOICE.

523. A few intransitive verbs take the passive form though used in an active sense. These are *not* passive verbs; as, He *is gone* [has gone]. The melancholy days *are come* [have come]. Babylon *is fallen* [has fallen]. But "Babylon *is destroyed*" is not the same as "Babylon *has destroyed*." The verb *fall* is not transitive; therefore, *is fallen* (not being formed from a transitive verb) is not passive. The verb *destroy* is transitive; therefore, *is destroyed* (being formed from a *transitive* verb) is passive, representing its *subject* as *receiving* the act.

524. A few intransitive verbs, taking the passive form, and combining in sense with a following preposition, are called **compound passive verbs**; as, You *will be laughed at* [ridiculed]. He *was smiled on* by Fortune [favored]. His arrival *was* anxiously *looked for* [expected]. He *was* unjustly *dealt with* [treated]. An honest man *is* well *thought of* [favorably *considered*]. The words in italics in each sentence form *one* verb.

Sentences for Parsing.

1. The bell rings merrily.
2. He is a wealthy man.
3. Our troops captured the enemy.
4. The enemy was captured by our troops.

525. Parsing Models.—*Rings* is an irregular, intransitive verb, in the present tense, and agrees with its subject *bell* in the third person, singular number. *Is* is an irregular neuter verb, in the present tense, and agrees with its subject *he* in the third person, singular number. *Captured* is a regular transitive verb, in the active voice, past tense, and agrees with its subject *troops* in the third person, plural number. *Was captured* is a regular transitive verb in the passive voice, past tense, and agrees with its subject *enemy* in the third person, singular number.

Direction.—Parse the verbs in the preceding lesson according to these models.

Direction.—After learning the omitted parts of lessons 61 and 92, determine which of the two words in brackets is the correct one, in each of the following sentences:

1. A large number of trees [was or were] planted.
2. A great variety of plants [grow or grows] in this latitude.
3. Plenty of oranges [are or is] brought from Florida.
4. I and not they [are or am] to blame.
5. Charles, as well as the others, [was or were] present.
6. The society refused [its or their] assent to this arrangement.
7. The society expressed [its or their] approbation by cheering.
8. The lady decided that politics [were or was] uninteresting to her.

INDEPENDENT ELEMENT. 175

CXLIII.—THE INDEPENDENT ELEMENT.

1. Shut that door.
2. William, shut that door.

Explanation.—Sentence 1 is imperative, and *you*, understood, is the subject. Sentence 2 is imperative, and also has *you* for its subject, thus: "William [you] shut that door." The noun *William* is *not* the subject of the sentence, this word being used simply to secure attention. I call to a person and say, **William**, then proceed to tell him what I wish to say. In this sentence, *you* is the subject, *shut* the verb, and *door* the object, modified by *that*, leaving *William* unnecessary to the sentence, or *independent of* it.

526. Whenever we call to, or *address*, any one (as in sentence 2, above), the name of the person addressed is never the subject* of the sentence, but is an *independent* noun. Such a noun is *associated* with the sentence as a whole, but it performs no grammatical office in it. *William* is therefore an *independent element*, and is called *independent by address*.

Remark.—In Latin, nouns independent by address are in the *vocative* case [Lat. *vocare*, to call], and some of these nouns have special forms for this use. But in English, all independent nouns are considered to be in the nominative case; they are names, and the name form of a noun is its nominative case.

527. Rule.—A noun or a pronoun used *independently* should be in the *nominative case*.

Direction.—Mention the subjects, also the *independent nouns*, in the following sentences. Parse each noun:

1. Thomas, bring that book to me.
2. Call the servant, Jane.
3. Move the chair quietly.
4. Mary, speak to the child more kindly.
5. James, have you a grammar?

Questions.—1. In what kind of sentences is the subject generally understood? 2. Is the name of a person *addressed* ever the subject of a sentence? 3. When is a noun independent? 4. What is the *case* of an independent noun? 5. In what sense does an independent noun belong to a sentence? 6. What office does it perform?

---

* A *noun* in the first or second person is never the subject of a verb.

528. When an address is made in an interrogative sentence, the subject is expressed; as,

    1. William, will *you* shut that door?

529. Independent nouns often occur in exclamatory expressions; as,

    1. Poor man! how he suffers!

Explanation.—In this sentence *man* is independent by exclamation, and is modified by *poor*.

530. Sometimes, on account of *repetition* for rhetorical effect, a noun is left without any grammatical relation in a sentence; as,

    1. The *boy*, oh, where was he!

A noun used like *boy* is in the nominative case, independent by pleonasm. *Pleonasm* means *redundancy of words*.

Models for Analysis.

    1. William, will you shut that door?

531. This is a simple interrogative sentence. The simple subject is *you*, the entire predicate, "will shut the door." The predicate verb *will shut* is completed by the object complement *door*, which is modified by the adjective *that*. William is *independent by address*.

    1. Poor thing! how hard she breathes!

This is a simple exclamatory sentence. The simple subject is *she*, the entire predicate "breathes how hard." The predicate-verb *breathes* is modified by the adverb *hard*, which is *itself* modified by the adverb *how*. *Thing* is *independent* by *exclamation*, and is modified by the adjective *poor*.

532. Punctuation Rule.—A noun independent by address, should with its modifiers be set off from the rest of the sentence by the comma.

533. Punctuation Rule.—An exclamatory expression should be followed by an exclamation point.

Direction.—Mention the independent nouns in the following sentences, analyze the sentences, then use them for a lesson in punctuation:

1. Sir, you can not have it.
2. Scotland! there is music in the sound.
3. "Flag of the seas! on ocean-wave
 Thy stars shall glitter o'er the brave."
4. "Auspicious hope! in thy sweet garden grow
 Wreaths for each toil, a charm for every woe."

Explanation.—*Hope*, in 6, partakes both of the nature of *address* and of *exclamation*.

CXLIV.—INTERJECTIONS.

534. Another kind of independent word is often used in exclamatory and other sentences; as,

1. O, may he never more be warm!
2. Ah! how dreary was the sound!
3. Oh! why did I not heed your counsel?

Explanation.—Such words as *O*, *ah*, and *oh*, are exclamations used to express different kinds of emotion. Each of these words is *independent* of the rest of the sentence. These words are called *interjections*.*

535. Definition.—An interjection is an exclamatory word used to express some strong or sudden emotion.

Interjections in common use.—Ah! aha! alas! adieu! bravo! fie! fudge! ha! ho! hail! all hail! hist! hello! hurrah! he, he, he! ha, ha, ha! O! oh! pshaw! pop! bang! tut! whew! whiz! heigh-ho!

536. Punctuation Rule.—An exclamation point usually follows an interjection; as,

1. Ah! how dreary was the sound!
2. Alas! no hope for me remains.

537. When the exclamatory idea extends through the whole sentence, a comma follows the interjection, and the exclamation point is placed at the end of the sentence; as,

1. O, may he never more be warm!
2. O, look at the sun!

---

* The word interjection [Lat. *inter-jectus*, thrown between] means *thrown between*, and these words are called interjections because they are *thrown in among words*, but do not make any essential part of the sentence; as, He died, alas! in early youth. An interjection is not the expression of an idea, but of a *feeling*.

INTERJECTIONS.

538. Sometimes in an interrogative sentence the exclamation point follows the interjection, and sometimes a comma is used instead; as,

    1. Oh! why did I not heed your counsel?
    2. O, where shall rest be found?

539 When an interjection is joined with an address, the punctuation point follows the address; as,

    1. O mother! will you not forgive?
    2. O sir, can this be true?

Direction.—Select the interjections used in sentences in this lesson, and give the rules for the punctuation marks used.

540. Sometimes the exclamatory expression is an elliptical sentence; as,

    1. O, for a lodge in some vast wilderness! [O, I wish for, etc.]
    2. Ah, how unfortunate! [he is].

541. Words that generally belong to other parts of speech are frequently used as interjections; as,

    1. Hush! my babe, lie still and slumber.
    2. There! you have set fire to the oil!

Remark.—These interjections *may* be parsed as other parts of speech by supplying ellipses; as, "*You* hush, my babe," etc., thus making *hush* a verb. It is better, however, to consider them as interjections.

Direction.—Select the interjections in the following sentences, mention those that are generally other parts of speech, and analyze the sentences:

1. What! are you angry? 2. A horse! a horse! my kingdom for a horse! [I will give a kingdom, etc.]. 3. Back! ruffians, back! 4. Strange! I had not heard of him. 5. The doctor came; but, alas! he came too late. 6. Magnificent! cried all at once. 7. Oh, save me, Hubert, save me! 8. Roll on, thou deep and dark blue ocean, roll! 9. Thou, too, sail on, O Ship of State!

Explanation.—Sentence 7 is simple, with a repeated predicate for rhetorical effect. Sentence 8 also has a repeated predicate.

542. The interjection *O* should always be a capital letter.

543. Many writers make the distinction of using *O* in an address, and *oh* to express emotion; as,

    1. O sir, can this be true?
    2. Oh! where shall rest be found?

INTERJECTIONS. 179

Model for Analysis.

1. Oh! why did I not heed your counsel?

This is a simple interrogative sentence. Simple subject, *I*. Entire predicate, "why did not heed your counsel"? The predicate-verb *did heed* is modified by the adverbs *why* and *not*, and is completed by the object complement *counsel*, which is modified by the possessive pronoun *your*. *Oh* is an interjection, and is *independent*.

Direction.—Punctuate the following sentences and give reasons. Punctuate sentence 7 so that *Lowell* shall be shown to be the genius; and again, so that *Parker* shall be shown to be the genius:

1. Please tell me sir how far it is to Baltimore
2. O what a beautiful collection of birds
3. My dear native hills shall I never see them again
4. What are there no enjoyments in life none
5. Galileo said nevertheless it does move
6. He said that he would soon make the point clear
7. Richard Green Parker says James Russell Lowell is a great genius.

CXLV.—ADJECTIVES IN DETAIL.

Note to Teachers.—The following lessons on adjectives and adverbs in detail, may be taken in connection with the work directly following. They are given for reference rather than to be learned in consecutive order.

544. Definition.—An adjective is a word used to describe or to limit the meaning of a noun or a pronoun.

Of the 8,000 adjectives in our language, the descriptive far exceed the limiting in number.

545. Definition.—A **descriptive adjective** qualifies or describes the meaning of a noun.

A descriptive adjective expresses some property or quality possessed by the object named by the noun; as, *sweet* orange; *strong* man; *hard* apple; *beautiful* flower.

546. Definition.—A **limiting adjective** is one that limits or restricts the application of a noun without describing it.

ADJECTIVES.

(1) Limiting adjectives point out, or express number or quantity; as, *an* orange; *the* sky; *some* people; *this* tree; *one* book; *two* boys; *first* man; *second* chapter; *much* rain.

(2) Those limiting adjectives that are used in numbering are called *numeral adjectives*; as, *one* apple; *two* pears; *first* row; *second* aisle.

547. Adjective Pronouns.—Some *limiting adjectives* are often used instead of nouns; that is, they are used like pronouns. When adjectives are so used, they are called **adjective pronouns**; as,

    1. All men seek happiness, but *all* do not find it.
    2. We ate a few apples, and we gave a *few* away.
    3. Some people were injured, and *some* escaped unhurt.
    4. Both ladies were invited, but *both* did not attend.

Note.—In sentence 1, *all* in the first member is a limiting adjective modifying *men*; in the second member it is an *adjective pronoun* and is the subject of *do find*.

548. Definition.—An adjective pronoun is a limiting adjective standing instead of the noun which it modifies.

549. List of Adjective Pronouns.—*All, any, another, both, each, either, enough, few, former, latter, last, little, many, much, neither, none, one, other, some, same, several, such, this, that, these, those.*

550. Adjectives used as Nouns.—A *descriptive adjective* denoting some prominent quality is sometimes (by ellipsis) used as a noun. An adjective so used is taken in a plural sense when it denotes persons, and is generally preceded by *the*; as,

    1. The *good* alone are great.
    2. The *rich* and the *poor* meet together.
    3. The *poor* suffer most in winter.
    4. They landed at *dead* of night.
    5. Providence rewards the *good* and punishes the *bad*.
    6. The *truly* wise are never selfish.
    7. The *young* are too often impatient.

Explanation.—In 1, *good* is a descriptive adjective used as a noun, third, *plural*, masculine (or feminine), nominative case, being the subject of the verb *are*.

INFLECTION OF ADJECTIVES.

551. Proper Adjectives.—Descriptive adjectives derived from proper names are called *proper adjectives*; as, *German* emigrants; *French* people; *English* ships [129].

Questions.—1. What is an adjective? 2. A descriptive adjective? 3. A limiting adjective? 4. A numeral adjective? 5. An adjective pronoun? 6. A proper adjective? 7. Mention three adjectives of each kind. 8. How should a proper adjective be written? 9. Mention the adjective pronouns given in the preceding list. 10. What kind of adjectives become adjective pronouns? 11. *How* do they become adjective pronouns? 12. What descriptive adjectives are sometimes used as nouns? 13. What form of verb must be used with a descriptive adjective used as a noun?

CXLVI.—INFLECTION OF ADJECTIVES.

552. Most descriptive adjectives change their form to express the *degree* of quality possessed by an object when compared with other objects having the same quality.

We speak of a *strong* man, a *sweet* orange, a *hard* apple, a *beautiful* flower. But all men do not possess the same *degree* of *strength*, nor all oranges the same *degree* of *sweetness*, nor do all flowers possess the same *degree* of *beauty*; i. e., the *same* quality may exist in *similar* objects in *different degrees*.

The same quality may also exist in *different* objects in *different degrees*; as, Honey is *sweeter* than sugar.

Comparison of Adjectives.

1. I have a *sweet* orange. [One object spoken of.]
2. You have a *sweeter* orange. [Two objects compared.]
3. She has the *sweetest* orange. [Three or more compared.]

In these sentences three degrees of the quality called *sweetness* are expressed, and *three forms* of the adjective *sweet* are used to indicate these degrees.

The form *sweet* is called the *positive* * degree.
The form *sweeter* is called the *comparative* degree.
The form *sweetest* is called the *superlative* degree.

---

* Some suppose that the *positive* form is improperly called a degree. But, when we speak of a *large* apple, we compare *one* apple with the *average size* of apples.

553. Comparison.—The change in the form of an adjective to express different degrees of quality or quantity is called comparison [inflection].

554. To compare an adjective is to mention properly the three degrees in their regular order.

Direction.—Compare the following adjectives and define *comparison*:

POSITIVE.	COMPARATIVE.	SUPERLATIVE.
tall.	taller.	tallest.
great.	greater.	greatest.
small.	smaller.	smallest.
warm.	warmer.	warmest.
short.	shorter.	shortest.

Questions.—1. How does the comparative degree of *tall* differ from the positive? 2. How is the superlative degree formed? 3. What is added to *great* to form its comparative degree? 4. What to form its superlative degree?

555. Definition.—The positive degree is expressed by the adjective in its simplest form.

556. Definition.—The comparative degree is expressed by adding *er* to the positive.

The comparative degree refers to two objects only, and shows that one of them possesses the quality in a greater or less degree than the other.

557. Definition.—The superlative degree is expressed by adding *est* to the positive.

The superlative degree refers to any number of objects greater than two, and shows that one of them possesses the quality in a greater or less degree than any of the others.

Direction.—Fill the blank spaces in the following sentences with the proper forms of *long, young, cold, large, tall, sweet,* using them in the order here given. Analyze each sentence:

1. My right arm is the ——.
2. She is the —— of the three sisters.
3. December is the —— month in the year.
4. My right hand is the ——.
5. The —— of those two boys is an excellent scholar.
6. I have an orange and you have one, but mine is the ——.

Questions.—1. How many degrees of comparison are there? 2. How is the positive degree expressed? 3. How the comparative? 4. The superlative? 5. What does the comparative degree show? 6. The superlative? 7. How many persons or things are spoken of when the comparative degree is used? 8. How many when the superlative degree is used?

CXLVII.—IRREGULAR COMPARISON.

558. Some adjectives can not be compared in any *regular* way; such adjectives are said to be irregularly compared; as,

POSITIVE.	COMPARATIVE.	SUPERLATIVE.	POSITIVE.	COMPARATIVE.	SUPERLATIVE.
good, well,	better,	best.	old,	{ older, elder,	oldest. eldest.
bad, ill, evil,	worse,	worst.	late,	{ later, latter,	latest. last.
			far,	farther,	farthest.
much, many,	more,	most.	[forth],	further,	furthest.
little,	less.	least.	near,	nearer,	{ nearest. next.

559. Older and **oldest** refer to either persons or things.

560. Elder and **eldest** refer to persons of the same family, and are considered, by many, preferable to *older* and *oldest*, unless they are followed by *than*; as,
    1. He is my *elder* brother.
    2. My brother is *older than* I am.

561. Farther, further.—*Farther* refers to *place* or *distance*; *further* refers to something *additional*; as,
    1. The *farthest* planet from the earth is Neptune.
    2. I have no *further* use for this book.

562. Forth is now used only as an adverb; therefore, *further* and *furthest*, as adjectives, have no *positive*. *Far* and *near*, and their variations, are also used as adverbs.

563. Last, latest.—Care should be taken in the use of *last* and *latest*. In speaking of a performance or of a production by a person now living, we should use *latest*; as,
    1. This book is his *latest* work [author living].
    2. This book is his *last* work [author dead].

Direction.—Write all the sentences in this lesson on the blackboard, omitting the adjectives in the comparative and superlative degrees, and require pupils to supply the proper word for each blank space and to give the reason for each choice of a word.

CXLVIII.—REGULAR COMPARISON.

564. Most adjectives that are regularly compared are words of one syllable; as,

POSITIVE.	COMPARATIVE.	SUPERLATIVE.	POSITIVE.	COMPARATIVE.	SUPERLATIVE.
cold,	colder,	coldest.	red,*	redder,	reddest.
sharp,	sharper,	sharpest.	sad,*	sadder,	saddest.
nice,*	nicer,	nicest.	wise,*	wiser,	wisest.
tame,*	tamer,	tamest.	fine,	finer,	finest.

565. Adjectives of two syllables may also be compared like monosyllables when they end in *le, re, w, y,* or *me*; as,

POSITIVE.	COMPARATIVE.	SUPERLATIVE.
able,	abler,	ablest.
sincere,	sincerer,	sincerest.
narrow,	narrower,	narrowest.
merry,	merrier,	merriest.
pretty,	prettier,	prettiest.
handsome,	handsomer,	handsomest.

566. Other dissyllables may be regularly compared if they can be easily pronounced after *er* and *est* are added; as,

POSITIVE.	COMPARATIVE.	SUPERLATIVE.
pleasant,	pleasanter,	pleasantest.
common,	commoner,	commonest.

567. Some adjectives can not be compared, because the qualities they express are not subject to change; as *true, square, round, straight, triangular, annual, eternal, absolute, preferable.*

Strictly speaking, these adjectives can not be compared. Good writers, however, defend the use of *truer, straighter, rounder,* etc., because, often when we speak of anything as *straight* or *round,* we do not have in mind

---

* For the rules for spelling the comparative and superlative degrees of these adjectives, see any speller.

perfect straightness or roundness; and thus we speak of other things as *straighter* or *rounder*; also *truer*; as, "A *truer* friend I never knew."

Direction.—Tell what adjectives may be compared by *er* and *est*, and why some adjectives can not be compared. Compare all the adjectives in this lesson.

CXLIX.—COMPARISON BY MORE AND MOST.

568. Different degrees of quality may also be expressed by joining the adverbs *more* and *most* to adjectives to express an increasing grade of quality, and the adverbs *less* and *least* to express a decreasing grade—thus making a kind of phrase-adjective; as,

POSITIVE.	COMPARATIVE.	SUPERLATIVE.
cheerful,	more cheerful,	most cheerful.
cheerful,	less cheerful,	least cheerful.
amiable,	more amiable,	most amiable.
amiable,	less amiable,	least amiable.

Although *more* and *most*, as here used, help to express different degrees of quality, yet the *form* of the adjective is not changed; therefore, *in a strict sense*, these adjectives are not compared.

569. Most adjectives compared in this way are those of more than one syllable, and *more* and *most* are *secondary adverbs*, modifying the adjectives with which they are used.

570. A few adjectives of *one* syllable, such as *wise, fit, fair, true*, may sometimes be compared by *more* and *most*; as, positive, *wise*; comparative, *more wise*; superlative, *most wise*.

571. When two qualities in the same person or thing are compared, or when the adjective follows its noun, this method of comparing adjectives of one syllable is alone used; as,

  1. He is more nice than wise.
  2. A man more kind I never knew.
  3. A sky more clear was never seen.
  4. A foot more light, a step more true, ne'er trod the earth.

Direction.—Compare such of the following adjectives as will admit of comparison, using both methods with those dissyllables that will admit of it:

Merry, handsome, worthless, virtuous, funny, hourly, contemptible, industrious, guilty, square, exact, high, remote, joyful, thick, eternal, happy, equal, daily, hourly, noble, successful, polite, useful, empty, full, universal, dead, gentle, spiteful, severe, feeble, truthful, profound.

Parsing Model.

1. A *truer* friend I never knew.

Truer is a descriptive adjective of the comparative degree, and modifies the noun *friend*. [The rule may be given or not.]

Rule.—An adjective may modify a noun or a pronoun.

CL.—PROPER USE OF ADJECTIVES.

572. Double Comparison.—Both methods of comparison should not be used at the same time. We should not say—

    1. I never heard a *more* wis*er* remark.
    2. This was the *most* unkind*est* cut of all.

573. Connected Adjectives.—When an adjective properly compared by *er* or *est* is connected with one compared by *more* or *most*, the smaller should be placed first, and the full form of comparison be used with each; or, both should be compared by one word (*more* or *most*), which should be used with the former adjective only, being understood with the latter; as,

    1. He chose the *wisest* and *most* advantageous course.
    2. He chose the *most* wise and advantageous course.
    3. Homer's imagination was by far the *most* wise and copious.

574. This, that.—Two adjectives, *this* (plural *these*) and *that* (plural *those*), change their form to express number. *This* and *that* can be used only with singular nouns; *these* and *those*, only with plural nouns.

Direction.—Use *this, that, these,* or *those* properly in the blank spaces in the following sentences; analyze and parse these, and the preceding sentences:

    1. —— kind of apples I like. 2. I have not seen him —— twenty years. 3. I dislike —— sort of berries. 4. —— memoranda are not correct. 5. I will take one of —— kind of knives. 6. —— phenomenon, the northern lights, is very beautiful. 7. I never liked —— sort of bonnets.

Remark.—We *may* say, "Thirty *head* of cattle"; "Three *yoke* of oxen"; but *not*, " We carted three *load* of hay."

CLI.—POSITION OF ADJECTIVES.

575. Position of Adjectives.—An adjective generally stands before its noun; as,

    1. A *diligent* man will succeed in business.

576. An adjective modified by an adverb or an adverbial phrase may follow its noun; as,

    1. The man, *innocent* of the offense, boldly faced his accuser.
    2. "A foot more *light*, a step more *true*,
        Ne'er from the heath-flower dashed the dew."

577. Two or more connected adjectives may follow the noun which they modify, and, in poetry, a single adjective; as,

    1. The poor woman, *weary* and *sad*, groaned pitifully.
    2. "Loose revelry and riot *bold*."

578. An adjective denoting a quality as the result of an action expressed by the verb follows its noun; as,

    1. Idleness makes a man *poor*.
    2. Labor makes a man *thrifty*.

579. An adjective follows the *pronoun* that it modifies; as,

    1. We found him *studious* and attentive.
    2. The doctor considers her very *sick*.

580. Predicate adjectives follow the nouns to which they relate, except in inverted sentences; as,

    1. The sky is *blue*.

581. *Alone, else, enough,* when they are adjectives, always follow their nouns, and *only* generally does.

582. Any adjective should be so placed that there can be no doubt to what noun it belongs; as,

    1. A pair of *new* shoes [not a *new* pair].
    2. A pair of *beautiful* vases [not a *beautiful* pair].

Direction.—Tell what noun or pronoun is modified by each of the italicised adjectives in the following sentences, and give reasons:

1. John *only* rowed the boat. 2. I have money *enough* for my wants. 3. He *alone* was *calm*. 4. Boys *only* occupy this floor, and *only* girls the lower floor. 5. Nobody *else* can go with me. 6. I consider the result *doubtful*. 7. They have food *enough* for three days *only*. 8. The flags, *bright* and *gay*, floated in the breeze. 9. *Only* a tyrant would act thus.

POSITION OF ADJECTIVES.

Direction.—Analyze the sentences found in this lesson. Also parse the adjectives, giving the degree of each.

Questions.—1. What is meant by double comparison? 2. How should connected adjectives be compared, and how should they be arranged [573]? 3. How should we parse adjectives used in the place of nouns? 4. What two parts of speech do adjectives modify? 5. What two adjectives have plural forms? 6. How must they be used? 7. When may an adjective follow its noun? 8. What special adjectives always follow their nouns? 9. What is a general rule for placing adjectives?

CLII.—USE OF SPECIAL ADJECTIVES.

583. Phrase-Adjectives.—In the expression "*a few* men," the words *a few* are taken together as *one* expression, and called a *phrase-adjective*. *A few* modifies the noun *men*.

Direction.—Mention the *phrase-adjectives* in the following expressions:

"*A little* food"; "*a hundred* men"; "*a great many* people"; "*many a* flower"; "*three hundred and sixty-five* days"; "*dark-blue* cloth." These expressions are idiomatic.

584. There is a difference in the use of *few* and *little* with *a*, and without *a*; as,

1. "*Few* men noticed it" = it was almost entirely overlooked.
2. "*A few* men noticed it" = some men surely noticed it.
3. "He had *little* cause for dissatisfaction" = almost no cause.
4. "He had *a little* cause for dissatisfaction" = had some cause.

585. No, none.—*No* means, *not any*; as, "*No* man cared for me" [no, adj.]. "I could go *no* farther" [no, adv. mod. the adv. *farther*]. *No* as a noun *refers to votes*; as, "The *noes* have it." *None* has nearly lost its adjective sense, and is now mostly used as a pronoun; as, "*None* pitied him." Formerly, however, *none* was used as an adjective; as, "Silver and gold have I *none*." Here *none* is an adjective modifying *silver* and *gold*. *None* standing for *quantity* is singular; as, "We searched for water, but *none has* been found." *None* standing for *number* is plural; as, "*None* of my friends *have* arrived."

586. Another.—The adjective pronoun *another* is used only in the singular; it forms the possessive case like a noun; as, "*Another's* grief he could not feel."

587. One, other.*—The adjective pronouns *one* and *other* form the plurals *ones* and *others*; as, "The nest was full of little *ones*"; "*Others* may take a different view." They form the possessive case in both numbers, but they are not used as adjectives in their plural forms; as, "I hear some *one's* footsteps"; "The boys destroyed the little *ones'* nest"; "He had a tear for others' woes"; "The other's child was sick." Used in this way *one's* and *other's* and *another's* are really *nouns* in the possessive case.

588. Only.—*Only* is often used as an adverb. Whether an adjective or an adverb, it should be placed as near as possible to the word or phrase it is intended to modify. When not so placed, a meaning is often given to the sentence not intended by the speaker or writer; as,

1. He only arrived yesterday [arrived only yesterday].
2. We only stopped for refreshments once [stopped only once].
3. We only staid three days [staid only three days].
4. He only copied the rules.
5. He copied the rules only [or, only the rules].

Only (in sentence 4) may modify any of the three words *he, copied,* or *rules,* according to the meaning given to the sentence by emphasis or rhetorical pause in reading it; as,

1. *He* only, copied the rules [no one else—*only* mod. *he*].
2. He only *copied* the rules [did nothing else—*only* mod. *copied*].
3. He copied only the *rules* [copied nothing else—*only* mod. *rules*].

This third meaning, however, is better expressed by placing *only* after *rules,* as in sentence 5, above.

Worth.—It is *worth* a dollar [*valuable* to the extent of a dollar]. To reign is *worth* ambition [*worthy* of ambition]. *Worth,* as here used, is an *adjective.*

589. Other words.—Care should be taken in placing such words as *merely, nearly, not, not only,* etc., so that there can be no doubt as to the words they are intended to modify.

Direction.—Justify the use of the words in italics in the following sentences, if correctly used; change their position if incorrectly placed; explain the use acquired by such change; change any that are correctly placed if by such change another correct use may be made:

---

* They love each other = They love, each [loves the] other, *each* being the subject of *loves* understood.

ADVERBS.—COMPARISON.

1. He *only* favors his friends. 2. I *only* spoke to him. 3. The French *nearly* lost three thousand men. 4. He *merely* mentioned the fact. 5. He was *only* elected twice. 6. I am *not* a man of much originality. 7. I saw *only* John and Henry. 8. I *only* saw John and Henry. 9. California *not only* produces gold in abundance, but quicksilver also.

CLIII.—ADVERBS.—COMPARISON, ETC.

590. A few adverbs are compared like adjectives, and these follow the same rules as adjectives in regard to terminations, number of syllables, etc.

Direction.—Compare *soon, fast, far, long, late, early, often, slowly, quickly, graceful.*

591. Position of Adverbs.—Adverbs should be so placed that they will most clearly express the meaning intended.

Direction.—Change the position of the adverb in each of the following sentences so that the meaning may be more clearly expressed:

1. We can not deprive them of merit wholly.
2. He did not see the reason for the movement clearly.
3. I understand my position fully.
4. The manufacture of silk originated in China unquestionably.
5. Tea chiefly comes from China and Japan.
6. The prisoner watched the expression on the face of the judge anxiously.

592. An adverb may modify a word, a phrase, or a whole sentence; as,

1. He ran *rapidly* toward the river.
2. He swam *almost* across the river.
3. *Perhaps* he made a mistake.

Explanation.—In 1, *rapidly* modifies *ran*; *almost* (in 2) modifies the phrase *across the river*; and *perhaps* (in 3) modifies the whole sentence *he made a mistake.* An adverb modifying a whole sentence is sometimes called a **modal** adverb.

Direction.—Read the first of the following sentences so that, by emphasis and rhetorical pause, and by changing the position of *only, three* different meanings may be expressed. Do the same with the second sentence, and tell what word or phrase *only* modifies according to each reading. Analyze and parse:

1. I only answered him.
2. I only study in school.
3. He only was firm.
4. Jane only sings to-night.

CLIV.—USE OF SPECIAL ADVERBS.

593. Double negatives.—*Two* negative words should not be used to express a negation; thus, "He does *not* know *nothing*."

Remark.—The adverbs *no, not, never,* and the nouns *nothing* and *nobody,* are the negative words to be used with care; also *scarcely, hardly,* and *but.* "He does *not* know *nothing*" = "He knows something"; i. e., two negatives are equal to an affirmative. Say, "He does not know anything," or "He knows nothing." *Especial care* should be taken to guard against the use of double negatives when one of them forms part of a contraction; as, "*Don't* say *nothing* about it." This should be, "Don't [do not] say anything about it," or "Say nothing about it."

594. Caution.—Do not say: 1. I can not by no means allow it. 2. Nobody never helps me. 3. He didn't say nothing to me. 4. I have not spoken to no one. 5. I'm not doing nothing at present. 6. There isn't hardly a breath of air. 7. We didn't have scarcely a minute to spare. 8. He doesn't do nothing but tease me. 9. I haven't but [only] one. 10. I can't hardly believe it. 11. We did not find scarcely any chestnuts.

595. An affirmative is sometimes delicately expressed by using two negatives, when one of them is a prefix; as, His language, though simple, is *not in*elegant; that is, It *is* elegant.

596. Rather.—In "I would *rather* stay at home," *rather* = *preferably,* and is an adverb modifying *would stay* [397].

1. It happened *twenty years ago.*
2. He staid *till a few minutes ago.*

597. Ago.—Some grammarians consider *ago,* in sentence 1, either an adjective in the sense of *past,* modifying *years,* or an adverb modifying *happened,* itself being modified by the adverbial objective *years* [377]. The latter is the better rendering of the word. But, it being very difficult, if not impossible, to supply the *ellipsis,* it is perhaps better to treat the expression *twenty years ago* as idiomatic, modifying *as a whole* the verb *happened.* The phrase *till a few minutes ago* may be disposed of in the same way without attempting to dispose of the separate words. The use of language as employed by good writers is of greater importance than the disposition of single words in idiomatic expressions.

598. There as an adverb generally means *in that place*. It is often used, however, merely to introduce a sentence for the sake of euphony; as, "*There* will be an eclipse of the moon to-night. When *there* is used in this way, the subject always follows its verb, *there* having little or no modifying force. Used in this way *there* should be called simply an *introductory adverb*.

599. Independent Adverbs.—Some adverbs are used independently; as, "*Well*, I can not help it"; "*Why*, that is not possible"; "*Yes*, you may go."

600. Yes and **no** are called **responsive adverbs**; as,
    1. Have you a knife? Yes.
    2. Did you bring the basket? No.

Here *yes* and *no* are independent. *Yes* or *no* may be considered to stand for a whole sentence. *Yes* = I have a knife. *No* = I did not bring the basket. *Yes*, *yea*, *ay*, and *amen*, are called *affirmative responsives*; *no* and *nay*, *negative responsives*.

601. Definition.—A *responsive* is a word used to reply to a question or a petition.

602. The.—In the sentence "The more he ate the fatter he grew," *the* intensifies the meaning of the adverb *more* and the adjective *fatter*; therefore *the*, as here used, is an adverb. For the purpose of analysis, the sentence should be transposed to read, "He grew the fatter *because* he ate the more," *because* being the connective. *The more* may be taken as a *phrase-adverb* instead of disposing of the words separately.

603. Idiomatic phrases.—Such phrases as *on high*, *of late*, *of old*, etc., are idiomatic, and each is used as an adverb [398]. *More than* is sometimes used in an idiomatic sense, and should be so parsed in such sentences as, He is *more than* willing to help you. Here *more than* is an idiomatic phrase, adverbial, and modifies the adjective *willing*.

604. Enough.—In the sentence "This is good enough for me," *enough* is an adverb modifying the adjective good. The expression *good enough* = *sufficiently good*. In the sentence "Have we bread enough?" *enough* is an adjective modifying *bread*. In the sentence "I have enough," *enough* is an adjective pronoun, and is the object of *have*.

605. Caution.—An adverb should not be used in place of an attribute complement. We should not say—
  1. The stars look *brilliantly* to-night.
  2. This velvet feels *smoothly*.

Questions.—1. What are *yes* and *no* called? 2. What is a responsive? 3. Which are the affirmative responsives? 4. The negative? 5. What is *amen* a reply to? 6. Why are *brilliantly* and *smoothly* incorrectly used in the above sentences?

CLV.—CLASSES OF ADVERBS.—FORMATION.

606. Adverbs may be separated into six general classes:

(1) **Time**—answering the questions when? how long? how often? as, *now, then, never, lately, sometimes.*

(2) **Place**—answering the questions where? whither? whence? as, *here, there, everywhere, forward.*

(3) **Manner**—answering the questions how? in what way? as, *fast, slowly, faithfully, together.*

(4) **Degree**—answering the questions how much? to what extent? as, *fully, mostly, scarcely, enough.*

(5) **Interrogative Adverbs**—used in asking questions; as, *how, where, whither, whence, when, why.*

(6) **Conjunctive Adverbs**—used to introduce clauses, and to connect them, like conjunctions, to preceding clauses; as, *how, where, whither, whence, when, why, as, before, after, till, until, however, wherever, whenever, while* [661].

Other classifications of adverbs are often made, but the class to which an adverb belongs is of very little importance.

Formations of Adverbs.

607. Adverbs in ly.—Many adverbs are formed by adding *ly* to adjectives; as, *closely* from *close; truthfully* from *truth; tastefully* from *tasteful; diligently* from *diligent; carefully* from *careful.*

608. Adjectives in ly.—Many adjectives also end in *ly,* generally formed from nouns, and these should not be mistaken for adverbs; as, a *motley* crowd; *costly* dress; *daily* toil; *queenly* airs; *manly* act; *womanly* trait; *quarterly* dues; *brotherly* love; *burly* man; *surly* boy; *wily* foe; *easterly* wind; *stately* carriage; *friendly* advice; *lively* debate; *princely* fortune; *cowardly* act; *holy* life; *lovely* disposition; *homely* features.

Questions.—1. What is an adverb of time? 2. Of place? 3. Manner? 4. Degree? 5. An interrogative adverb? 6. From what are most adverbs formed? 7. How are adjectives ending in *ly* formed?

CLVI.—VARYING PARTS OF SPEECH.

609. Nouns used as Adjectives.—Some nouns, especially those denoting the *metals* and *other materials*, are often used as adjectives; as,

1. The builder erected a *stone* cottage.
2. The farmer gathered his *wheat* harvest.

610. Adjectives used as Nouns.—A noun that would naturally follow an adjective is frequently omitted to avoid repetition [550]. In such cases, the adjective assumes the place and office of the omitted noun, and is called an adjective used as a noun; as,

1. The French speak the French language [French *people*].
2. The English speak the English language [English *people*].
3. Many people like mountain scenery, and *many* like the sea-shore [adj. pron. used as a noun].
4. The *rich* and the *poor*, the *weak* and the *strong*, have one common Father [rich *people*].

611. Same Word as Adjective or Adverb.—Some words are adjectives in some constructions and adverbs in others; as, *hard, ill,* far, fast, much, less, little, so, all, early, only, the, well* [89].

Direction.—Determine the part of speech of the words just given, as found in the following sentences:

1. The farmer works *hard*. 2. The farmer plows the *hard* soil. 3. He has a *fast* horse. 4. We walked very *fast*. 5. How *far* did you walk? 6. He went to a *far* country. 7. I *only* answered him. 8. I answered him *only*. 9. You should work *more* and play *less*. 10. *More* work and *less* play will produce better results. 11. *All* men desire happiness. 12. *All* † bloodless lay the untrodden snow. 13. *The* longer we live, *the* wiser we grow.

---

* *Illy* is sometimes improperly used for *ill* when it is an adverb.
† *All* = *entirely*, an adverb modifying the adjective *bloodless*.

612. But.—A conjunction, "We looked, *but* we could not find it." An adjective or an adverb [meaning *only*], "I am *but* a man"; "I have *but* one orange." A preposition [meaning *except*], "All *but* him had fled."

613. Like.—An adjective, "My book is *like* yours." An adverb, "The Assyrian came down *like* a wolf on the fold" [380]. A verb, "All people *like* fair play." A noun, "*Like* begets *like*." *Like*, however, should not be used as a conjunction. Do not say, "She walks *like* you do" [427].

614. Same Word as Verb and Noun:
   1. Tall trees *shade* the lawn.
   2. This *shade* protects us from the sun.
   3. Artists *paint* pictures.
   4. *Paint* preserves wood.
   5. *Man* the life-boat with trusty *men*.

615. Nouns used as Adverbs.—A noun used as an adverb is called an *adverbial objective* [377]. The ellipsis may be supplied, however, thus forming an adverbial phrase; as,
   1. We came *home Friday* [*to* our home *on* Friday].
   2. I don't care a *fig* [*to* the extent *of* a fig].

616. Adverbs used as Nouns:
   1. Every *why* hath a *wherefore*.
   2. Thou hast kept the good wine until *now* [this time].

617. So, as Adverb and Adjective.—In "I did not expect you *so* soon," *so* is an adverb. In "He is not wealthy, yet he may become *so*," *so* = *wealthy*, and is an adjective.

618. Yet, as Adverb and Conjunction.—In "Does my father *yet* live?" *yet* is an adverb. In, "He is not wealthy, *yet* he may become so," *yet* is a conjunction.

619. Hence, thence, and whence.—*Hence* = *from* this place; therefore *from* should not be used before this word. For the same reason *from* should not precede *thence* and *whence*.

Direction.—Use each of the following words in two sentences so that it shall be one part of speech in the first, and another in the second: *run, walk, play, dream, mountain, gold, iron, burn, cut, paint, enough, fast, more, much, each, milk, shovel, cook, only, copper, tin, good, all.*

620. Caution.—An adjective should not be used when an *adverb* derived from it is required. Do not say—

1. She walks very graceful. 2. He does not read good. 3. The day was dreadful hot. 4. He is a real kind man. 5. Do not walk so slow. 6. James behaves very rude. 7. He is in tolerable good health. 8. We were real hungry. 9. I was awful angry. 10. I caught a remarkable fine trout.

CLVII.—INFINITIVES.

1. William *studies* for improvement.
2. William studies *to improve*.
3. He has flowers *to sell*.
4. I am anxious *to return*.

Explanation.—A **finite** verb is a verb limited [confined] to a subject, of which it makes an affirmation, as *studies*, in sentence 1. The word *finite* means *limited* or *confined within bounds*. An **infinite** verb [an infinitive] is one *not* limited to a subject; i. e., a verb that has not a direct subject, and makes no affirmation. The verb *to improve* (in 2) is an *infinite* verb because it is not used with a direct subject; it is used in an adverbial sense, like the phrase *for improvement* (in 1) to tell *why* about the finite verb *studies*. The word *to*, used with the root-verb *improve*, becomes a part of the verb, and "*to improve*," taken as a whole, is called an *infinite verb* or an **infinitive**. In 3, the infinitive *to sell* is used like an adjective to modify the noun *flowers*. In 4, the infinitive *to return* is used as an adverb to modify the adjective *anxious*. In sentence 2, by the use of the infinitive *to improve*, an act is expressed *indirectly* of the person named by the subject of the principal verb *studies*.

621. Definition.—An infinitive is a verb that expresses action in a general way, without affirming it of a subject.

622. Infinitives take the same modifiers and complements as *finite* verbs.

623. Infinitive phrase.—Any combination of an infinitive with its modifiers and complements forms an **infinitive phrase**; as,

1. They endeavored *to act cautiously*.
2. He is anxious *to succeed in business*.
3. I have a desire *to visit Europe*.
4. He endeavored *to be a good boy*.
5. She made an effort *to be agreeable*.

INFINITIVE PHRASES. 197

Explanation.—In sentence 1, the infinitive phrase *to act cautiously* is composed of the infinitive *to act*, combined with the adverb *cautiously*. The phrase is adverbial, modifying *endeavored*.

In 2, the phrase = the infinitive plus an adverbial phrase.
In 3, the phrase = the infinitive plus an object complement.
In 4, the phrase = the infinitive plus an attribute complement [noun].
In 5, the phrase = the infinitive plus an attribute complement [adj.].

Direction.—Tell whether the phrases in these five sentences are *adjective* or *adverbial* in their use, and give the definition of an infinitive, and of an infinitive phrase.

CLVIII.—ANALYSIS OF INFINITIVE PHRASES.

Direction.—Select the infinitive phrase in each of the following sentences, determine its office, and tell how each is composed. Analyze and parse according to the models given below:

1. He strove to do his work in the best manner.
2. They endeavored to act in harmony.
3. Some people always endeavor to be honest in their dealings.
4. It is exceedingly hard to please some people.
5. Our parents always tried to make us happy.
6. Will you be kind enough to move your chair?
7. The young man had a great desire to be an artist.
8. He ought to have known better.
9. Then he proceeded to explain the point with great clearness.
10. We went to the river to catch some fish.
11. No one likes to be forced into an unpleasant position.
12. The whole party went to the woods to gather berries.
13. This incident afforded us an opportunity to study human nature.
14. The old man expressed a strong wish to visit the home of his childhood.
15. We should always endeavor to speak truthfully, and to be careful of other people's feelings.

Models for Analysis.

1. Some people always endeavor to be honest in their dealings.

624. This is a simple declarative sentence. The entire subject is "Some people," and the predicate is "always endeavor to be honest in their dealings." The simple subject *people* is modified by the adjective *some*. The predicate-verb *endeavor* is modified by the adverb *always*, and also by the complex infinitive phrase *to be honest in their dealings*. The principal word of this phrase, the infinitive *to be*, is completed by the adjective complement *honest*, which is modified by the adverbial phrase *in their dealings, dealings* being the principal word, modified by the possessive pronoun *their*.

625. Parsing Model.—In parsing *to do* (in 1) say, *to do* is an infinitive, irregular, transitive, and with its phrase modifies the verb *strove*.

626. *Infinitives* are sometimes called **verbals**.

CLIX.—SUBSTANTIVE PHRASES.

Remark.—Only single words have been used, so far, as *subjects*, or as *object* and *attribute* complements. In this lesson it will be seen that an *infinitive* or an *infinitive phrase* is often used in place of a *noun*. Afterward it will be seen that a whole sentence (called a *clause*) is also used as a noun. When a phrase or a clause is used as a noun it is called a *substantive phrase* or a *substantive clause*.

627. The term *substantive* is a name given to a noun or to any word, phrase, or clause used in place of a noun.

628. As a **substantive**, an *infinitive* or an *infinitive phrase* may be used—

(1) As the subject of a finite verb:
  1. *To retreat* was impossible [*to retreat* is sub. of was].
  2. *To retreat with safety* was impossible [*inf. ph.*, sub. of *was*].
  3. *To hesitate now* is folly.
  4. *To teach idle pupils* is disagreeable work.

(2) As the object of a verb or of the preposition *about*:
  1. He wished *to sleep*.
  2. A refined mind loves *to contemplate the works of Nature*.
  3. I know *how to draw a map*.*
  4. He was about *to retreat to his defenses*.

---

* In this sentence, *how to draw a map* is the object phrase, *how* modifying *to draw a map* as a whole; and yet most authors say that the infinitive *to draw* depends on *how*. Say, *To draw* is an infinitive, and with its phrase is the object of the verb *know*.

SUBSTANTIVE PHRASES. 199

(3) As an attribute complement:
1. To be good * is *to be happy* [*goodness* is *happiness*].
2. His great desire was *to be wealthy.*
3. Cæsar seems *to have been ambitious.*
4. His intention was *to sail for Europe.*

(4) As an appositive term:
1. Delightful task! *to rear the tender thought.*

(5) As an independent term:
1. *To confess the truth,* † I was in fault.

Direction.—Determine the *use* of each infinitive phrase in the following sentences, and tell how each is composed: 1. His hands refuse to labor. 2. In his haste to be wealthy, he fell into temptation. 3. To die for one's country is glorious. 4. To speak plainly, I think you are dishonest. 5. To obey is to enjoy. 6. To conceal the truth is often highly criminal. 7. I have walked far enough to weary me. 8. A good man loves to do good. 9. The wisest course is always to speak the truth.

Questions.—1. What is a substantive? 2. What is a substantive phrase? 3. In what different ways have infinitive phrases been used in preceding lessons? 4. What uses are made of such phrases in this lesson? 5. What is an infinitive? 6. What is an infinitive phrase?

CLX.—ANALYSIS AND PARSING.—MODELS.

Remark.—These models cover only what is new to pupils. The analysis should be completed according to previous models.

1. To look at thee unlocks a warmer clime.

629. The subject is the infinitive phrase "To look at thee." The principal word in this phrase is the infinitive *to look* modified by the adverbial phrase *at thee.*

Parsing Model.—*To look* is an *infinitive, regular, intransitive,* and with its phrase is the subject of the verb *unlocks.*

---

* The adjective *good*, being used in a subject phrase, does not *definitely* refer to any preceding word; it is, therefore, called an indefinite adjective complement.

† This use of the infinitive phrase seems analogous to that of the *modal adverb* in "Certainly, I was in fault," and the phrase seems rather to modify the rest of the sentence. It is generally classed, however, as above.

2. Some people wished to crown Washington king.

The predicate is "wished to crown Washington king." The predicate-verb *wished* is completed by the object phrase *to crown Washington king.* The principal word in this phrase is the infinitive *to crown*, completed by the object *Washington*, which is modified by the appositive noun *king.**

Parsing Model.—*To crown* is an *infinitive, regular, transitive*, and with its phrase is the object of the verb *wished.*

3. To be good is to be happy [*goodness* is *happiness*].
4. To become a good scholar requires hard study.

This (No. 3) is a simple declarative sentence. The subject is the infinitive phrase "To be good," and the predicate, "is to be happy." The principal word in the subject phrase is the infinitive *to be*, completed by the *indefinite* adjective complement *good.* The predicate-verb *is* is completed by the attribute complement *to be happy.* The principal word in this phrase is *to be*, completed by the attribute complement *happy.*

Parsing Model.—*To be* (in *to be happy*) is an *infinitive, irregular, intransitive*, and with its phrase is the *attribute complement* of *is.*

Explanation.—The attribute *good*, in 3, and *scholar*, in 4, completing an infinitive in a *subject phrase*, do not refer *definitely* to anything preceding; they are used *indefinitely.* *Scholar* is called independent, and is considered in the nominative case. Some, however, prefer to suppose an ellipsis, thus: "*For me* to be good"; "*For me* to become a good scholar." This makes *scholar* an attribute, referring to *me* as an object. *Scholar*, here, is therefore considered to be an *attributive object.*

CLXI.—ELLIPTICAL INFINITIVES.

630. There is generally an ellipsis of the sign *to* before all but the first of two or more infinitives in the same construction; as, *To* eat, drink, and sleep seemed to be his only enjoyment.

631. There is generally an ellipsis of the sign *to* before infinitives following the verbs *bid, dare* (meaning *venture*), *feel*

---

* Some authors prefer to consider this *elliptical*; thus, Some people wished to crown Washington [to be] king, making *king* the attribute complement of *to be.* Washington being an object complement, king is considered to be an objective, and, thus used, it is called an attributive object, completing, with Washington, the infinitive *to crown.*

(when transitive), *hear, let, make, need,* and *see* (when trans.); as, He *dare* not speak; Did you *hear* it *thunder*? Let me *see* your new watch. After the *passive voice* of these verbs, the sign *to* is generally expressed; as, He was made *to* obey.

Note.—The reason for the omission of the sign *to* before infinitives is one of *euphony*; therefore, *to* may be used after these verbs *bid, dare,* etc., when harshness will not thereby be produced; as, This book needs *to be revised*; Dare *to be true*, nothing can need a lie; He will never dare *to come*. *To* is occasionally omitted after *observe, behold, watch, help,* and *have*.

632. An infinitive, or an infinitive phrase, is sometimes used as explanatory of *introductory* **it**; as,

  1. It is my duty *to caution you*.

The real *subject-thought*, however, is expressed by the phrase *to caution you*, and the sentence may be written, *To caution you* is my duty. But *euphony* requires *it** as a subject to round out the sense and improve the sound.† In this kind of sentence, and also in—

  1. For you to deceive me is highly criminal,

there is a transposition of elements which should be adjusted mentally before analysis; as,

  1. It, *to caution you*, is my duty [inf. phrase modifies *it*].
  2. *To deceive me* is highly criminal *for you* [*for you* mod. *criminal*].

633. Sometimes there is an entire ellipsis of the infinitive; as, I consider him [to be] honest. This ellipsis is not generally considered in analysis, the adjective *honest* being directly referred to *him*.

634. The sign *to* must not be separated from the remainder of the infinitive by an adverb; as, "To describe *accurately* this scene would be impossible"; *not* "To *accurately* describe this scene."

Caution.—Avoid the use of *and* instead of *to*; also the superfluous use of *with* in connection with an infinitive; as, "Come *and* see me often"; "Try *and* come early"; "To begin *with*, we started in the rain." Say, "Come *to* see me"; "Try *to* come early"; "To begin, we started in the rain."

---

* *It* as here used is sometimes called the *anticipative* subject.
† *It* or *there* in "It is my duty to caution you," and "There is a delightful breeze," is an introductory word called an *expletive*. An *expletive* is a word used in such a way as to give fullness to a sentence, or to render it agreeable to the ear.

635. In such sentences as "I have walked far enough to become weary," and "I regard you too highly to offend you intentionally," the infinitive phrases modify, severally, *far enough* and *too highly*, taken together, rather than either word separately.

Direction.—Fill out the following incomplete sentences by inserting into the blank spaces the following words, using them in the order here given: *throw, call, hastily, carry, go, pass, tremble, purposely, sit*. With each of these words use *to* when correct to do so:

1. I saw him —— the ball. 2. He heard his father —— him. 3. It is not wise —— form an opinion. 4. Help me —— this basket. 5. They would not have us —— with them. 6. Please —— the bread. 7. I could feel the earth ——. 8. I regard you too highly —— offend you. 9. He would not let me —— near him.

Direction.—Analyze the following sentences, and parse the infinitives and any other words that may be thought desirable:

Sentences for Analysis.

1. To know her is to love her.
2. It is a difficult task to root out old errors.
3. I have a work to do, and courage to perform it.
4. They are not strong enough to conquer.
5. I am in haste to return to my native land.
6. It was impossible to please him.
7. He was heard to make a very unpleasant remark.
8. To eat and drink seemed to be his only enjoyment.
9. For him to do such an act is shameful.
10. To speak plainly, I consider you dishonest.
11. Hope comes with smiles the hour of pain to cheer.
12. They are ready to find fault, and hard to please.
13. This industrious youth is anxious to become an engineer.
14. He would not let me sit near him.
15. The way to acquire knowledge is to labor for it.
16. We could feel the earth tremble beneath our feet.
17. He determined to live on vegetables only.
18. The sailors furled the sails so as to be prepared for the storm.
19. To become a good scholar requires close application and hard study.
20. James Smith, a careful student, at last thought how to begin his composition.

CLXII.—PARTICIPLES.*

636. We have learned [467] that the simple participles are used with auxiliaries to form real verbs; as, William *is driving* too fast, and he *has driven* in this way for a mile.

637. Participles are also used *without* auxiliaries to *assume* an act, state, or position [assume = to take for granted]; as,
   1. The gentleman *rowing* is my uncle.
   2. The lady *sitting* in the bow of the boat is my aunt.
   3. A vessel, *laden* † with coal, has just entered the harbor.
   4. *Scaling* yonder peak, I saw an eagle rise.

Explanation.—In sentence 1, the participle *rowing* merely *assumes* an act. By its use we understand (or take for granted) that the person *is rowing*, but this fact is not *asserted*. The only *assertion* made is, "This gentleman is my uncle." In 2, the participle *sitting* merely *assumes* the *position* of the lady—does not assert it. In 3, the participle *laden* assumes the *condition* or *state* of the vessel, and *scaling* (in 4) assumes an *act*. A participle *assumes* an act or state of some person or thing considered as an indirect subject; but it does not *affirm* anything of that subject. The participle as a modifying element relates to its subject.

638. Position of Participles.—Participles usually follow the nouns or pronouns to which they relate. In an inverted sentence, the participle precedes the noun or pronoun, as *scaling* (in 4), which relates to *I*.

639. Participles may take the same modifiers and complements as the verbs from which they are derived; as,
   1. A word, *once* uttered, can never be recalled [part. with adv.].
   2. A vessel, **laden** *with coal*, has entered the harbor [p. with adv. ph.].
   3. **Scaling** *yonder peak*, I saw an eagle rise [part. with obj. comp.].
   4. **Being** *president*, he did not choose to vote [part. with att. comp.].
   5. **Being** *weary*, I retired early [part. with att. comp.—adj.].

640. Definition.—Any combination of a participle with its modifiers and complements is called a **participial phrase**.

---

* Participles and infinitives are, by some authors, called **verbals**.
† For the principal parts of irregular verbs not already given, see complete list of irregular verbs [704].

Explanation.—In 1, of the first set of sentences above, *rowing* modifies the noun *gentleman* by showing which person is referred to. In 2, the participial phrase *sitting in the bow of the boat* modifies the noun *lady* in the same way. In 3, the participial phrase *laden with coal* modifies *vessel* by showing its condition or state. In 4, the participial phrase *scaling yonder peak* modifies the pronoun *I*.

641. Use of Participles.—A *participle* or a *participial phrase* may modify a noun or a pronoun.

Direction.—In the following sentences (and also in the preceding) select the participial phrases, tell what word each modifies, and whether the participle in each is a present or a past participle:

1. The road, winding through the forest, leads to a beautiful lake.
2. The window, broken by the explosion, fell with a loud crash.
3. Forsaken by his friends, he despaired of success.
4. Placing my gun on my shoulder, I started for the woods.

Note.—In 2, the participle *broken* assumes the receiving of an act, and is, therefore, passive in meaning.

642. A present participle is generally *active* in meaning; but a past participle is always *passive* in meaning.

Questions.—1. Do participles *assert* an act? 2. What is meant by the word *assume*? 3. In what respect are participles like verbs? 4. In what respect are they unlike verbs? 5. What may a *participle* or a *participial phrase* modify? 6. What is a participial phrase? 7. What position does a participle generally occupy? When does it not occupy this position? 8. Is a past participle *active*, or *passive* in meaning?

CLXIII.—PARTICIPIAL ADJECTIVES.

643. Participles often modify *nouns* by being placed directly before them to *describe* some condition, characteristic, or habit. Used in this way they lose, either partly or wholly, their *verbal* meaning; as,

1. The soldier, *wounded* by a shell, was carried to the rear [part.].
2. The *wounded* soldier was carried to the rear [adj.].
3. The little rill, *rippling* over its pebbly bottom, pursued its course, *winding* its way to a larger stream [participles].
4. The little *rippling* rill pursued its *winding* way to a larger stream.

PARTICIPIAL ADJECTIVES.

Explanation.—In 1, *wounded* assumes the receiving of an act, and is a participle. But *wounded*, in 2, loses its verbal meaning and simply *describes* a *condition*; it is therefore called a *participial adjective*. In 3, *rippling* and *winding* imply action, and are participles; but (in 4) they describe a habit, or a settled condition, and therefore are called *participial adjectives*.

Direction.—Select the participial adjective, the participle, or the participial phrase, in each of the following sentences, tell what word each modifies, then analyze each sentence and parse each participle according to the following models:

1. The commander, riding ahead, encouraged his troops.
2. I found my old friend seated in his easy chair.
3. The frightened horse dashed down the street.
4. Turning our horses, we rode back to the fort.
5. The wind blew with increasing violence till midnight.
6. In a thickly settled country, the farms are small.
7. With wan, fevered face tenderly lifted to the cooling breeze, he looked out wistfully upon the ocean's changing wonders.
8. This gently flowing stream, winding its course between the hills, finally empties into a beautiful lake.

Remark.—It is sometimes difficult for the beginner to distinguish the past participle from the past tense; but if the pupil will remember that the past participle is *passive* in meaning, and that the noun which it limits is represented as *receiving the action*, no difficulty will arise. Besides, the noun or pronoun that may *seem* to be the subject of the participle, will be found to have another relation in the sentence, as in 7, where *face*, the object of *with*, may at first seem to be the subject of *lifted*.

644. Model for Analysis.—Sentence 8 is a simple declarative sentence. The entire subject is, "This gently flowing stream, winding its course between the hills." The predicate is "finally empties into a beautiful lake." The simple subject *stream* is modified by the pronominal adjective *this*, and the participial phrase *winding its course between the hills*, in which the present participle *winding* is the principal word, completed by the object complement *course*, and modified by the adverbial phrase *between the hills*, etc.

645. Parsing Model.—Wounded (in the first set above) is the *past participle* of the verb *wound*, and, with its phrase, it modifies the noun *soldier*; principal parts—*wound, wounded, wounding, wounded*. Wounded (in 2) is a *participial adjective*, and modifies the noun *soldier*.

CLXIV.—PARTICIPIAL NOUNS.—SUBSTANTIVE PHRASES.

646. A participle, or a participial phrase, may be used as a noun. In this substantive use it may be:

(1) The subject of a verb; as,
   1. *Skating* is a healthful recreation.
   2. *Reading steadily* injures the eyes.
   3. *Reading at twilight* is bad for the eyes. [*Bad*, adj., mod. subj. phrase.]
   4. *Chopping wood* is good exercise.
   5. *Becoming a good man* did not atone for past misdeeds.

(2) The object complement of a verb; as,
   1. I like *bowling*.
   2. I dislike *rising early*.
   3. We enjoyed *riding in the park*.
   4. I dread *crossing the ocean*.

(3) The attribute complement of a verb; as,
   1. Earning is *having*.
   2. Love is the *fulfilling* of the law [fulfillment].
   3. This is *surprising* [wonderful—*adj.*, simply].

(4) The object of a preposition; as,
   1. I am fond of *reading*.
   2. By *doing nothing*, we learn to do ill.
   3. In *praising a man*, avoid injuring him.
   4. It is folly to think of *assisting them* in *capturing the fort*.

647. A participial noun used as the name of an occupation or a habit, or one preceded by *the* or other adjective, loses its verbal sense and is simply a participle used as a noun. [*Participial* in *form* only]; as,
   1. *Smoking* is an injurious habit.
   2. *Reading* is taught in school, yet good *reading* is rare.
   3. *Fishing* is an important industry of the State of Maine.

648. A participle often performs a twofold office; as,
   1. The venerable orator, rising slowly, addressed the audience.
   2. Reading steadily injures the eyes.
   3. Chopping wood is good exercise.
   4. We enjoy riding in the park.
   5. By laboring industriously we achieve success.

PARTICIPIAL NOUNS. 207

Explanation.—In 1, *rising* partakes of the nature of a verb and of an adjective. As a verb, it is modified by the adverb *slowly*, and as an adjective it modifies the noun *orator*. In 3, *chopping* partakes of the nature of a verb, and of a noun. In its verbal sense, it is completed by the object complement *wood*, and as a noun it is (with the rest of the phrase) the subject of the verb *is*. In 5, *laboring* is a participial noun. As a participle it is modified by the adverb *industriously*, and as a noun it is the object of the preposition *by*. (*Laboring* is not, however, in the objective case.) In parsing, say, "*Laboring* is a present participle used as a noun, and is the object of the preposition *by*." ("*By laboring industriously*" is a prepositional phrase.)

649. Definition.—A participle is a form of the verb that merely assumes an act or state, and partakes of the nature of a verb and of an adjective or noun.

Direction.—Define a participle. Select from all the sentences in this lesson the participles, or the participial phrases; tell the use of each; mention each of the three general ways in which they are used; also the four uses they have as nouns; and analyze each sentence.

CLXV.—PARTICIPLES—SIMPLE AND COMPOUND.

650. Definition.—A simple participle is a single word derived from a verb.

Remark.—The *present* and the *past participles* are the *simple participles*.

651. The simple participles *being*, *been*, and *having* (used as auxiliaries), are combined with those derived from other verbs to form the compound participles:

Simple Participles.

PRESENT PARTICIPLE.　　　　　　PAST PARTICIPLE.
　　Driving.　　　　　　　　　　　Driven.

Compound Participles.

{ Being driving,　　　　　　　{ Being driven,
{ Having been driving.　　　　{ Having driven,
　[Seldom used.]　　　　　　　{ Having been driven.

652. Definition.—A **compound participle** is a combination of a simple participle with either of the auxiliary participles *being, having,* or *having been.*

Direction.—Select the participles in the following sentences, tell whether they are present or past, simple or compound; mention the phrases, then analyze and parse:

1. Having been censured for idleness, he resolved to do better.
2. Passing the Rubicon, Cæsar marched on to Rome.
3. Having received assistance from my friends, I carried out my plans.
4. A city, set on a hill, can not be hid.
5. Having been expecting him for several days, his arrival did not surprise us.
6. By endeavoring to please all, we fail to please any.
7. The thief, caught in the act of stealing, confessed his crime before the judge.
8. Approaching the coast, they saw it covered with a multitude of people.
9. I found my old friend sitting in his easy chair.
10. He soon began to be weary of having nothing to do.
11. Having finished his speech, he descended from the platform.

653. Comma Rule.—A participial phrase used as an adjective should be set off by the comma, unless used in a restrictive sense;* as,

1. The deer, *suddenly lifting its head,* detected our presence.
2. The deer *standing nearest the lake* is looking toward us.

Explanation.—In sentence 1, the participial phrase is used in a parenthetical sense to refer to *deer,* but it is not used to distinguish a particular deer from *any others.* In 2, the phrase is used to explain *deer* by distinguishing it from others; a phrase used in this way is said to be *restrictive.*

Direction.—Justify the punctuation of the preceding sentences, and also those in the three preceding lessons.

Questions.—1. What is a simple participle? 2. Which two participles are simple? 3. What is a compound participle? 4. What are the different uses of participles and participial phrases? 5. What is the rule for setting off participial phrases?

---

* Sometimes a *participle* is set off by the comma; as, "The flower, fading, lost its charm."

CLXVI.—USE AND ARRANGEMENT OF PARTICIPLES.

654. A participle, or a participial phrase (unless used as a noun), should always refer to some noun or pronoun *expressed* in the sentence.

FAULTY USE.

1. Riding to the edge of the cliff, a merry yachting party was seen.
3. While standing on deck, the most beautiful landscapes passed in succession before *our* eyes.

IMPROVED.

2. Riding to the edge of the cliff, *we* saw a merry yachting party.
4. While standing on deck, *we* beheld a succession of the most beautiful landscapes.

Explanation.—In sentence 1, no noun or pronoun is used to which the participle with its phrase can refer; therefore, the sentence must be reconstructed, as in sentence 2, where the participial phrase refers to *we*. In 3, there is no word except the possessive *our* to which the participial phrase can refer; but we can not properly say that *our* were *riding to the edge of the cliff*. The sentence must be reconstructed, as in 4.

655. A participle or a participial phrase should be so placed that there can be no doubt as to the noun or pronoun intended to be modified.

FAULTY ARRANGEMENT.

1. A gentleman will let his house going abroad for the summer to a small family containing all the improvements.

IMPROVED.

1. A gentleman, going abroad for the summer, will let his house, containing all the improvements, to a small family.

656. By means of participles, we are enabled to express more smoothly and forcibly in a single sentence what would otherwise require two or more sentences.

SEPARATE SENTENCES.

1. His body was found two days after. It was stretched upon the ground. His faithful horse was still standing by his side.
2. The hunter returned to his tent. He had killed the deer. He was satisfied.

CONDENSED.

1. His body was found two days after, stretched upon the ground, with his faithful horse still standing by his side.
2. Having killed the deer, the hunter returned to his tent satisfied.

PARTICIPLES.

Direction.—Improve the following sentences:
1. She walked with the lamp across the room still burning.
2. I saw twenty meteors sitting on my porch the other evening.
3. Climbing to the top of the hill, the Atlantic Ocean was seen.
4. Standing on the summit of the mountain, a scene of unparalleled beauty met our view.

Direction.—Condense each of the following sets of statements into a single sentence, by using participial phrases:
1. I had transacted my business. I wished to be at home the next day. I left the city by the midnight express.
2. The husbandman was stripped of his harvest. He was driven from his fields. He abandoned himself to idleness.
3. The warriors gathered the bodies of the slain. They strapped them across their pack-horses. They returned to the village.
4. The general was confronted by a superior force of the enemy. He was without ammunition. He was compelled to surrender.

CLXVII.—PARTICIPLES MODIFIED BY A POSSESSIVE.

657. A participle in its use as a noun may be modified by a possessive noun or pronoun; as,

1. Much depends on *his** obeying the rules [his obedience].
2. *His* having decided against you is no proof of malice on his part.
3. *His* being a faithful student † increases his chances for promotion.
4. *His* being called a wit did not make him one.

Explanation.—In 1, *obeying* partakes of the nature of a verb and of a noun. In its use as a *verb* it takes the object *rules*; in its use as a *noun* it is modified by the possessive pronoun *his*.

658. Caution.—Do not mistake an adjective or a noun ending in *ing*, for a present participle; as,

---

* This use of the possessive is practiced by the best writers; and indeed it is sometimes preferable to the objective form of the pronoun, as it often prevents ambiguity, i. e., the use of doubtful language. In "I am sure of *him* being a shrewd politician," the participle may refer to *I* or to *him*. But if I say, "I am sure of *his* being a shrewd politician," it is plain that *being* does not refer to *I*. A better expression, however, would be, "I am sure that he is a shrewd politician."

† Here the noun *student*, being used as the attribute complement in a subject phrase, does not refer to any preceding noun or pronoun; it is, therefore, used *indefinitely*, but is considered to be in the nominative case.

PARTICIPLES.   211

1. He is an *enterprising* man.
2. He is *willing* to go. [Not from the verb *to will*.]
3. In the country, the *evening* paper is received on the next *morning*.

Promiscuous Sentences for Analysis and Parsing.

1. "He is but a landscape-painter,
   And a village maiden she."
2. "Ah, well! for us all some sweet hope lies
   Deeply buried from human eyes."
3. "Rock of Ages, cleft for me,
   Let me hide myself in thee."
4. "Full many a flower is born to blush unseen,
   And waste its sweetness on the desert air."
5. By teaching others, we improve ourselves.
6. His being a foreigner prevented his election.
7. Having been riding all day over a rough road, I gladly accepted my friend's hospitality.
8. Let the conceited simpleton learn the hard lessons of experience.
9. We traveled thence to Oxford, stopping on the way at Woodstock to visit Blenheim Palace.
10. At daybreak, the combined fleets were distinctly seen from the Victory's deck, formed in close line of battle ahead, about twelve miles to leeward, and standing to the north.

CLXVIII.—CONJUNCTIVE ADVERBS.—COMPLEX SENTENCE.—ADVERBIAL CLAUSE.

1. The wind blew and the sea roared.
2. We will start *at sunrise*.
3. We will start *when the sun rises*.

Explanation.—Sentence 1 is compound, consisting of two co-ordinate sentences; i. e., two members of *equal rank*, the second being joined to the first as something *additional*. In the simple sentence 2, the phrase *at sunrise* is adverbial, and modifies the verb *will start*. *At sunrise* = *when the sun rises*; therefore, in 3, the whole sentence *when the sun rises* is adverbial in use, denoting *when*, and modifying the verb *will start*. The adverb *when* connects *the sun rises* to the verb *will start*, and also modifies the verb *rises*, thus performing a twofold office, that of *con-*

nective and also of *adverbial modifier*. *When* is therefore called a *conjunctive adverb*.

The sentence "We will start" is the principal part of the sentence, but *when the sun rises*, being adverbial in use, is a dependent element. These two elements, one of which is *principal*, and the other *dependent*, are called *clauses* instead of *members*, as in a compound sentence.

Sentence 3, being composed of a *principal* and a *dependent* (modifying) clause is called a *complex sentence*.

659. Definition.—A **complex sentence** is one composed of a principal clause, and one or more dependent clauses.

660. Definition.—A **conjunctive adverb** is one that modifies the verb in the clause of which it forms a part, and joins such clause to some word in the principal clause.

661. Conjunctive Adverbs.—*How, why, where, when, while, whence, whither, wherefore, as, before, after, till, until, however, wherever, whenever, since, therefore, because, as soon as, as far as,* etc.

Direction.—Determine which of the following sentences are simple, which complex, which compound, and give reasons. Also tell which word in the principal clause is modified by the adverbial clause:

1. He drove the horse before he bought him. 2. I answered him when he spoke to me. 3. I will listen to you, but I will not dispute with you. 4. The book remains where I left it. 5. Our army went into winter quarters, the enemy retreated beyond the river, and the country was again quiet. 6. I love him because he is kind to me. 7. When I was a boy, I used always to choose the wrong side of the debate. 8. As I drew near the camp, I heard a loud shout. 9. The man, thoroughly frightened, fled from the house. 10. He has written some things hard to be understood. 11. While the band played, the soldiers rested. 12. Washington retreated from Long Island because his army was outnumbered.

Note.—Sentence 7 is inverted. The dependent clause, standing first, requires a comma after it.

Comma Rule.—When a subordinate clause introduces a sentence, it should be set off by the comma.

Questions.—1. What is a compound sentence? 2. What does co-ordinate mean? 3. What are members? 4. What is a complex sentence? 5. What are clauses? 6. What is a conjunctive adverb? 7. Mention the conjunctive adverbs? 8. What kind of element is an adverbial clause?

CLXIX.—ANALYSIS OF COMPLEX SENTENCES.

662. In analyzing a complex sentence, state—
1. The *class*.
2. The *principal clause*.
3. The *dependent clause*.
4. The *connective*.
5. The *analysis* of the *separate clauses*.

Model for Oral Analysis.

1. The farmer smoked his pipe of clay while he sat in his easy chair.

663. This is a complex declarative sentence. The principal clause is, "The farmer smoked his pipe of clay," and the dependent clause, "while he sat in his easy chair," the connective being the conjunctive adverb *while*. The simple subject of the principal clause is *farmer*, modified by *the*. The predicate-verb is *smoked*, modified by the dependent clause *while he sat*, etc. The object complement *pipe* is modified by the possessive pronoun *his* and the adjective phrase *of clay*. The subject *he* in the dependent clause is unmodified. The predicate-verb *sat* is modified by the adverb *while* and the adverbial phrase *in his easy chair*.

Model for Written Analysis.

2. The farmer smoked his pipe of clay while he sat in his easy chair.

Class.....................	Complex declarative.
Principal clause..........	The farmer smoked his pipe of clay.
Dependent clause.........	While he sat in his easy chair.
Connective...............	*While*, a conjunctive adverb.
Simple sub. in prin. clause	*Farmer*, modified by *the*.
Predicate-verb in prin. cl.	*Smoked*, mod. by the dep. cl. *while he sat*, etc.
Object complement........	*Pipe*, mod. by *his* and the adv. phrase *of clay*.
Simple sub. in dep. clause	*He*, unmodified.
Predicate-verb in dep. cl.	*Sat*, mod. by *while* and the phrase *in his easy chair*.

DIAGRAM.

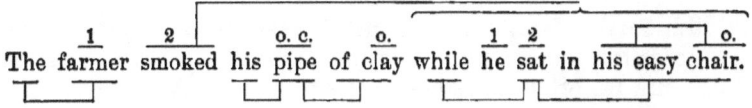

Model for Oral Analysis.

1. Our weakened forces feared to move forward while the enemy, encamped beyond the river, were closely watching us.

This is a complex declarative sentence. The principal clause is, "Our weakened forces feared to move forward," and the dependent clause, "while the enemy, encamped beyond the river, were closely watching us," the connective being the conjunctive adverb *while*. The simple subject in the principal clause is *forces*, modified by the possessive pronoun *our*, and by the participial adjective *weakened*. The predicate-verb is *feared*, which is completed by the infinitive object phrase *to move forward*, in which the principal part is the verb *to move*, modified by the adverb *forward* and by the dependent adverbial clause *while the enemy*, etc. The subject *enemy*, in the dependent clause, is modified by *the* and by the participial phrase *encamped beyond the river*. The predicate-verb *were watching* is modified by the adverb *closely*, and completed by the object complement *us*. In the participial phrase, *encamped* is the principal word, modified by the adverbial phrase *beyond the river*.

Sentences for Analysis.

1. Fools rush in where angels fear to tread. 2. When the morning dawned, all doubts and fears were dispelled. 3. We arrived at the landing after the steamer had left. 4. She is far from the land where her young hero sleeps. 5. When the western sky is red in the evening, we may expect pleasant weather. 6. When Nature removes great men, the people explore the horizon to find a successor. 7. While the world lasts, fashion will continue to lead it by the nose. 8. Speak well of the absent whenever you have the opportunity. 9. America can not be reconciled till the troops of Britain are withdrawn. 10. The ostrich is unable to fly because it has not wings in proportion to the size of its body. 11. When snow accumulates on the ground in winter, it is useful in keeping the earth at a moderate degree of cold. 12. When Columbus had finished speaking, the sovereigns sunk upon their knees.

Direction.—After analyzing these sentences, parse each conjunctive adverb according to the following model:

664. Parsing Model.—In sentence 1, *where* is a conjunctive adverb. As a conjunction it connects the dependent clause "where angels fear to tread" with the principal clause "Fools rush in." As an adverb it modifies the verb *fear*.

RELATIVE PRONOUNS. 215

Abbreviation of Complex Sentences.

665. A complex sentence is often changed to a simple one by abridging the adverbial clause into a participial phrase; as,
1. When Columbus had accomplished his object, he returned to Spain.
2. Columbus, *having accomplished his object*, returned to Spain.

Direction.—Change the following complex sentences to simple ones:
1. When we reached the hotel, we dismounted.
2. When we reached the top of the hill, we saw the beautiful Hudson.
3. When the war was ended, the army was disbanded.
4. As we walked along, we came suddenly upon a nest of quails.
5. I did not attend the meeting because I was ill.
6. When night came on we gave up the chase.
7. Since he was a worthless man he could not be respected by his subjects.

CLXX.—RELATIVE PRONOUNS.—COMPLEX SENTENCES.

1. Large enterprises require men, *and the men* must be wealthy.
2. Large enterprises require men *who* are wealthy.
3. I have sold the house *which* stands on yonder hill.
4. My father planted the tree *that* shades the lawn.

Explanation.—In the compound sentence 1, *men* is repeated unnecessarily. In 2, *who* takes the place of the three words in italics, thus making the sentence shorter, and the language smoother. *Who* being used more especially instead of the noun *men* is a pronoun, and is the subject of the verb *are*. *Who*, then, forms a part of the clause *who are wealthy*, and it also joins its clause to the antecedent *men* in the principal clause. In 3, *which* is the subject of the clause *which stands on yonder hill*, and also joins the clause to the antecedent *house*. In 4, *that* is the subject of the clause *that shades the lawn*, and also joins the clause to the antecedent *tree*.

666. We see, then, that *who*, *which*, and *that* are used in these sentences as *connectives*, and also as *pronouns*; they are, therefore, sometimes called *conjunctive pronouns*. They are, however, usually called **relative pronouns.**

RELATIVE PRONOUNS.

Adjective Clauses.

667. As has already been learned, a *modifying* element may be a *word*, a *phrase*, or a *clause*:
  1. Large enterprises require *wealthy* men.
  2. Large enterprises require men *of wealth*.
  3. Large enterprises require men *who are wealthy*.

Explanation.—In 1, *wealthy* is an adjective modifying *men*. In 2, the phrase *of wealth* also performs an adjective office. In 3, the clause *who are wealthy* performs the same office as *of wealth* in 2, or *wealthy* in 1; therefore *who are wealthy* is an adjective clause modifying the antecedent *men* in the principal clause. Sentence 3 is a *complex sentence*, being composed of a principal and a dependent clause.

Questions.—1. Which is the relative pronoun in 2 of the first set of sentences? 2. What is its antecedent? 3. What is the office of the clause *who are wealthy*? 4. What kind of sentence is 3? 5. Why? 6. What kind of sentence is 4? 7. Why? 8. What part of speech is *that* in 4? 9. What is its antecedent? 10. What two offices does it perform? 11. What kind of element is *who are wealthy*, in sentence 3 [667]?

CLXXI.—RELATIVE PRONOUNS.

668. Definition.—A relative pronoun is a pronoun used to relate to an antecedent word and to connect with it a dependent clause.

Note.—The clause, of which the relative forms a part, is called a *relative clause*; it performs an adjective office, modifying the antecedent of the relative pronoun.

669. Position of the Relative Clause.—The relative pronoun, with its clause, should stand as near as possible to its antecedent.

This rule of arrangement often places the relative clause between the subject and predicate of the principal clause; as, "He *that steals my purse* steals trash." Sometimes a *word* or a *phrase* modifying the antecedent, properly separates it from the relative clause; as, "In a moment my pursuers appeared on the *bank* above me, *which here rose to the height of twenty feet.*"

RELATIVE PRONOUNS. 217

Direction.—Improve the following sentences by a re-arrangement of clauses, and by other necessary changes:
1. The figs were in small wooden boxes, which we ate.
2. He should first count the cost, who intends to build a house.
3. Some streams are entirely dry in summer, that are roaring torrents in winter.
4. A young man recently cut his foot while bathing with a clam-shell.
5. A great river was discovered by De Soto, which the Indians named Mesa-seba.
6. I have bought a house, located in a pleasant village, which has a bay-window in front.
7. The couple left for the East on the night train, where they will reside.
8. The farmer went to his neighbor and told him that his* cattle were in his fields.

Questions.—1. What is a relative pronoun? 2. What is a relative clause? 3. What is the proper position of a relative in a sentence? 4. Where is a relative clause generally placed when it modifies the subject of a verb? 5. What word does each relative clause modify in the sentences just corrected? 6. In which sentence is *that* not a relative?

CLXXII.—RELATIVE PRONOUNS.—DECLENSION.

670. The **simple relative pronouns** are *who, which, that, as,* and *what*.

671. The **compound relatives** are *whoever, whosoever, whichever, whichsoever, whatever,* and *whatsoever*. [Also, *whoso* by abbreviation.]

672. Who, which.—*Who* is used to represent *persons* only. *Which* is used to represent *things*, and *animals* inferior to man; as,
 1. Longfellow is the *poet who* wrote "Evangeline."
 2. *He who* labors faithfully will be rewarded.
 3. The *horse which* threw his rider galloped away.
 4. I had a *dream, which* was not all a dream.

Remark.—The antecedent of *who* is sometimes understood; as, [He] "who steals my purse steals trash."

---

* *Any pronoun* should be so used that no doubt can arise as to which word is its antecedent.

15

RELATIVE PRONOUNS.

673. *Who* and *which* have case forms; the other simple relatives have none.

SING. AND PLURAL.	SING. AND PLURAL.
Nom. Who,	*Nom.* Which.
Poss. Whose,	*Poss.* Whose.
Obj. Whom,	*Obj.* Which.

674. That *may be used* in place of *who* or *which* to represent persons, animals, or things.

675. That is *preferred* to *who* or *which*:

(1) After two antecedents, one requiring *who* and the other *which*; as, The *lady* and her *dog that* just passed us, walk out together every day.

(2) After a collective noun denoting unity; as, The *army that* was defeated suffered great privations.

(3) After the superlative degree; as, These are the *best* apples *that* grow on this farm.

(4) After *who*, as an interrogative, to avoid repetition; as, *Who that* knows him will doubt his honesty?

(5) When it introduces a restrictive clause [680]; as, People *that* live in glass houses should not throw stones.

(6) Generally, after *all, any, each, every, no, same,* or *very*; as, This is the *same* lesson *that* we had yesterday.

Remark.—*That* is a relative only when *who, whom,* or *which* can be substituted for it. When *that* is not a relative, it is a conjunction, an adjective, or an adjective pronoun.

676. As is a relative pronoun when it follows *such, same,* or *many*; as, He selected *such* apples *as* pleased him [the apples *that* pleased him].

677. What.*—*What* is used to represent *things* only, and has no antecedent expressed; as,

    1. I know *what* troubles you.
    2. He told you *what* he needed.

---

* *What* may be a limiting adjective; as, We know *what* master laid thy keel.
What may be an interrogative adjective; as, *What* books did you buy?
What may be an interjection; as, *What*! does he expect to frighten me?
What may be an adverb meaning *partly*; as, *What* by force and *what* by stratagem he finally accomplished his purpose; here *what* modifies the phrases *by force* and *by stratagem*.

RELATIVE PRONOUNS. 219

Explanation.—In sentence 1, the clause "what troubles you" is the object of the verb *know*. *What*, generally considered a relative, is really an *adjective pronoun* [what *thing*], used as a noun, and is the subject of the verb *troubles*. *What*, in 2, is the object of *needed*. Many authors, however, consider *what* a double relative equivalent to *that* [thing] *which*, the antecedent part *that* being an adjective pronoun, the object of *know*, and *which* the relative part, the subject of *troubles*.

Questions.—1. Which are the simple relative pronouns? 2. Which are the compound relatives? 3. What names may the relative *who* represent? 4. What names may the relative *which* represent? 5. For what names may the relative *that* be used? 6. Which of the simple relatives have case forms? 7. Which are the singular case forms of *who*? 8. Which, the plural? 9. Mention the plural case forms of *which*. 10. When is the relative *that* preferred to *who* or *which*? 11. Is *that* always a relative pronoun? 12. When *that* is a relative, what other relatives may be substituted for it? 13. What kind of pronoun is *what* generally considered to be? 14. What is a better way of considering its use? 15. For how many different parts of speech may *what* be used?

Direction.—Insert the correct relative pronoun in the blank spaces, in each of the following sentences, and give reasons; mention the relative clauses and their antecedents after the relative has been supplied:

1. We do not respect people —— do not respect themselves.
2. In his hand was a torch —— lighted up the cave.
3. The vultures —— live among the Alps often carry off lambs.
4. Let those —— stand take heed lest they fall.
5. Even the ox, —— is a very patient animal, can be enraged.
6. Hannibal was the deadliest enemy —— Rome ever had.
7. He is the same man —— met us on the bridge.
8. He does all —— he can to help his father.
9. Men —— make the laws should not break them.
10. A story is told of another fox —— displayed great sagacity in getting out of an equally bad scrape.

CLXXIII.—RELATIVE PRONOUNS.—CASE RELATIONS.

678. The relative may be, in its clause, the *subject*; the *object* complement; the *object* of an *infinitive, participle*, or *preposition*; a *possessive* modifier.

RELATIVE PRONOUNS.

(1) The subject of the clause:
  1. The man who feels truly noble will become so.
  2. I have destroyed the letter that was sent to me.
  3. I have found the book which was lost.

(2) An object complement:
  1. The man whom we met, is our neighbor [we met *whom*].
  2. The book which I lost, has been found [I lost *which*].
  3. This is the book that I borrowed [I borrowed *that* (or book)].

(3) The object of an infinitive, participle, or preposition:
  1. The man whom I wish to meet may not be present [to meet whom].
  2. The man whom I was fearful of offending was my best friend.
  3. He is a boy whom I am proud of [am proud of whom].
  4. He is a man in whom I have little confidence.
  5. The property that I spoke of yesterday was sold this morning [I spoke of that].

(4) The relative, a possessive modifier:
  1. I venerate the man whose heart is warm.
  2. This is the lady whose husband was injured.

Direction.—Select the relative in each of the above sentences, tell its case and why, and mention the word that is modified by the relative clause.

Direction.—Fill the blank spaces in the first five of the following sentences with one of the forms of *who*, giving the reason for the use of each pronoun. Fill the blank spaces in the others with any simple relative, being careful to use *that* where it is preferable:

1. The lady —— you saw at our house, lives in Boston.
2. There goes the man —— house was burned.
3. The gentleman —— you spoke to is my uncle.
4. It is hard to oppose those —— you know are in the right.
5. Washington was the man —— the colonies needed.
6. This is the longest lesson —— we have yet had.
7. This is the same lesson —— we had yesterday.
8. The men and the tools —— you sent for, have arrived.
9. I am happy to know that it was his horse and not the general —— fell in battle.
10. The passengers and baggage —— arrived at this point were transported across the river.

ANALYSIS. 221

CLXXIV.—ANALYSIS.

Direction.—Analyze the following sentences (also those in the preceding lesson) according to the models here given:

Models for Written Analysis.

679. 1. A sharp tongue is the only edged tool that grows keener with constant use.

Class..................	Complex declarative.
Principal clause.........	A sharp tongue is the only edged tool.
Dependent clause (relative)	That grows keener with constant use.
Connective.............	*That*, a relative pronoun.
Simple sub. in prin. clause	*Tongue*, modified by *a* and *sharp*.
Predicate-verb in prin. cl.	*Is*, unmodified.
Attribute complement...	*Tool*, mod. by *the*, *only*, *edged*, and the dep. cl.
Simple sub. in dep. clause	*That*.
Predicate-verb in dep. cl..	*Grows*, mod. by the phrase *with constant use*.
Attribute complement....	*Keener*, relating to *that*.

2. The police found the man whom they were looking for.

Class..................	Complex declarative.
Principal clause.........	The police found the man.
Dependent clause........	Whom they were looking for.
Connective.............	*Whom*, a relative pronoun.
Simple sub. in prin. clause	*Police*, modified by *the*.
Predicate-verb in prin. cl.	*Found*, unmodified.
Object complement......	*Man*, mod. by *the* and the dependent clause.
Simple sub. in dep. clause	*They*, unmodified.
Predicate-verb in dep. cl..	*Were looking*, mod. by the phrase *for whom*.

DIAGRAM.

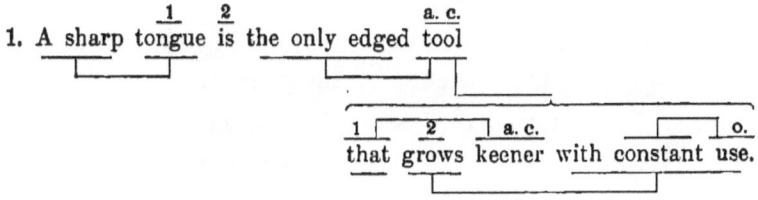

Sentences for Analysis.

1. Men that are old and wise should be consulted by the young.
2. The diamond, which is pure carbon, is a brilliant gem.
3. Read thy doom in the flowers, which fade and die.
4. The detective found the man whom he was looking for.
5. He was the same person that I saw on the platform.
6. He recovered, a result* which was not expected.
7. The criminal fled from the country whose laws he had broken.

CLXXV.—RESTRICTIVE CLAUSES.

680. Relative clauses are classed as restrictive and non-restrictive; as,

1. The diamond that I lost was a birthday present.
2. The diamond, which is pure carbon, is a brilliant gem.

Explanation.—In sentence 1, the clause "that I lost" is necessary to the sense; without this clause we should not know *what* diamond is meant. Not *any* diamond is here meant, but the *lost* diamond. A relative clause used in this way limits or *restricts* the meaning of the antecedent, and is called a **restrictive clause.** In 2, the clause "which is pure carbon" *adds* a thought in an explanatory way in regard to *diamonds in general*—not to any *particular diamond*; it is, therefore, a **non-restrictive clause.** The relative *which* as here used is equivalent to *and it*; thus, "The diamond is a brilliant gem, *and it* is pure carbon."

681. Definition.—A restrictive clause is one whose limiting sense is necessary to distinguish the antecedent.

682. Definition.—A non-restrictive clause adds a thought, or makes an explanation in a parenthetical sense.

Note.—The relative in a non-restrictive clause is generally equivalent to *and he, and they, and it,* etc.

683. Comma Rule.—A non-restrictive clause must be set off from the rest of the sentence by the comma.

684. The relative *that* should be used *only* in restrictive clauses; *who* or *which*, in non-restrictive clauses. Many rep-

---

* Here *result* is in apposition with the clause "He recovered."

SYNTHESIS. 223

utable writers, however, use *who* and *which* in clauses that are restrictive.

Direction.—Determine the two different kinds of clauses in the following sentences, and punctuate them according to the rule just given:

Sentences for Punctuation and Analysis.

1. Happy is the man that findeth wisdom. 2. The man that fell overboard was drowned. 3. Maize which is another name for Indian corn grows in America. 4. I gave the umbrella to John who handed it to the owner. 5. They ascended to the platform which fell with a crash. 6. People that live in glass houses should not throw stones. 7. I had a dream which was not all a dream. 8. Columbus who was a Genoese discovered America. 9. A fierce spirit of rivalry which is at all times a dangerous passion had now taken full possession of him.

Direction.—Supply the proper pronoun for the blank spaces:

1. I went down to the river —— I found greatly swollen. 2. The fish —— we caught furnished an excellent dinner. 3. The fish —— were very small were caught in large numbers. 4. Peace at any price —— these orators seem to advocate means war at any cost. 5. The gentleman —— lives next door has gone to California.

CLXXVI.—SYNTHESIS.

685. Direction.—Combine the following statements into a complex sentence containing one relative clause, one participial phrase, one appositive phrase, arranging the phrases properly:

  Columbus saw at a distance a light.
  This was about two hours before midnight.
  Columbus was standing on the forecastle.
  He pointed the light out to Pedro.
  Pedro was a page of the queen's wardrobe.

Direction.—Combine these same statements into a complex sentence containing an adverbial clause, a relative clause, an appositive phrase. Then combine them into a simple sentence containing a compound participial phrase and an appositive phrase.

Direction.—Combine the following statements into a complex sentence, arranging phrases and clauses properly:

Edward J. Gladdis was drowned at Jamesport.
Jamesport is on Long Island.
The accident happened on Monday of last week.
Gladdis was an assistant book-keeper.
He was employed by Theodore Starr.
Mr. Starr is a jeweler.
His store is on Broadway, New York.
Gladdis lived with his aunts.
They lived in East Seventieth Street.
He was making an effort to save the lives of two young ladies.
He was successful in saving them.
They were the daughters of Mrs. Hamilton.
She lives in this city.

Direction.—Combine the following into a simple sentence containing a compound predicate, an appositive phrase, and a participial phrase:

Frederick Muller fell overboard.	It happened yesterday.
He lived in this city.	The lighter was lying at Pier No. 20.
He was mate of a lighter.	
The name of the lighter was George Henry.	This pier is on the North River.
	Muller was drowned.

CLXXVII.—RELATIVES UNLIKE PERSONAL PRONOUNS.

686. A *personal* pronoun may stand directly for the name of an individual in a simple sentence; as, "I will go with you." A personal pronoun may stand directly for an antecedent, and it may be replaced by the antecedent without destroying the sense; as,

 1. The lady called James and *he* obeyed *her*.
 2. The lady called James and James obeyed the lady.

687. A *relative* pronoun can not *personate*, and thus be used in a simple sentence; nor can it be used in the principal clause of a complex sentence. A *relative* does not stand directly for an antecedent; it only *represents* an antecedent, which the entire relative clause modifies; as,

 I saw the man who invented the telephone,

in which *who invented the telephone*, taken as a whole, tells *what* man. A relative pronoun does not show person by its form.

688. Attributing gender to a relative is of very little importance, but it is necessary to consider its person and number by reference to its antecedent in order to be able to use the proper form of the verb with the relative as a subject.

689. The form of a verb having a relative for its subject depends upon the person and number of the antecedent.

Direction.—Justify the choice of the relative pronoun, and also of the form of the verb in the relative clause, in each of the following sentences:

1. He that speaks rashly is not wise.
2. The men that have just passed us are going to California.
3. I, who have always told you the truth, am not lying now.
4. The boy who teases his little sister should be punished.
5. I, that speak to you, am he.
6. You, who know better, are most in fault.
7. It is you who do all the talking.
8. I pity you, who make this man your enemy.

690. A relative pronoun shows neither *gender*, *person*, nor *number* by its form; yet, because a relative represents an antecedent, it is considered to have the same gender, person, and number as its antecedent. Hence, for the sake of uniformity, the following general rule is given for pronouns:

691. Rule for Construction.—A pronoun must represent its antecedent in gender, person, and number.

692. Parsing Model.—In 4, *who* is a relative pronoun, representing its antecedent, the noun *boy*, in the masculine gender, third person, and singular number; it is in the nominative case, being the subject of the verb *teases*.

Position of the Relative.

693. The relative *that*, as an object in a prepositional phrase, is always separated from the preposition, the latter being placed at the end of the clause. *Whom* or *which* may accompany the preposition or be separated from it. A relative, when used as an object complement of a verb, *precedes* both the subject and the verb [678 (2)].

Direction.—Insert prepositional phrases having relatives as objects, in the following sentences, placing the preposition and the relative together or separately, as the blank spaces may indicate:

1. This is the house —— my friend resides.
2. There goes the man —— I spoke a moment ago.
3. There is no better material —— I know ——.
4. The friend —— I spoke —— has just returned from Europe.
5. He made a statement —— I was astonished.
6. This is the worst case —— I ever heard ——.
7. This is a matter —— I know nothing.
8. The friend —— I staid is my cousin.

CLXXVIII.—INTERROGATIVE PRONOUNS.

694. Besides their use as relatives, *who* (*whose, whom*), *which*, and *what* are used in asking questions. When so used they are **interrogative pronouns**, and are declinable the same as when they are relatives; as,

1. Who went with you?
2. Whom do these pagans worship?
3. Which of these do you prefer?
4. What have you in your hand?

Remark.—*Which* and *what*, when used with nouns, are interrogative adjectives; as, "Which book did you select?" [348].

Note.—In parsing interrogative pronouns, the gender, being indefinite and unimportant, need not be mentioned.

Direction.—Tell what kind of pronoun introduces each of the above sentences, what its relation is in the sentence, and parse it according to the following models:

695. Parsing Models.—*Who* (in 1) is an interrogative pronoun, third, singular, nominative, being the subject of the verb *went*.

Whom (in 2) is an interrogative pronoun, third, singular, objective, being the object of the verb *do worship*.

Direction.—Insert the correct form of *who* in the blank space in each of the following sentences, tell its part of speech, and give the reason for its use:

1. —— do you sit with?
2. I know —— you are.
3. I know —— you love.
4. —— do you think that I am?
5. —— book have I?
6. Do you know —— I fear?
7. —— did your father take with him?

Responsive Pronouns.

1. He will not tell who robbed him.
2. I know who broke the window.
3. I do not know what was said.
4. I know who you are.

696. Explanation.—As used in these four sentences, *who* and *what* are neither relatives nor interrogatives. They are used in *response* to an *implied* question, and are therefore called **responsive pronouns**. *Who*, in 1, is a responsive pronoun, and is the subject of the verb *robbed*; the clause "who robbed him" is the object of the verb *will tell*.

CLXXIX.—OFFICE OF THE RELATIVE CLAUSE.

697. A relative clause may be the subject of a verb; the object or attribute complement; the object of a preposition; as,

1. *What I want* can not be found.
2. I have *what you want*.
3. This medicine is *what you need*.
4. Sell it for *what you can get*.

Ellipsis of the Relative Pronoun.

698. There is frequently an ellipsis of a relative pronoun in the objective case; as,

1. There goes the man we met yesterday [*whom* we met].
2. Show me the exercise you have written [*that* you have written].

Direction.—Analyze the following sentences, being careful to notice any ellipsis. Parse the relative pronouns in this and in preceding lessons according to the models given:

Sentences for Analysis and Parsing.

1. The man who was injured has not fully recovered. 2. Moses was the meekest man that we read of in the Old Testament. 3. The men and things that he has studied have not improved his morals. 4. They who seek wisdom will certainly find it. 5. Whoever wishes to excel must study diligently. 6. The man whose mind is cultured sees beauty in Nature's works. 7. You shall have whatever you ask for.

ABBREVIATED CLAUSES.

699. Parsing Model.—*Whoever*, in sentence 5, is a compound relative pronoun introducing the subject clause "Whoever wishes to excel"; it is in the nominative case, being the subject of the verb *wishes*.

Note.—Some, however, prefer to consider *whoever* equivalent to *he who*, making *he* the subject of *must study*, and *who* the subject of the verb *wishes*. The method given in the model is, however, less cumbersome, and therefore preferable.

CLXXX.—ABBREVIATED CLAUSES.

700. A participial phrase introduced by a *past participle* is often an abbreviated clause. The ellipsis, however, should not be supplied in analysis and parsing; as,

1. The window, which was broken by the explosion, fell with a crash.
2. The window, ————— broken by the explosion, fell with a crash.

Explanation.—The passive verb *was broken* is composed of the past participle *broken* and the auxiliary *was*. By striking out the subject *which* and the auxiliary *was*, there remains the past participle *broken*, introducing the phrase, *broken by the explosion*, which modifies *window*.

Direction.—Change each of the following complex sentences to a simple sentence by abbreviating the relative clause:

1. A city that is set on a hill can not be hid.
2. A task that is well done is twice done.
3. A gun that is loaded to the muzzle is a dangerous weapon.
4. A word that has once been spoken can never be recalled.
5. Principles which are based on Christianity are our best support in trials.

Direction.—Supply the omitted relative in each of the following sentences and give its relation:

1. The question you asked I could not answer.
2. The friends we expected have all arrived.
3. I did not have the book you sent for.
4. The vessel we sailed on was stanch and safe.
5. The harbor we entered was large and beautiful.
6. Annie lost the book I loaned her.
7. Few were the privileges we had.
8. The fish we caught afforded an excellent meal.

CLXXXI.—SYNTHESIS.

701. Direction.—Combine the following statements into two separate unconnected sentences, the first to contain a principal clause, a dependent object clause, which clause must be the object of a present participle formed from the verb in the sixth statement; the principal clause must contain two appositive phrases, and one participial phrase containing a past participle derived from the verb in the fourth statement, the phrase being introduced by the conjunctive adverb *while*. The second sentence to contain a principal, and a dependent adjective clause explanatory of *impression* in the eighth statement; the principal clause to contain a compound predicate. The second sentence must include only the last four statements:

  Charles Furman was an old citizen of De Sola.
  He was a prominent citizen of that place.
  De Sola is in Wisconsin.
  Furman was intoxicated last Tuesday night.
  In this condition he attempted to enter the house of Chas. Worth.
  Furman supposed the house was his own.
  Worth was Furman's neighbor.
  Worth acted under an impression.
  This was that Furman was a burglar.
  Therefore he shot Furman.
  He mortally wounded him.

Direction.—Combine the following statements into a complex sentence. Principal clause must contain an appositive phrase, a participial phrase, prepositional phrases, three of which are to be elliptical; the dependent *relative* clause to contain a participial phrase introduced by *while*. *Body* to be the subject of the principal clause, modified by the relative clause.

  Captain Webb was a famous English swimmer.
  He lost his life.
  He lost it on the 24th inst.
  It was in the afternoon.
  He was attempting to swim through the whirlpool rapids.
  These rapids are in the Niagara River.
  His body was found near Lewiston.
  It was found at ten o'clock this afternoon.
  It was floating in the river.
  Lewiston is four miles from the head of the rapids.

CLXXXII.—ABBREVIATION.—NOMINATIVE ABSOLUTE.

702. In changing an adverbial clause to a participial phrase, the subject of the clause is often retained; as,

1. When the *war* was ended, the army was disbanded.
2. The *war* being ended, the army was disbanded.

Explanation.—The noun *war*, in 1, is the subject of the finite verb *was ended*. In 2, *war* is set free [absolved] from its relation as subject of a *finite* verb, and is simply associated with the *participle* without having any grammatical relation to it. Being thus associated with the participle, *war* is not really independent, but is used *absolutely* in the nominative case with the participle *being ended*. The whole phrase "The war being ended" is called an *absolute phrase*, and, being a condensed adverbial clause, it retains something of its modifying force as an adverbial. In parsing say, *war* is in the nominative case used *absolutely* with the participle *being ended*.

Direction.—Abbreviate the following sentences so that each may contain a noun in the *nominative case absolute*; mention such noun, and the participle with which it is used:

1. When shame is lost, all virtue is lost.
2. While the enemy was approaching, we prepared for battle.
3. When the President had given his consent, the bill became a law.
4. Because the rain poured in torrents, we were obliged to stay at home.
5. When their ammunition was exhausted, the troops surrendered.

703. Pleonasm.—A noun or a pronoun introduced for the sake of emphasis, and then left independent of the rest of the sentence, is used in the nominative case; as,

1. The *boy*, oh! where was he?
2. *He* that cometh, let him come quickly.

Note.—*Boy* and *he* thus used are said to be in the nominative case independent by *pleonasm*. By *pleonasm* is meant the superfluous use of words.

Review Questions.—1. When is a noun in the nominative case absolute? 2. When in the nominative case by pleonasm? 3. Why does it require more thought to use the pronoun *he* in its various relations in a sentence than to use a *noun* for which *he* may stand? 4. Why does it require more care to use the relative *who* than the relative *that*? 5. Can

CONJUNCTIONS. 231

a relative pronoun be used in a simple sentence? 6. In how many ways may possession be expressed? 7. How many uses of the nominative case can you mention?

CLXXXIII.—CONJUNCTIONS.

704. Conjunctions may be separated into two classes: *co-ordinate* and *subordinate*.

705. A **co-ordinate conjunction** is one that connects parts of equal rank; as, *and, or, nor, but,* and sometimes *for, yet.*

706. A co-ordinate conjunction connects the members of a compound sentence; two words of the same part of speech; two phrases or two clauses having a common dependence; as,

1. Heat expands metals **but** *cold contracts them.*
2. The *sun* **and** *moon* give light.
3. We found him *studious* **and** *attentive.*
4. The valleys rejoiced *in sunshine* **and** *in shower.*
5. This is the house *where he lived* **and** *where he died.*
6. Do as you are told, **for** much depends on it.

707. A **subordinate conjunction** is one that introduces a subordinate [dependent] clause and joins it to a principal clause; as, *if, because, since, lest, unless, except, though, although, for, that, than, as, so that, in order that,* etc.

Note.—Generally, when a conjunction introduces a sentence, it does so by inversion. *And, but,* or *for,* however, often introduces a sentence, simply making a tacit reference to what has been said in the preceding sentence, in order to render what follows more forcible. Used in this way they are considered merely as *introductory* conjunctions. *And yet,* taken as a whole, is used as *one* conjunction; *but if,* and *but that,* are used in the same way.

708. Correlatives.*—Certain conjunctions are used in pairs, the former suggesting the latter and assisting it to connect the same elements. The two taken together are called *correlatives.* They are sometimes called *corresponsives.*

---

* *Correlative* = *having mutual relation.*

The Corresponding Word, a Conjunction.

Both—and: With him lay dead *both* hope *and* pride.
Either—or: *Either* you *or* I will be benefited.
Neither—nor: *Neither* you *nor* I will be benefited.
Whether—or: I care not *whether* it rains *or* snows.
If—then: *If* this be treason, *then* make the most of it.
Though—yet: *Though* it is winter, *yet* we find it very pleasant.

The Corresponding Word, an Adverb.

So—that: It was *so* dark *that* I could not see the path.
As—as: His word is *as* good *as* his bond.
As—so: *As* thy day is, *so* shall thy strength be.
So—as: He is not *so* tall *as* I am.
Not only—but also: *Not only* the boys, *but also* the girls, were present.

Caution.—Do not say, "Either he or I am right"; "Neither James nor his brothers have come," although sanctioned by most grammarians. Say, rather, "He is right, or I am"; "James has not come, nor have his brothers."

Note.—Care should be taken to use *as—as* in making an *equal* comparison, and *so—as* in making an *unequal* comparison.

Explanation.—In the first example above, *both* corresponds to *and*, the two uniting to connect *hope* and *pride*. In the last example but one, *so* corresponds to *as*, but *so* is an adverb, modifying *tall*, and *as* connects the two clauses. In the example before this, the sentence is inverted; *so* is an adverb, modifying *shall be*, and *as* is a conjunction, connecting the clauses.

CLXXXIV.—THE KINDS OF DEPENDENT CLAUSES.

709. A dependent, or **subordinate clause**, used as an **adverbial element**, may be connected with a principal clause by a *conjunctive adverb* or any *subordinate conjunction*; as,

1. I left the book *where I found it*.
2. I will go *if you will accompany me** [conditionally].
3. The result was better *than we had expected* [sub. clause mod. *better*].

---

* Clauses like "If you will accompany me" are called *conditional* clauses.

DEPENDENT CLAUSES.—CLASSES. 233

4. He is much taller *than you* [are tall].
5. He is not so tall *as I am* [tall].
6. He is as tall *as you* [are tall].
7. He was so ill *that he could not raise his head.*
8. He acted *as if he were afraid.*
9. He loved her *as though she had been his own daughter.*
10. *The more he ate* the fatter he grew.

Explanation.—In 2, the adverbial clause in italics modifies the verb *will go*. The subordinate conjunction *if* introduces the clause and connects it with the principal sentence. In 4, the dependent clause modifies the adjective *taller*. In 5, the adverbial clause in italics modifies the expression *so tall*. In 8, there is an ellipsis of a clause between *as* and *if*, supplying which the sentence is, He acted as [he would act] if he were afraid. The conjunctive adverb *as* is the connective of the first and second clauses, and *if*. of the second and third. Sentence 8 = He grew the fatter [when] he ate the more. *The more*, a *phrase-adverb*, modifying *ate* and *grew*.

710. A dependent clause used as an **adjective element** may be connected with a principal clause by a relative pronoun, the subordinate conjunction *that*, or by the relative adverbs *where*, *when*,* etc.; as,

1. I have found the money *which was lost.*
2. This is the house *in which my friend resides.*
3. This is the house *where my friend resides.*
4. The report, *that he was killed*, is not true.
5. It is true *that I was unsuccessful.*

Remark.—In 4, the adjective clause is explanatory of *report* in the sense of an *appositive*, and is therefore sometimes called an *appositive clause*. In 5, the adjective clause modifies the introductory *it*.

711. A subordinate clause may be used as a **substantive element**; that is, it may perform the office of a **noun**:

(1) As the subject of a sentence; as,

1. *How plants grow* has puzzled many a brain.
2. *That plants do grow* is learned from observation.
3. *When he will come* has not been ascertained.

---

* *Where*, *when*, *whence*, or *whither* is sometimes used to introduce a clause modifying a noun, as in 3, above. When so used these are called **relative adverbs**. In 3, *where* = *in which*.

(2) As an *object complement*; as,
  1. We have learned *that the earth is round.*
  2. We learn by observation *that plants do grow.*
  3. He knows *where the melons grow.*

(3) As an *attribute complement*; as,
  1. The fact is, *that plants do grow.*
  2. His order was, *that he should flank the enemy.*

(4) As the *object* of a *preposition*; as,
  1. That depends upon *how long you can stay.*
  2. Give careful attention to *what you read.*

712. A complex sentence may contain an abridged dependent clause, in which the predicate-verb is an infinitive, with its *subject* in the objective case; as,
  1. I know him *to be* an honest man [that he is an honest man].
  2. I desire it *to be* done neatly [that it shall be done neatly].
  3. We believed it *to be* him.
  4. He made a sign for me *to leave* you.

Explanation.—Most authors treat these sentences as simple, and say that *him* is the *direct object* of *know*, and that the phrase *to be an honest man* relates to *him* as the *indirect subject* of the infinitive. But the entire object of *know* is, *him to be an honest man*, which (as is indicated in the brackets) is equivalent to a *clause.* It is better, therefore, to consider *him to be an honest man* an *object clause*, *him* being its subject, *to be* the predicate-verb, and *man* an attribute in the objective case. See rule [501]. In either way of treating these sentences, the attribute is in the objective case. This is more clearly seen in sentence 3, where the attribute takes the form *him* instead of *he.*

Direction.—In the following sentences distinguish the subordinate clauses, and mention the relation that each bears to the sentence in which it is used:
  1. Forgive us our debts as we forgive our debtors.
  2. Whoso keepeth the law is a wise son.
  3. Have you heard why my brother went to England?
  4. Life is what we make it.
  5. We know that Whitney invented the cotton-gin.
  6. Persevere in whatever you undertake.
  7. I am glad to learn that you are doing well.
  8. That the earth is a sphere has been proved.

COMPLEX SENTENCES.—ANALYSIS. 235

9. "On Linden, when the sun was low,
All bloodless lay the untrodden snow."
10. "Not a soldier discharged his farewell shot
O'er the grave where our hero was buried."
11. He wondered, as he looked around, how long he had slept.
12. We attend to what we hear more closely than to what we read
[than *we attend* to what, etc.].

Questions.—1. What is a co-ordinate conjunction? 2. Subordinate conjunction? 3. What are *correlatives*? 4. When should *so—as* be used? 5. When *as—as*? 6. Mention the three kinds of subordinate, or dependent clauses. 7. In how many relations may a substantive clause be used?

CLXXXV.—ANALYSIS OF COMPLEX SENTENCES.

Direction.—Analyze the sentences in the preceding lesson according to the following models:

Models for Analysis.

713. 1. That plants do grow, is learned from observation.

This is a complex declarative sentence. The dependent clause being substantive, the principal clause is the entire sentence. The subject of the principal clause is the substantive clause, *That plants do grow*, introduced by the conjunction *that*. The predicate *is learned* is modified by the adverbial phrase *from observation*. In the dependent clause, the simple subject is plants, and the predicate-verb, *do grow*.

2. We have learned that the earth is round.

This is a complex declarative sentence. The dependent clause being substantive, the principal clause is the entire sentence. The simple subject of the principal clause is *we*, and the predicate-verb is *have learned*, completed by the substantive object clause *that the earth is round*, introduced by the conjunction *that*. The simple subject *earth*, in the dependent clause, is modified by the limiting adjective *the*, and also by the predicate adjective *round*. The predicate verb *is* is completed by the adjective *round*.

3. That depends on who can run the fastest.

This is a complex declarative sentence. The dependent clause being substantive, the principal clause is the entire sentence. The simple subject of the principal clause is the adjective pronoun *that*, and the predicate-verb is *depends*, modified by the prepositional adverbial phrase *on who can run the fastest.* The phrase *on who can run the fastest* contains the dependent clause *who can run the fastest* as the object of the preposition *on.* The simple subject in the dependent clause is *who,* the predicate-verb, *can run,* modified by the phrase-adverb, *the fastest.*

CLXXXVI.—COMPLEX SENTENCES.—CLASSIFICATION.*

Direction.—Separate into their elements the following sentences according to the several classifications:

714. Complex sentences may be separated into classes containing:

(1) One principal and one dependent clause; as,
1. No man is so wise that he can not learn more.
2. Flowers are like familiar friends that we love to meet.
3. As we roam about the fields and woods, it is pleasant to see here and there a flower.
4. How much we should miss flowers if they did not come every year!
5. A little girl, finding a wild violet, exclaimed, "How glad I am to see you again!"
6. The bluebird, which seems to be the harbinger of spring, has come to us from the south.

(2) Principal clause simple, dependent clause complex; as,
1. One writer tells us that it was the grand morality of his nature which brought him success.
2. I was grieved when I heard how he had obtained the character that he bore.
3. As my heart was entirely subdued by the captivating strains, [that] I had heard, I fell at his feet.

(3) Principal clause complex, dependent clause simple; as,
1. Where is the child that would forget the most tender of parents, though to remember be but to lament?
2. When I was in Grand Cairo, I picked up several manuscripts, which I have still by me.
3. When we passed the corners of the streets, we were always saluted by some beggars who were congregated there.

---

* This classification of complex sentences is not intended to be exhaustive.

COMPLEX SENTENCES.—CLASSIFICATION. 237

(4) A principal clause, and dependent clauses occurring in succession, each modifying some part of the preceding clause; as,

    1. Columbus was the first European who set foot upon the soil of the new world which he had discovered.
    2. The crocodile is so difficult to kill that people are apt to imagine that the scales have resisted their bullets.
    3. We must be as courteous to a man as we are to pictures which we are willing to give the advantage of a good light.
    4. " Happy are they who thus can choose
       Such blameless themes, that oft amuse
       And oft improve."

(5) A principal clause, in which the subject and some word in the predicate are each modified by an adjective clause; as,

    1. He that can not forgive others, breaks the bridge over which he himself must pass.
    2. People who make puns are like wanton boys that put coppers on the railroad tracks.

(6) A principal clause, and a compound dependent clause; as,

    1. He was admitted into this institution by a gentleman who had been his father's oldest friend, and who had long watched over his interests.
    2. I know that the eye of the public is upon me, and that I shall be responsible for every act.

CLXXXVII.—COMPOUND SENTENCES.—CLASSIFICATION.

Direction.—Separate into their elements the following sentences according to the several classifications:

715. A compound sentence may have one or more of its members complex; as,

    1. He was a great and good man, and he left behind him an influence that told on the actions of men.
    2. He that observeth the winds shall not sow, and he that regardeth the clouds shall not reap.
    3. Mirth is the flash of lightning that breaks through the clouds, but cheerfulness is the daylight that fills the mind with a perpetual serenity.

716. A compound sentence may have one or more of its *members* compound; as,

1. The hours passed heavily along, but they passed; and I was watching the last rays of my last sun when I perceived a cloud rise suddenly in the direction of Rome.
2. The seasons come and the seasons go, but the sun shines on with unchangeable warmth and splendor.
3. The sea licks your feet, its huge flanks purr very pleasantly for you; but it will crack your bones and eat you for all that.

The following sentence is compound if we supply a subject for *stored* in the third line; otherwise it is complex:

1. "In harvest, when the glad Earth smiled with grain,
Each carried to his home one half the sheaves,
And stored them with much labor in his barn."

717. Some compound sentences may be changed to complex sentences; as,

1. Govern your passions, or they will govern you [compound].
2. If you do not govern your passions, they will govern you [complex].

Direction.—Change the following compound sentences to complex sentences:

1. Drive your work, or your work will drive you.
2. We grow older and we grow wiser.
3. Take care of the pennies, and the dollars will take care of themselves.
4. Train up a child in the way he should go, and when he is old he will not depart from it.
5. This pianist converses, and at the same time he plays a difficult piece of music.

CLXXXVIII.—ELLIPTICAL SENTENCES.

718. Sentences are often elliptical for the sake of brevity. Clauses of comparison and sentences containing conditional clauses are frequently elliptical. In the following, the words in brackets show the ellipses in the original sentences.

Direction.—Determine which of the following sentences contain clauses of comparison, and which conditional clauses; analyze and parse:

ELLIPTICAL SENTENCES.

1. The best [that] I have is not too good for you.
2. He is not so tall as his brother [is tall].*
3. He sailed up the Hudson as far as Troy † [is].
4. What can be worse than [it is] to live in slavery?*
5. One has as good a right to the property as the other [has].
6. He is as happy as [he would be] if he were a king.
7. "Do not look for wrong and evil [for],
   You will find them if you do" [look].
8. As a bird [is] that wandereth from her nest, so is a man that wandereth from his place.

Direction.—Supply the ellipses in the following sentences; analyze and parse:

1. He acts as if he owned the whole establishment.
2. It is better to suffer wrong than to do wrong.
3. Lives of great men all remind us,
   We can make our lives sublime.
4. I came to bury Cæsar, not to praise him.
5. She is as handsome as ever.
6. He is but a landscape painter,
   And a village maiden she.
7. Stone walls do not a prison make,
   Nor iron bars a cage.
8. The words I utter, let none think flattery.
9. There's not a joy the world can give
   Like that it takes away.
10. As a door turneth upon its hinges, so does a slothful man upon his bed.

CLXXXIX.—SENTENCES FOR ANALYSIS.

719. Direction.—Before analyzing each sentence, be careful to supply any needed ellipsis. But do not supply an ellipsis to expand an appositive or participial phrase into a clause:

1. Many things lawful are not expedient.
2. Wisdom is better than wealth.
3. A kind deed often drives away sorrow.
4. The faster you go, the sooner you will reach home.
5. Nitrous oxide, or laughing gas, produces insensibility.

---

* Clause of comparison.   † Or, *as far as*, a phrase preposition.

6. No man is so fortunate as always to be successful.
7. He never lends an umbrella, although he has a dozen.
8. Sin has many tools, but a lie is a handle which fits them all.
9. We know what we are, but we know not what we may be.
10. From the lowest depths there is a path to the loftiest height.
11. The largest and most delicious fruits grow on the most thrifty trees.
12. She sat on the sea shore as if in a dream, while by her side lay the dead body of her boy.
13. "Nothing," says Quintilian, quoting from Cicero, "dries sooner than tears."
14. Whither thou goest, I will go, and where thou lodgest, I will lodge.
15. I am not solitary while I read and write, though nobody is with me.
16. We look for a new heaven and a new earth wherein dwelleth righteousness.
17. Murmur not, O man! at the shortness of time, if thou hast more than is well employed.
18. The rosy-fingered morn, mother of dews, opes wide the pearly gates of day.
19. We venture to say, that no poet has ever had to struggle with more unfavorable circumstances than Milton.
20. The greatest pleasure I know is to do a good action by stealth, and to have it found out by accident.
21. We may not be able to accomplish all we desire, but shall we therefore sit still with folded hands?
22. "Let me make the ballads of a nation," says Fletcher, "and I care not who makes the laws."
23. A teacher who is qualified for his office is a blessing to the community, but a time-server is a disgrace to the profession.
24. It is true that the glorious sun pours down his golden flood as cheerily on the poor man's cottage as on the rich man's palace.
25. In this march, we traversed almost the whole circuit of the hills around Jerusalem, and I then had the opportunity that I had longed for, to see the force with which we were contending.
26. The Chinese pitcher-plant is quite common in Ceylon, where it is called the monkey-cup, because the monkeys sometimes open the lid and drink the water when there is no spring of water where they can quench their thirst.
27. Pure, simple, unassuming, kindly, touched with sadness and relieved with mirth, but never stained with falsehood or treachery, or any hint of shameful act, his heart was as tender as his life was grand.

28. I have a son, a third, sweet son, whose age I can not tell,
   For they reckon not by years and months where he has gone to dwell.
29. 'Tis with our judgments as with our watches; none
   Go just alike, yet each believes his own.
30. Do not look for wrong and evil,
   You will find them if you do;
   As you measure for your neighbor,
   He will measure back to you.
31. The farmer sat in his easy chair,
   Smoking his pipe of clay,
   While his dear old wife, with busy care,
   Was clearing the dinner away.
32. Spake full well, in language quaint and olden,
   One who dwelleth by the castled Rhine,
   When he called the flowers, so blue and golden,
   Stars, that in earth's firmament do shine.

CXC.—BAD CONSTRUCTION IMPROVED.

720. Direction.—Compare, with the class, the bad construction with the improved, giving reasons for the need of reconstruction, then (books being closed) dictate one or more of the badly constructed exercises for pupils to re-write and improve. These selections have been made from original compositions; teachers will be able to collect many others for use as exercises in the correction of language:

BAD CONSTRUCTION.	IMPROVED.
1. A seal that was carried by Washington was found which was probably shot from his watch-chain after a lapse of eighty years in a field.	1. A seal that was carried by Washington, and that was probably shot from his watch-chain, was found in a field, after a lapse of eighty years.
2. About four o'clock one afternoon the three boys that were staying on the island that I did and myself had boat races between ourselves in which I was the winner of two of them.	2. I was spending the summer on an island with three other boys. About four o'clock one afternoon we had a number of boat races among ourselves, in two of which I was the winner.

BAD CONSTRUCTION.

3. In your letter you remarked of having a very cold passage across the ocean. It may be cold enough here yet as we have got two good winter months yet to get.

I was too busy to answer your letter on Monday so I thought the nearest time I had a chance would do. Please remember me to your parents and I wish them a happy New Year and include yourself.

4. I went about the 12th of July to the country. My uncle is situated in a town about eighty miles from where we live.

All day long my cousin and I were either on the lake fishing or shooting and all other sports.

Very near by there is a very large river flows by the village where we went sailing every day and there was also a beach where we went bathing every once and awhile.

5. We spent four weeks in this place and then returned feeling much better and a little darker in color.

Swimming was the leading occupation of the boys. They went in at an average of five times a day.

One day we decided to make a trip to the falls which took about a ride of an hour. After returning I took a walk to the river with a neighboring gentleman.

IMPROVED.

3. In your letter you spoke of having a very cold passage across the ocean. It may yet be cold enough here, as we have two full winter months before us.

I was too busy to answer your letter on Monday, but I thought the first chance I had would do. Please remember me to your parents in "A happy New Year," including yourself in the wish.

4. About the 12th of July, I went to visit my uncle who resides in a town about eighty miles distant.

All day long my cousin and I were either shooting, or on the lake fishing, or enjoying other sports.

A very large river flows by the village, on which we went sailing every day; and besides, there was a fine beach from which we went in bathing every once in a while.

5. We spent four weeks in this place, and then returned a little darker in color, and feeling much better.

The chief sport of the boys was swimming, which they indulged in on an average of five times a day.

One day we made a trip to the Falls, which made a ride of about an hour. After returning, I took a walk to the river with a gentleman living near.

Direction.—Teachers should place on the blackboard, for a general exercise, passages selected from compositions for reconstruction.

CXCI.—PUNCTUATION.—SEMICOLON.

721. Rule 1.—The semicolon is used to separate the members of a compound sentence that are not very closely connected in sense ; as,

1. She presses her child to her heart; she drowns it in her tears; her fancy catches more than an angel's tongue can describe.
2. Wisdom is the principal thing; therefore get wisdom; and with all thy getting get understanding.

722. Rule 2.—The semicolon is used to separate the members of a compound sentence when either contains elements separated by commas, especially when the connective is omitted ; as,

1. Errors, like straws, upon the surface flow;
   He who would search for pearls must search below.
2. Now abideth faith, hope, charity; but the greatest of these is charity.
3. When the million applaud, you ask what harm you have done; when they censure, what good.

723. Rule 3.—The semicolon is used to separate the members of a compound sentence when the latter is added for the sake of contrast, or as a reason or inference; as,

1. The world will little note nor long remember what we *say* here; but it can never forget what *they did* here.
2. His subjects must have despised him; for he was a bad man.
3. The ground is wet; therefore it must have rained.
4. He who tells a lie is not sensible how great a task he undertakes; for he must be forced to invent twenty more to maintain the one.

724. Rule 4.—The semicolon is generally used to separate a series of clauses or phrases having a common dependence upon some other clause or word ; as,

1. Here let us resolve that they shall not have died in vain; that this nation shall, under God, have a new birth of freedom; and that the government *of* the people, *by* the people, and *for* the people, shall not perish from the earth.

2. The light that led them on was composed of rays from the whole history of the race; from the traditions of the Hebrews in the gray of the world's morning; from the heroes and sages of republican Greece and Rome; from the example of Him who died on the cross for the life of humanity.

725. Rule 5.—A semicolon is used before *as* and *namely* when they introduce an example, or an enumeration of particulars; as,

1. Nouns change their form to distinguish gender; as, count, countess.
2. Five great enemies are constantly harassing us; namely, avarice, ambition, envy, anger, and pride.

Sentences for Punctuation.

1. A man's first care should be to avoid the reproaches of his own heart his next to escape the censures of the world.
2. I was impatient to see it come upon the table but when it came I could scarcely eat a mouthful my tears choked me.
3. When the righteous are in authority the people rejoice but when the wicked beareth rule the people mourn.
4. Phillips speaks as well as Sumner but he does not reason so well.
5. Some writers divide the history of the world into four ages viz. the golden age the silver age the bronze age and the iron age.
6. Philosophers assert that Nature is unlimited in her operations that she has inexhaustible treasures in reserve that knowledge will always be progressive and that all future generations will continue to make discoveries.
7. If we think of glory in the field of wisdom in the cabinet of the purest patriotism of the highest integrity public and private of morals without a stain of religious feeling without intolerance and without extravagance—the august figure of Washington presents itself as the personification of all these.

The Colon.

726. Rule 1.—The colon is used *before* a direct quotation; *before* a sentence added by way of inference when not introduced by a conjunction; *after* the words *following, as follows, this, these,* etc.; as,

1. Holmes says: "Sin has many tools, but a lie is the handle that fits them all."
2. Apply yourself to study; for it will redound to your honor. Apply yourself to study: it will redound to your honor.
3. The committee will meet on the following days: Mondays, Wednesdays, and Saturdays.

CXCII.—VERBS.—MODES.

727. Definition.—A verb is a word used to assert something of its subject.

728. A verb may be *used*:
1. To affirm; as, William *speaks* distinctly.
2. To ask a question; as, *Does* William *speak* distinctly?
3. To express a command; as, *Speak* (thou, ye, or you) distinctly.
4. To express possibility; as, He *may have spoken* once.
5. To express necessity; as, You *must speak* distinctly.
6. To express obligation; as, You *should speak* distinctly.
7. To express condition; as, I can hear you if you *speak* distinctly.
8. To express supposition; as, If I *speak* distinctly, you will not listen.

729. These different uses of a verb arise from the different kinds of thoughts and feelings that we wish to express.

Modes of the Verb.

730. We have *moods* [states of mind] caused by surrounding circumstances, or as the result of observation and thought. When we wish to speak or write, our *moods* require the use of such forms of a verb as will properly express our thoughts. *Mood* [manner of thought] being thus shown in the *forms of the verb* used to express thought, these *forms*, themselves, have come to be considered the moods or **modes** *of the verb.*

731. Definition.—**Mode** is that form or use of a verb which shows the manner of thought of the speaker or writer.

732. There are four modes, the *indicative*, the *potential*, the *subjunctive*, the *imperative*.

733. Indicative mode.—The form of a verb used in a sentence to affirm or to declare something as an actual occurrence or fact, is said to be in the *indicative mode*, because such a verb indicates or asserts positively what is in the mind of the speaker or writer with reference to the subject; as, "The mocking bird *sings* with great sweetness, and readily *imitates* the songs of other birds."

Questions.—1. What is a verb? 2. What does the verb express in "William speaks distinctly"? 3. Teacher should read the other sentences and ask questions. 4. What is *mode* in grammar? 5. What is the indicative mode? 6. Why is it so called?

CXCIII.—THE INDICATIVE MODE.

734. Definition.—The indicative mode is that form of a verb used to assert something as an actual occurrence or fact.

The indicative mode may be used—

(1) To make an affirmation; as,

1. The stars *shine* brightly (or *do shine*—emphatic form).
2. We *saw* Venus last evening (or *did see*—emphatic form).
3. I *have seen* Niagara Falls this summer.
4. I *had seen* Niagara Falls before.
5. I *will begin* this work immediately.
6. I *shall have finished* the work by to-morrow noon.

(2) To ask a question; as,

1. Have you seen Niagara Falls?
2. Will they start to-morrow?

Tenses of the Indicative Mode.

735. There are *six* tenses in the indicative mode: the *present*, the *past*, and the *future*, which are the *primary* tenses; also the *present perfect*, the *past perfect*, and the *future perfect*, which are the *secondary* tenses.

736. Auxiliaries.*—In the active voice, the auxiliaries used in this mode are *do* and its past tense *did* (*helping* to make the emphatic forms of the present and past tenses); *have* and its past tense *had*; also *shall* and *will*.

Note.—The verbs formed by using the auxiliaries *have*, *had*, and *shall have* or *will have*, make the perfect tenses of this mode, because such

---

* These helping verbs aid in forming the compound tenses.

CONJUGATION OF THE VERB "SEE." 247

verbs represent an act or event as *perfected* or finished at or before some particular time indicated in the sentence.

Direction.—After carefully reading this note, point out the verbs in the six sentences above, that are in the perfect tenses. Read the definition of the *present perfect* tense found in the next lesson, then point out a verb in this tense. Proceed in this way with the other two perfect tenses.

737. The *arrangement* in the following lesson shows the *tense forms* of the verb *see*, in a *sample sentence*, abbreviated by omitting all the words after the verb. This arrangement is called *conjugation*.

738. Conjugation.—*Conjugation* is the orderly arrangement of the various verb-forms, *showing their use with subjects* in the different persons and numbers in all the modes and tenses.

CXCIV.—CONJUGATION OF THE VERB "SEE."

Principal Parts.

PRESENT TENSE.	PAST TENSE.	PRESENT PARTICIPLE.	PAST PARTICIPLE.
See.	Saw.	Seeing.	Seen.

Indicative Mode.

PRESENT TENSE.

739. The *present tense** is that form of a verb used to represent incomplete action in present time; as, I *see* the stars.

SINGULAR.	PLURAL.
1. I see.	1. We see.
2. You see (thou *seest* †).	2. You see.
3. He, she, or it sees.	3. They see.

Note.—In its simple form, this tense is the present, or *root-form* of the verb; but in its emphatic form, *do* is joined to *see*; as, I *do see*. *See* is either a singular or a plural form, but is changed to the special singular form *sees* in the third person singular.

---

* The present tense is also used to express general truths, and also habits and customs; as, Vice *produces* misery; Charles *smokes*; Mary *dresses* neatly; The sun *rises* every morning and *sets* every evening.

† *Seest* is the form used with *thou*, the old style personal pronoun of the second person.

CONJUGATION OF THE VERB "SEE."

Past Tense.

740. The *past tense* is that form of a verb used to represent an act or event as completed* in time now wholly past; as, I *saw* John early *this morning, yesterday, last week, last month, last year,* etc.

SINGULAR.
1. I saw.
2. You saw (thou *sawest*).
3. He saw.

PLURAL.
1. We saw.
2. You saw.
3. They saw.

Note.—This tense in its simple form is the past tense of the verb; but in its emphatic form, *did* is joined to the present tense *see*; as, I *did see* the stars. There is no change in the form of the verb for person and number in this tense.

Direction.—Conjugate these two tenses in the emphatic form. Mention the only special singular form of the verb found in either of these two tenses. Tell which of these tenses has no change of form. Mention the forms used with *thou* as a subject.

Future Tense.

741. The *future tense* is that form of a verb used to represent an act or event as yet to take place; as, I *shall see* my brother *next week*.

SINGULAR.
1. I shall see.
2. You will † see (thou *wilt* see).
3. He will see.

Or,
1. I will see.
2. You shall see (thou *shalt* see).
3. He shall see.

PLURAL.
1. We shall see.
2. You will see.
3. They will see.

1. We will see.
2. You shall see.
3. They shall see.

Note.—This compound tense is formed by joining the auxiliary *shall* or *will* to the root-form of the verb.

---

* The progressive form of the verb in this tense represents the act or event as continuing in time wholly past.

† **Shall and Will.**—*Shall* used with a subject in the *first person* denotes *intention*. *Will* used with a subject in the *second* or *third person* also denotes intention. In order to carry the idea of *intention* through all three of the persons, the change in the auxiliary is made from *shall* in the *first* person to *will* in the *second* and *third*.

Will used with a subject in the *first* person denotes *determination*. *Shall* used with a subject in the *second* and *third* persons also denotes determination; therefore a similar change is made in the second arrangement of the future tense to carry the idea of *determination* through the three persons.

CONJUGATION OF THE VERB "SEE."

Present Perfect Tense.

742. The *present perfect tense* is that form of a verb used to represent an act or event as *perfected*, or *completed*, yet connected with present time; as, I *have seen* my brother *this evening*; I *have written* many letters *this month*,* *this year*, or *since I returned from Europe*.

SINGULAR.
1. I have seen.
2. You have seen (thou *hast*).
3. He has seen.

PLURAL.
1. We have seen.
2. You have seen.
3. They have seen.

Note.—This compound tense is formed by joining the auxiliary *have* to the past participle of the verb. *Have* is changed to the special singular form *has* in the third person singular.

Past Perfect Tense.

743. The *past perfect tense* is that form of a verb used to represent an act or event as finished at or before some specified past time; as, I *had seen* the agent *before I received your letter*.

SINGULAR.
1. I had seen.
2. You had seen (thou *hadst*).
3. He had seen.

PLURAL.
1. We had seen.
2. You had seen.
3. They had seen.

Note.—This compound tense is formed by joining the auxiliary *had* to the past participle of the verb. There is no change in the verb in this tense for person and number.

Future Perfect Tense.

744. The *future perfect tense* is that form of a verb used to represent that an act or event will be completed at or before some specified future time; as, I *shall have seen* the agent *by twelve o'clock to-morrow*.

SINGULAR.
1. I shall have seen.
2. You will have seen (thou *wilt*).
3. He will have seen.

PLURAL.
1. We shall have seen.
2. You will have seen.
3. They will have seen.

Note.—This compound tense, which is seldom used, is formed by joining the auxiliaries *shall have* or *will have* to the past participle of the verb. The change from *shall* in the first person to *will* in the *second* and *third* is made for the same reason as in the *future tense*.

---

* The phrase *this month* connects the *completed act* with a period of time *yet present*.

POTENTIAL MODE.

Direction.—Conjugate other verbs in this mode, stating how the verb is formed in each tense. For *synopsis*, see [762].

Questions.—1. What is mode? 2. What is the indicative mode? 3. For what may this mode be used besides making an affirmation? 4. How many tenses in this mode? 5. Which of the tenses of this mode are generally simple in form? 6. Which are always compound in form? 7. What auxiliary is always the sign of the three perfect tenses? 8. What is the special name of each of the perfect tenses? 9. Why is *shall* changed to *will* in the second and third persons of the future tenses? 10. When are the verb forms, *seest, hast, wilt*, etc., used?

CXCV.—POTENTIAL MODE.

745. Definition.—The *potential mode* is that form of a verb used to assert something as *possible, necessary*, or *obligatory*.

1. **Something Possible.**—I *may be* wrong. He *can write* rapidly (having the power). You may return now (having permission).

2. **Something Necessary.**—I *must go* now. You *must write* better. He *must study* more.

3. **Something Obligatory.**—I *should have gone* before. You *should study* more. He *should be* more careful.

Note.—This mode may also be used in asking questions; as, *May I go* with you?

PRESENT TENSE.

746. Auxiliaries, **may, can,** or **must.**

SINGULAR.
1. I may see.
2. You may see (thou *mayst*).
3. He may see.

PLURAL.
1. We may see.
2. You may see.
3. They may see.

Note.—The tenses of the potential mode do not correspond with the time of the act or event as exactly as those of the indicative mode.

PAST TENSE.

747. Auxiliaries, **might, could, would,** or **should.**

SINGULAR.
1. I might see.
2. You might see (thou *mightst*).
3. He might see.

PLURAL.
1. We might see.
2. You might see.
3. They might see.

POTENTIAL MODE.

Present Perfect Tense.

748. Auxiliaries, **may have, can have, must have.**

SINGULAR.
1. I may have seen.
2. You may have seen.
3. He may have seen.

PLURAL.
1. We may have seen.
2. You may have seen.
3. They may have seen.

Past Perfect Tense.

749. Auxiliaries, **might have, could have, would have, should have.**

SINGULAR.
1. I might have seen.
2. You might have seen.
3. He might have seen.

PLURAL.
1. We might have seen.
2. You might have seen.
3. They might have seen.

Direction.—Define the potential mode. Give the auxiliaries belonging to each tense. Tell how each tense is formed. Conjugate, first with *may* and *might*, and then with *must* and *could*. Ask a question with a verb in this mode.

Parsing Model.

1. He *has caught* a fine trout.
2. I *may go* to Albany to-morrow.

Has caught is an irregular transitive verb, *indicative*, present perfect, and agrees with its subject *he* in the third, singular.

May go is an irregular intransitive verb, *potential*, present, and agrees with its subject *I* in the first, singular.

Direction.—Parse any of the verbs in the preceding lessons according to the model here given.

CXCVI.—SUBJUNCTIVE MODE.

750. The *form* of a verb used to express a fact is often different from that of the same verb used to express a future uncertainty, or a supposition contrary to fact; as,

1. It *rains* very fast [fact].
2. If it *rain* to-morrow, I shall not go to Albany [future uncertainty].
3. He *was* here yesterday [fact].
4. If he *were* here, I should be glad [supposition].

SUBJUNCTIVE MODE.

The forms *rain* and *were*, as used in 2 and 4 with singular subjects, are said to be in the *subjunctive mode* because each is used in a *subjoined* clause to express something as uncertain or as a supposition.

Modern usage, however, almost entirely discards this distinction in the use of *active* verbs, and many grammarians encourage this usage. The present usage is to say:

1. If it *rains* to-morrow, I shall not go to Albany.
2. If he *works* steadily, I will increase his wages.
3. Unless the physician *arrives* soon, the patient will die.
4. If help *comes*, all will be well.

And yet, the grammarians who favor this would hardly change the verbs in the following sentences to the indicative form:

1. Though he *slay* me, yet will I trust in him.
2. If thy brother *offend* thee, rebuke him; and if he *repent*, forgive him.

751. Formerly *active* verbs used in sentences indicating future uncertainty (as in the four sentences above) were invariably in the subjunctive form; i. e., the form without the *s*; as, If it *rain* [shall rain]; If he *work* [shall work]; Unless the physician *arrive* [shall arrive], each of these subjunctive forms being considered a sort of elliptical future. The use of these special forms is still adhered to by some of the best authors.

752. The use of the verb *be* or *am* in its various forms in conditional clauses requires more attention than that of other verbs.

753. The conjunction *if, though, lest, unless*, or *whether*, is generally used to introduce a conditional clause; but it is the *future uncertainty* that calls for the subjunctive form *in the present tense*, and the *supposition* of a state of things, for the subjunctive form *in the past tense*. *The verb in a conditional clause may be in the indicative, or in the potential mode.*

754. Definition.—The subjunctive mode is that form of a verb used in a conditional clause, when it expresses a future uncertainty or a supposition with indefinite time, or a supposition implying the contrary to be true.

Questions.—1. What is the subjunctive mode? 2. When should the verb in a conditional clause be in the subjunctive form? 3. What conjunctions generally introduce conditional clauses?

IMPERATIVE MODE.

Indicative Mode. *Subjunctive Mode.*

PRESENT TENSE.   PRESENT TENSE.

SINGULAR.	PLURAL.	SINGULAR.	PLURAL.
1. I see.	1. We see.	1. (If) I see.	1. (If) we see.
2. You see.	2. You see.	2. (If) you see.	2. (If) you see.
3. He **sees**.	3. They see.	3. (If) he **see**.	3. (If) they see.

PAST TENSE.   PAST TENSE.

SINGULAR.	PLURAL.	SINGULAR.	PLURAL.
1. I saw.	1. We saw.	1. (If) I saw.	1. (If) we saw.
2. You saw.	2. You saw.	2. (If) you saw.	2. (If) you saw.
3. He saw.	3. They saw.	3. (If) he saw.	3. (If) they saw.

Note.—As all the *forms* peculiar to the *subjunctive mode* are found only in the present and past tenses, this mode is considered to have but *two* tenses. By placing, side by side, the conjugation of the active verb *see*, it is plainly shown that there is only *one form* in the present tense *subjunctive*, different from the forms of the indicative mode; and also that there is no difference whatever in the forms in the past tense. In the conjugation of the verb *be*, however, there are changes in both tenses. [See 757].

CXCVII.—IMPERATIVE MODE.

755. Definition.—The imperative mode is used to make a command or a request, or to give permission.

PRESENT TENSE.

SINGULAR.   PLURAL.

2d Per. See [*thou* or *you*].   *2d Per.* See [*you* or *ye*].

Note.—This mode has only one tense. The subject of a verb in this mode being always *thou, you,* or *ye* (generally understood), the verb can be used only in the second person.

Verbals.

Infinitives.—*Present.* To see. *Present Perfect.* To have seen.

Participles.—*Pres.* Seeing. *Past.* Seen. *Past Perfect.* Having seen.

756. Definition.—A verbal is a form of the verb that assumes, or expresses in a *general* way, an act or state without *affirming* it of a subject.

757. *Conjugation of the Verb* "**Be.**"

PRESENT.	PAST.	PRESENT PARTICIPLE.	PAST PARTICIPLE.
Be or **am**.	Was.	Being.	Been.

Indicative Mode.

Present Tense.

SINGULAR.
1. I **am**.
2. You **are** (thou **art**).
3. He **is**.

PLURAL.
1. We **are**.
2. You **are**.
3. They **are**.

Past Tense.

1. I **was**.
2. You were (thou *wast*).
3. He **was**.

1. We were.
2. You were.
3. They were.

Future Tense.

1. I shall be.
2. You will be (thou *wilt*).
3. He will be.

1. We shall be.
2. You will be.
3. They will be.

Present Perfect Tense.

1. I have been.
2. You have been (thou *hast*).
3. He has been.

1. We have been.
2. You have been.
3. They have been.

Past Perfect Tense.

1. I had been.
2. You had been (thou *hadst*).
3. He had been.

1. We had been.
2. You had been.
3. They had been.

Future Perfect Tense.

1. I shall have been.
2. You will have been.
3. He will have been.

1. We shall have been.
2. You will have been.
3. They will have been.

Potential Mode.

Present Tense.

1. I may be.
2. You may be.
3. He may be.

1. We may be.
2. You may be.
3. They may be.

Past Tense.

Singular.	Plural.
1. I might be.	1. We might be.
2. You might be.	2. You might be.
3. He might be.	3. They might be.

Present Perfect Tense.

1. I may have been.	1. We may have been.
2. You may have been.	2. You may have been.
3. He may have been.	3. They may have been.

Past Perfect Tense.

1. I might have been.	1. We might have been.
2. You might have been.	2. You might have been.
3. He might have been.	3. They might have been.

*Subjunctive Mode.**

Present Tense.

1. If I **be**.	1. If we **be**.
2. If you **be**.	2. If you **be**.
3. If he **be**.	3. If they **be**.

Past Tense.

1. If I **were**.	1. If we were.
2. If you **were** (thou *wert*).	2. If you were.
3. If he **were**.	3. If they were.

Imperative Mode.

Present Tense.

2. Be [*thou* or *you*].	2. Be [*you* or *ye*].

Verbals.

Infinitives.

Present. To see.	*Present Perfect.* To have seen.

Participles.

Present. Seeing.	*Present Perfect.* Having seen.

---

* The forms of the subjunctive mode, different from those of the indicative in the present and past tenses, are shown by the full-face type. *Am, is, are* are indicative forms. *Be* and *were* are used in the subjunctive without change in both the singular and plural.

CXCVIII.—CONDITIONAL CLAUSES.

758. Some conditional clauses require a verb in the indicative form. The following statements will be a guide to the learner:

Indicative Mode.

A condition may be—

(1) Assumed as a fact; as,
  1. Though wealth *is* desirable, it is not essential to happiness.
  2. If his work *was* satisfactory, why did you discharge him?
(2) May express a present uncertainty; as,
  1. If he *is* guilty, his punishment will be severe.
  2. I will go and see if he *is* at home.
(3) May express a future uncertainty with *definite* time; as,
  1. If I *am* not there by noon, do not wait for me.
  2. If he *starts* at nine o'clock, he will get there in time.

759. Some conditional clauses require a verb in the subjunctive form:

Subjunctive Mode.

A condition—

(1) May express a future uncertainty with *indefinite* time; as,
  1. If he *be* convicted, his punishment will be severe.
  2. Withdraw thy foot from thy neighbor's house, lest he *be* weary of thee.
(2) May express a supposition with *indefinite* time; as,
  1. If I *were* you, I would not go.
  2. If it *were* not so, I would have told you.
(3) May express a supposition implying the contrary to be true; as,
  1. If he *were* near enough, I would speak to him [but he is not].
  2. If he *were* honest, he would pay me [but he is not].
(4) May express a wish implying the contrary, or an intention unfulfilled; as,
  1. I wish I *were* at home.
  2. O, that thou wert as my brother!
  3. The sentence is, that you be imprisoned.

CONDITIONAL CLAUSES.

Direction.—Choose the correct form of the two inclosed in brackets in the following sentences, and give reasons:

1. If he [be or is] here, ask him to come to me.
2. Kiss the son, lest he [is or be] angry.
3. Though he [were or was] industrious, he continued very poor.
4. If the book [be or is] in print, I can get it for you.
5. If he [is or be] not there at the appointed time, do not wait for him.
6. If my friend [was or were] now present, I should be happy.
7. If the snow [was or were] four feet deep, it would not prevent my going.

760. A condition is sometimes expressed without a subordinate conjunction; as,

1. Had I the wings of a dove, how soon would I see you again!
2. Could he have remained, I should have been greatly pleased.
3. Were I in your place, I should not do it.

The question as to whether *had* (in 1) or *could have remained* (in 2) should be considered as belonging to the indicative and potential moods, respectively, or to the *subjunctive*,* is one on which grammarians do not agree. Indeed, it is of little importance, as the form of these verbs in conditional clauses is not different from their form in clauses not conditional, and consequently no mistake is likely to occur in their use.

CXCIX.—VERBS.

761. Progressive Form.—The present participle joined to the verb *be* as an auxiliary in all the modes and tenses makes the progressive form of the verb; as, I **am freezing** the cream.

Passive Form.—The past participle of a transitive verb is joined to the verb *be* as an auxiliary in all the modes and tenses to make the passive form of the verb; as, The cream **is frozen.**

---

* Whatever the subjunctive mode may have meant in the past, or however comprehensive was its grasp of conditional clauses in general, the fact, as to its present use, seems to be, that it is fading out of our language—about the only remnant left being the forms of the verb *be* in the present and past tenses. The tendency seems to be to refer to the indicative and potential modes all verbs in conditional clauses whose forms correspond to the forms of those modes.

VERBS—PROGRESSIVE AND PASSIVE FORMS.

Conjugation of Progressive and Passive Forms.

Remark.—Only two tenses are here given. The pupil should finish the conjugation of this and of the other modes, first using one form throughout, and then the other.

Indicative Mode.

PRESENT TENSE.

SINGULAR.
1. I am
2. You are } seeing.
3. He is

PLURAL.
1. We are
2. You are } seeing.
3. They are

1. I am
2. You are } seen.
3. He is

1. We are
2. You are } seen.
3. They are

PAST TENSE.

SINGULAR.
1. I was
2. You were } seeing.
3. He was

PLURAL.
1. We were
2. You were } seeing.
3. They were

1. I was
2. You were } seen.
3. He was

1. We were
2. You were } seen.
3. They were

762. Synopsis.—Giving a synopsis is making a selection from the conjugation of a verb, of a particular person in each tense, in either number. *Synopsis* means a *collective view*.

Synopsis of See, Active Voice.

1. Synopsis of the Indicative Mode, *I* being the subject:

Present. I see.
Past. I saw.
Future. I shall see.
Pres. Perf. I have seen.
Past Perf. I had seen.
Fut. Perf. I shall have seen.

2. Synopsis of the Indicative Mode, *he* being the subject:

Present. He sees.
Past. He saw.
Future. He will see.
Pres. Perf. He has seen.
Past Perf. He had seen.
Fut. Perf. He will have seen.

3. Synopsis of the Indicative Mode, *they* being the subject:

Present. They see.
Past. They saw.
Future. They will see.
Pres. Perf. They have seen.
Past Perf. They had seen.
Fut. Perf. They will have seen.

Potential Mode.

Model for giving the synopsis of a number of verbs at one time:

Present.	He may	sit,	set,	rise,	raise,	lie,	lay.
Past.	He might	sit,	set,	rise,	raise,	lie,	lay.
Pres. Perf.	He may have	sat,	set,	risen,	raised,	lain,	laid.
Past Perf.	He might have	sat,	set,	risen,	raised,	lain,	laid.

CC.—SELECTIONS OF POETRY FOR ANALYSIS.

763. Poetic License.—For the purpose of accommodating words to the measure of a line of poetry, they are changed in various ways: 1. Words are contracted by an elision [omission] of one or more letters; as, *o'er* for *over*; *'gainst* for *against*; *'tis* for *it is*; *tho'* for *though*. 2. An adjective is used for an adverb; as, "So *sweet* she sung" [sweetly]. 3. Words are shortened or lengthened; as, *morn* for *morning*; *darksome* for *dark*; *bedimmed* for *dimmed*. 4. Special words are used; as, *rife, vasty, yore.* Such use of words is called *poetic license*, because it is employed chiefly by poetical writers.

Direction.—In the following selections, mention each word that is used by *poetic license*; then analyze and parse. Also use the selections as exercises in changing poetry to prose:

1. Night, sable goddess! from her ebon throne,
   In rayless majesty now stretches forth
   Her leaden scepter o'er a slumbering world.—*Young.*

2. There was tumult in the city,
   In the quaint old Quaker town,
   And the streets were rife with people
   Pacing restless up and down.—*Anon.*

3. Then we kissed the little maiden,
   And we spoke in better cheer;
   And we anchored safe in harbor
   When the morn was shining clear.—*J. T. Fields.*

4. Howe'er it be, it seems to me
   'Tis only noble to be good.
   Kind hearts are more than coronets,
   And simple faith than Norman blood.—*Tennyson.*

5. Ring in the valiant man and free,
   The larger heart, the kindlier hand;
   Ring out the darkness of the land,
   Ring in the Christ that is to be.—*Tennyson.*

6. He that filches from me my good name,
   Robs me of that which not enriches him,
   And makes me poor indeed.—*Shakespeare.*

7. If I were a voice,—a persuasive voice,—
   That could travel the wide world through,
   I would fly on the beams of the morning light,
   And speak to men with a gentle might,
   And tell them to be true.
   I'd fly, I'd fly o'er land and sea,
   Wherever a human heart might be,
   Telling a tale or singing a song,
   In praise of the right—in blame of the wrong.—*Mackay.*

8. Thou, too, sail on, O ship of State!
   Sail on, O Union, strong and great!
   Humanity with all its fears,
   With all the hopes of future years,
   Is hanging breathless on thy fate!
   We know what Master laid thy keel,
   What workmen wrought thy ribs of steel,
   Who made each mast, and sail, and rope,
   What anvils rang, what hammers beat,
   In what a forge, and what a heat,
   Were shaped the anchors of thy hope.—*Longfellow.*

TO-DAY.

9. Here hath been dawning another blue day,
   Think, wilt thou let it slip useless away?

   Out of eternity this new day was born;
   Into eternity at night must return.

   See it aforetime no eye ever did,
   So soon it again from all must be hid.

   So, here hath been dawning another blue day,
   Think, wilt thou let it slip useless away?—*T. Carlyle.*

CCI.—LIST OF IRREGULAR VERBS.

764. The following list contains most of the irregular verbs in the language. Those in italics are obsolete, or now but little used. Those marked with an R may also be used as regular verbs; and, when the R is in heavy type, it indicates that the regular form is preferable. The present participle is here omitted, as it is always formed by adding *ing* to the root-verb:

Pres. T.	Past T.	Past P.	Pres. T.	Past T.	Past P.
Abide	abode	abode	Cast	cast	cast
Am	was	been	Catch	caught, R.	caught, R.
Arise	arose	arisen	Chide	chid	{ chidden
Awake	awoke, R.	awaked			{ chid
Bake	baked	baked, *baken*	Choose	chose	chosen
Bear (*to bring forth*)	bore, *bare*	born	Cleave,* (*to split*)	{ clove { cleft	cloven cleft
Bear, *for-* (*to carry*)	bore, *bare*	borne	Cling	clung	clung
			Clothe	clad, **R.**	clad, **R.**
Beat	beat	beaten, beat	Come, be-	came	come
Begin	began	begun	Cost	cost	cost
Bend	bent, R.	bent, R.	Creep	crept	crept
Bereave	bereft, R.	bereft, R.	Crow	crew, **R.**	crowed
Beseech	besought	besought	Cut	cut	cut
Bet	bet, R.	bet, R.	Dare †	durst, **R.**	dared
Bless	blest, **R.**	blest, **R.**	(*to venture*)		
Bid	bid, bade	bidden, bid	Deal	dealt	dealt, R.
Bind	bound	bound	Dig	dug, R.	dug, R.
Bite	bit	bitten, bit	Dive	dove, R.	dived
Bleed	bled	bled	Do	did	done
Blow	blew	blown	Draw	drew	drawn
Break	{ broke { *brake*	broken *broke*	Dream	dreamt, R.	dreamt, R.
			Dress	drest, **R.**	drest, **R.**
Breed	bred	bred	Drink	drank	{ drank, { drunk
Bring	brought	brought			
Build	built, R.	built, R.	Drive	drove	driven
Burn	burnt, **R.**	burnt, **R.**	Dwell	dwelt, R.	dwelt, R.
Burst	burst	burst	Eat	ate, *ĕat*	eaten
Buy	bought	bought	Fall, be-	fell	fallen

---

* Cleave, *to adhere*, is *regular*.   † Dare, *to challenge*, is *regular*.

IRREGULAR VERBS.

Pres. T.	Past T.	Past P.	Pres. T.	Past T.	Past P.
Feed	fed	fed	Let	let	let
Feel	felt	felt	Lie (*recline*)	lay	lain
Fight	fought	fought	Light	lit, R.	lit, R.
Find	found	found	Lose	lost	lost
Flee	fled	fled	Make	made	made
Fling	flung	flung	Mean	meant	meant
Fly	flew	flown	Meet	met	met
Forsake	forsook	forsaken	Mow	mowed	mown, R.
Freeze	froze	frozen	Pass	past, R.	past, R.
Get	got	got, gotten	Pay, *re-*	paid	paid
Gild	gilt, R.	gilt, R.	Pen	pent, R.	pent, R.
Gird	girt, R.	girt, R.	(*to inclose*)		
Give, *for-*	gave	given	Put	put	put
Go, *under-*	went	gone	Quit	quit, R.	quit, R.
Grave*	graved	graven	Rap	rapt, R.	rapt, R.
Grind	ground	ground	Read	rĕad	rĕad
Grow	grew	grown	Rend	rent	rent
Hang †	hung	hung	Rid	rid	rid
Have	had	had	Ride	rode	ridden, *rode*
Hear	heard	heard	Ring	rang, rung	rung
Heave	hove, R.	hoven, R.	Rise	rose	risen
Hew	hewed	hewn, R.	Rive	rived	riven, R.
Hide	hid	hidden, hid	Run	ran, *run*	run
Hit	hit	hit	Saw	sawed	sawn, R.
Hold, *be-*	held	held, *holden*	Say	said	said
Hurt	hurt	hurt	See	saw	seen
Keep	kept	kept	Seek	sought	sought
Kneel	knelt, R.	knelt, R.	Seethe	sod, R.	sodden, R.
Knit	knit, R.	knit, R.	Sell	sold	sold
Know	knew	known	Send	sent	sent
Lade	laded	laden, R.	Set	set	set
Lay	laid	laid	Shake	shook	shaken
Lead, *mis-*	led	led	Shape	shaped	shapen, R.
Leave	left	left	Shave	shaved	shaven, R.
Lean	leant, R.	leant, R.	Shear	sheared	shorn, R.
Leap	leapt, R.	leapt, R.	Shed	shed	shed
Lend	lent	lent	Shine	shone, R.	shone, R.

* Engrave is *regular*.
† Hang, *to take life by hanging*, is *regular*.

IRREGULAR VERBS.

Pres. T.	Past T.	Past P.
Shoe	shod	shod
Shoot	shot	shot
Show	showed	shown, R.
Shrink	shrunk, shrank	shrunk
Shred	shred	shred
Shut	shut	shut
Sing	sang, sung	sung
Sink	sunk, sank	sunk
Sit	sat	sat
Slay	slew	slain
Sleep	slept	slept
Slide	slid	slidden, slid
Sling	slung, slang	slung
Slink	slunk	slunk
Slit	slit	slit
Smite	smote	smitten
Sow	sowed	sown, R.
Speak	spoke, spake	spoken
Speed	sped	sped
Spend	spent	spent
Spin	spun, span	spun
Spit	spit, spat	spit
Split	split	split
Spread	spread	spread
Spring	sprang, sprung	sprung
Stand	stood	stood
Stay	staid, R.	staid, R.
Steal	stole	stolen
Stick	stuck	stuck
Sting	stung	stung
Stride	strode, strid	stridden, strid

Pres. T.	Past T.	Past P.
Strike	struck	struck, stricken
String	strung	strung
Strive	strove	striven
Strow	strowed	strown, R.
Swear	swore, sware	sworn
Sweat	sweat	sweat, R.
Sweep	swept	swept
Swell	swelled	swollen, R.
Swim	swam, swum	swum
Swing	swung	swung
Take	took	taken
Teach	taught	taught
Tear	tore, tare	torn
Tell	told	told
Think	thought	thought
Thrive	throve	thriven, R.
Throw	threw	thrown
Thrust	thrust	thrust
Tread	trod, trode	trodden, trod
Wax	waxed	waxen, R.
Wake	woke	woke, R.
Wear	wore	worn
Weave	wove	woven
Wed	wed	wed, R.
Weep	wept	wept
Wet	wet, R.	wet, R.
Whet	whet, R.	whet, R.
Win	won	won
Wind	wound, R.	wound
Work	wrought, R.	wrought, R.
Wring	wrung	wrung
Write	wrote	written

A number of regular verbs are sometimes spelled in an abbreviated form, with *t* instead of *ed*; as, *spelt, spilt, learnt, smelt, blent, spoilt, crept, knelt.*

765. Definition.—A redundant verb is one whose past tense or past participle is formed both regularly and irregularly. The verbs marked R in the list of irregular verbs are redundant.

766. Definition.—A defective verb is one that has at most only two of the principal parts—the *present* and *past.* Some of the defective verbs have only the *present.*

List of Defective Verbs.

Pres. T.	Past T.	Pres. T.	Past T.
Beware,	——.	Shall,	should.
Can,	could.	Will,	would.
May,	might.	Wis,	wist.
Must,	——.	Wit,	——.
Ought,	——.	Wot,	——.
——,	quoth.		

CCII.—USES OF THE INFINITIVE.

767. The time of the act or state expressed by an infinitive may be *subsequent to, correspondent with,* or *prior to,* that expressed by the principal verb; as,

1. He intended *to see* you about the matter [time, subsequent].
2. He appeared *to enjoy* his visit [time, correspondent with].
3. I happened *to have seen* him once before [time, prior to].

768. When the time of an act or state expressed by an infinitive is *subsequent to,* or *correspondent with,* that expressed by the principal verb, the *present* infinitive must be used; as,

1. I intended *to go* with you yesterday [not *to have gone*].
2. I expected *to be* in Chicago to-day [not *to have been*].
3. He seemed *to enjoy* the lecture last evening [not *to have enjoyed*].

769. When the time expressed by the infinitive is *prior* to that expressed by the principal verb, the *perfect* infinitive must be used; as,

1. He believed his friend *to have been* wronged.
2. He appeared *to have seen* better days.

USES OF THE INFINITIVE.

Direction.—Correct the use of the infinitive in such of the following sentences as need correction, and give reasons:

1. I meant, when I first came, to have bought all Paris.
2. It was my intention to have collected many interesting specimens.
3. I meant to have written to you before to-day.
4. He was proud to be born in France.
5. I should have been glad to see him before I left.
6. I expected to see you early this morning.

Direction.—Insert the proper form of the infinitive of the verb in brackets at the end of each of the following sentences:

1. When I arrived, I expected [ ] you waiting. [find.]
2. I should be proud [ ] so fine a book as this. [write.]
3. I should like very much [ ] him. [see.]
4. He appeared [ ] the book before. [see.]
5. He intended [ ] a good impression, but failed. [make.]
6. He knew better than [ ] his case. [present.]
7. We happened [ ] present when the President arrived. [be.]
8. He appeared [ ] from the country. [come.]
9. I intended [ ] him go with me. [let.]
10. They seemed [ ] themselves. [enjoy.]
11. He was known [ ] guilty of the crime. [be.]
12. He expected [ ] last week. [return.]

CCIII.—USES OF "SHALL" AND "WILL."

770. When a person *determines* for *himself*, or for himself with others, *will* is used, and the subject is in the first person; as,

1. *I will* help you to-morrow.
2. *We will* attend to the matter very soon.
3. *I will* write to Washington to-day.

But when a person *determines* for *another*, *shall* is used, and the subject is in the second or third person; as,

1. *You shall* obey me.
2. *He shall* not go with us.
3. *They shall* feel my power.

Note.—*Shall* here implies duty or obligation on the part of the subject, and also implies power outside of the subject to enforce the obligation.

771. When a person *foretells* for himself [expresses intention], or simply announces what is to happen, *shall* is used with a subject in the first person; as,

    1. *I shall* start in the morning.
    2. *We shall* see you again to-morrow.
    3. When *shall we* have fair weather again?

But when a person foretells for another [indicates another's intention], or announces what is to happen to him, *will* is used with a subject in the second or third person; as,

    1. I am sure *you will* help me.
    2. *He will* stay in Chicago a month.
    3. *They will* be in town next week.

772. In interrogative sentences, *shall* is used with a subject in the first or the second person to indicate mere intention [probability] on the part of the one of whom the question is asked; as,

    Shall I hear from you soon?
    Shall you be in your office to-morrow?

But *will* is used with a subject in the second person when the question partakes of the nature of a *request*; as,

    Will you be in your office to-morrow?

773. Should and would.—*Should* and *would* are the *past tenses* of *shall* and *will*, and the same principles are applied in their use as to the present tense.

Direction.—In the following, correct the complete sentences, and supply *shall* or *will* in the incomplete. Give reasons for corrections:

    1. Will I put some coal on the fire?
    2. I will drown; nobody shall save me.
    3. I have sometimes asked, will we ever be satisfied?
    4. Will I be allowed to occupy this seat?
    5. I will suffer, if I do not wear my overcoat.
    6. Would we hear a good lecture if we would go?
    7. I [ ] see my father this afternoon.
    8. We [ ] then be obliged to retreat.
    9. [ ] I find you here when I return?
    10. I fear I [ ] be too late for the train.
    11. [ ] I bring you a glass of water?

CCIV.—RULES FOR CAPITAL LETTERS.

774. Rules for capitals are scattered throughout the preceding lessons. For the sake of convenience, they are here repeated, and a few others added.

Begin with capital letters:

(1) Every sentence and every line of poetry.

(2) Proper nouns and proper adjectives.

(3) The names of objects strongly personified; as,

"War flings his torch into the doomed hamlet; Peace strews her blossoms o'er the plain."

(4) Names of the Deity; as,

God; Creator; the Almighty; the Supreme Being.

Note.—Many authors say that a pronoun standing for the name of Deity should also begin with a capital letter. But in the authorized editions of the English Bible such pronouns do not begin with capitals.

(5) Titles of office, honor, and respect; as,

The Honorable William M. Evarts, Senator from New York; Alexander the Great; Peter Cooper, Esq.

(6) The first word of a direct quotation; as,

Coleridge says, "Experience is the best schoolmaster."

Note.—But an indirect quotation should not begin with a capital letter nor be set off by a comma; as, Coleridge says that experience is the best schoolmaster.

(7) Every *noun, adjective, verb,* and *adverb* in the titles of books, headings of compositions, chapters, etc.; as,

"What a Blind Man Saw in Europe"; "The Decline and Fall of the Roman Empire"; "My Trip to Niagara Falls."

(8) The names of the months and of the days of the week; as,

The concert was given on Monday evening, the 23d of January.

(9) The pronoun *I* and the interjection *O* should always be capitals.

(10) Words denoting events, eras, written instruments, or institutions of special importance; as,

The Centennial Exhibition; the Fourth of July; the Revolutionary War; the Constitution of the United States; the City Hall; the College of the City of New York; Independence Hall.

CCV.—RULES OF SYNTAX.

775. Rule 1.—A noun or pronoun used as the subject of a finite verb must be in the nominative case.

Rule 2.—A noun or pronoun used as the complement of an intransitive or of a passive verb must be in the same case as the subject to which it refers. See [501].

Note.—When the attribute complement of an infinitive means the same as a preceding noun or pronoun in the objective case, the complement must be in the objective case; as, "They took *me* to be *him*."

Rule 3.—A noun or pronoun used independently or absolutely must be in the nominative case.

Rule 4.—A noun or pronoun used as the object of a transitive verb, of a verbal, or of a preposition, must be in the objective case.

Rule 5.—A noun or pronoun used in apposition must be in the same case as the noun or pronoun which it explains.

Rule 6.—A noun or pronoun used to limit another noun by denoting possession, origin, or fitness, must be in the possessive case.

Rule 7.—A pronoun must represent its antecedent in gender, person, and number.

Rule 8.—An adjective is used to modify a noun or a pronoun.

Note.—An adjective is sometimes used indefinitely, or absolutely, as the complement of an infinitive in a subject phrase.

Rule 9.—A verb must agree with its subject in person and number.

Rule 10.—An adverb is used to modify a verb, a verbal, an adjective, or another adverb.

Rule 11.—A conjunction is used to connect words, phrases, clauses, or members.

Note.—A conjunction is sometimes used simply as an introductory word. It may connect a word element to a like phrase element.

Rule 12.—A preposition is used to introduce a phrase and to join it to the word which the phrase modifies.

Rule 13.—A verbal is used as a substantive, or as a modifying element.

Rule 14.—An interjection is used independently.

CCVI.—SUBJECTS FOR COMPOSITION.

776.

Poetry.
The importance of trifles.
The boat-race.
Advantages of order.
Base-ball.
A day's fishing.
Shall I study for a profession?
The power of habit.
How I got left.
Self-denial.
The power of fashion.
American humor.
Seeing the managerie.
Boys I don't like.
The self-made man.
Our Saturdays.
The Pratt Institute.
Real heroes.
My forgetfulness.
Gains in literary work.
Why I don't carry an umbrella.
Some old fashions.
Variety of flowers.
The ideal country.
Importance of mathematics.
The work of the blind.
What I know of maple sugar.
Voices in our ears.
The art of writing.
Things that cost nothing.
Scotland in the 17th century.
The study of nature.
Making the best of things.
A day in the woods.
Deserve success if you would have it.
What I know of the signal service.
Politeness.
Scott and Dickens compared.
Common sense.
Class distinctions in America.
Horseback-riding.
Valentines.
Coming to school in a street-car.
Girls I like.
Silk manufacture.
Our postman's trials.
The feelings of a tardy girl.
Animal instinct.
Shall I learn short-hand?
Lawn-tennis.
True business principles.
A candy-pull.
The peppered cream tart.
Why I was tardy.
Our Friday afternoons.
Books I like best.
French or German, which?
Variety of trees.
Making bread.
A woman's education.
The imagination.
House-cleaning.
Shall we ever have another war?
The surprise party.
Building a fire.
To-day's good things.
Life on a farm.
The microscope.
A day's boating.
Rewards of merit in life.
Why I don't like a mouse.
Queen Elizabeth as a woman.
What I know of the life-saving service.

Subjects for Short Exercises.

1. Write a ten-word telegraph message.
2. Write a message of ten words making three statements.
3. Write a circular advertising your business. (Choose that of a grocer, dry-goods merchant, clothier, hatter, or coal-dealer.)
4. Write an advertisement for a house you have to rent, to occupy one inch, single column.
5. Write five local news items for your paper, each to occupy not more than five printed lines.
6. Write a notice, for publication, of your church festival.
7. Write an application for a position as clerk in a dry-goods house.
8. Write a business card suitable for a general merchant just beginning business in your village.
9. Write a courteous circular letter to your customers, requesting them to pay up.
10. Write a description, for publication, of some accident to which you were an eye-witness.
11. Write an invitation to Mr. and Mrs. Chas. J. Martin to dine with you, and also a proper acceptance of such invitation.
12. Write a notice, for publication, of a change in location of your business.

Note.—In these subjects for compositions, the capitals for particular words are omitted; they must be supplied by pupils according the rule under [774 (7)].

APPENDIX.

CCVII.—DIRECTIONS FOR DIAGRAMMING.

777. If possible, use paper sufficiently wide to contain the whole sentence on one line. When more than one line is needed, place a *whole* phrase, clause, or member on a second line. Mark a—

Subject *word*,	1 ;	subject *phrase* or *clause*,	1
Predicate-verb,	2 ;	infinitive or participle v.	= verbal.
Object comp. (word),	o. c. ;	object *phrase* or *clause*,	o. c.
Attribute comp. (word),	a. c. ;	attribute *phrase* or *clause*,	a. c.
Object in a phrase,	o. ;	attribute in a phrase,	a.
Appositive *word*,	ap. ;	adverbial objective,	ad. o.
Independent word,	ind. ;	independent *phrase* or *clause*,	ind.
Introductory adv. or conj.,	int.		—

Adjective or adv. clause, ⌒ ; also a dependent phrase in a complex phrase, or whenever necessary to make the relation clear.

Join *modifying* to *principal* elements by straight lines. (See next page.)

Join *as one* two or more adjectives or adverbs standing together and modifying the same word.

Underline the *connective* between *members* with *one* line, and between *clauses*, *phrases*, and *words* with *two* lines.

Indicate an omission of a preposition or of the sign of the infinitive by the caret (∧); the omission of subject, verb, object, or attribute by a mark over the caret, $\overset{1,\ 2,\ \text{etc.}}{\wedge}$

After a little practice, an article standing next to its noun need not be joined to it, especially in phrases.

Inverted sentences may be transposed when written for diagramming (see diagram 34).

Construction of brackets.

272   APPENDIX.

Simple Sentences.

1. An old sailor soon mended the ragged sail.

2. Fine groves of oranges lined the banks of the river.

3. A large flock of wild geese flew directly over our heads.

4. He dived to the bottom of the river for pebbles.

5. During the early part of the day, dark clouds arose above the horizon.

6. The grocer sold ∧ him a bushel of potatoes.

7. That unfortunate old blind man fell into the river. [459.]

8. London, the capital of the British Empire, and the largest city in the world, is situated on the Thames, a river in England.

9. Hope, the balm of life, soothes us under every misfortune.

10. California produces not only gold in abundance, but ∧ quicksilver also.

DIAGRAMMING.—SIMPLE SENTENCES. 273

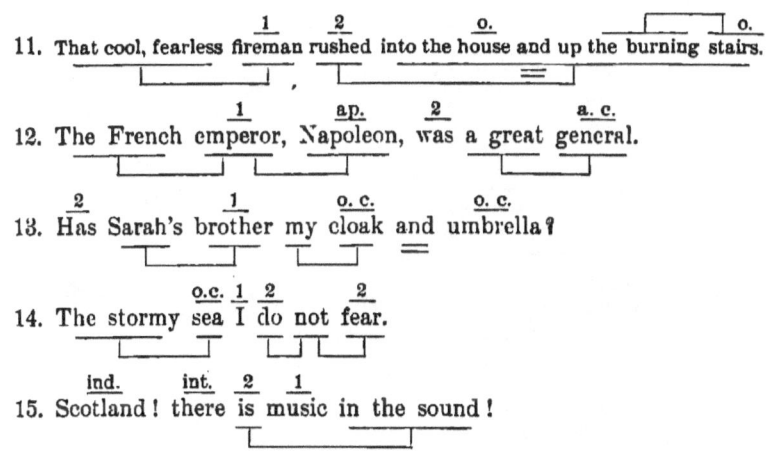

11. That cool, fearless fireman rushed into the house and up the burning stairs.

12. The French emperor, Napoleon, was a great general.

13. Has Sarah's brother my cloak and umbrella?

14. The stormy sea I do not fear.

15. Scotland! there is music in the sound!

Some consider that the phrase *in the sound* refers to *music* rather than to *is*. The question depends upon whether the verb *is*, as here used, is a *copula*, or is a *complete* verb denoting mere existence [511, 512].

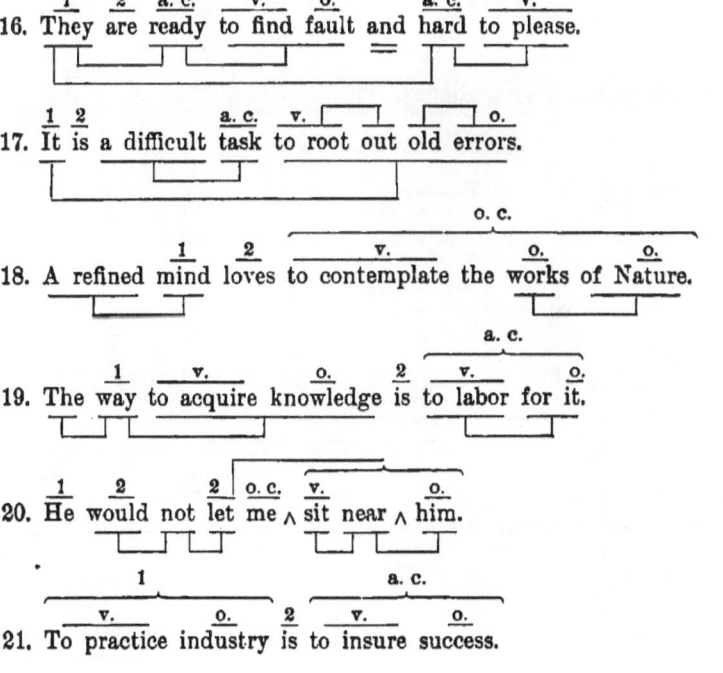

16. They are ready to find fault and hard to please.

17. It is a difficult task to root out old errors.

18. A refined mind loves to contemplate the works of Nature.

19. The way to acquire knowledge is to labor for it.

20. He would not let me ∧ sit near ∧ him.

21. To practice industry is to insure success.

274   APPENDIX.

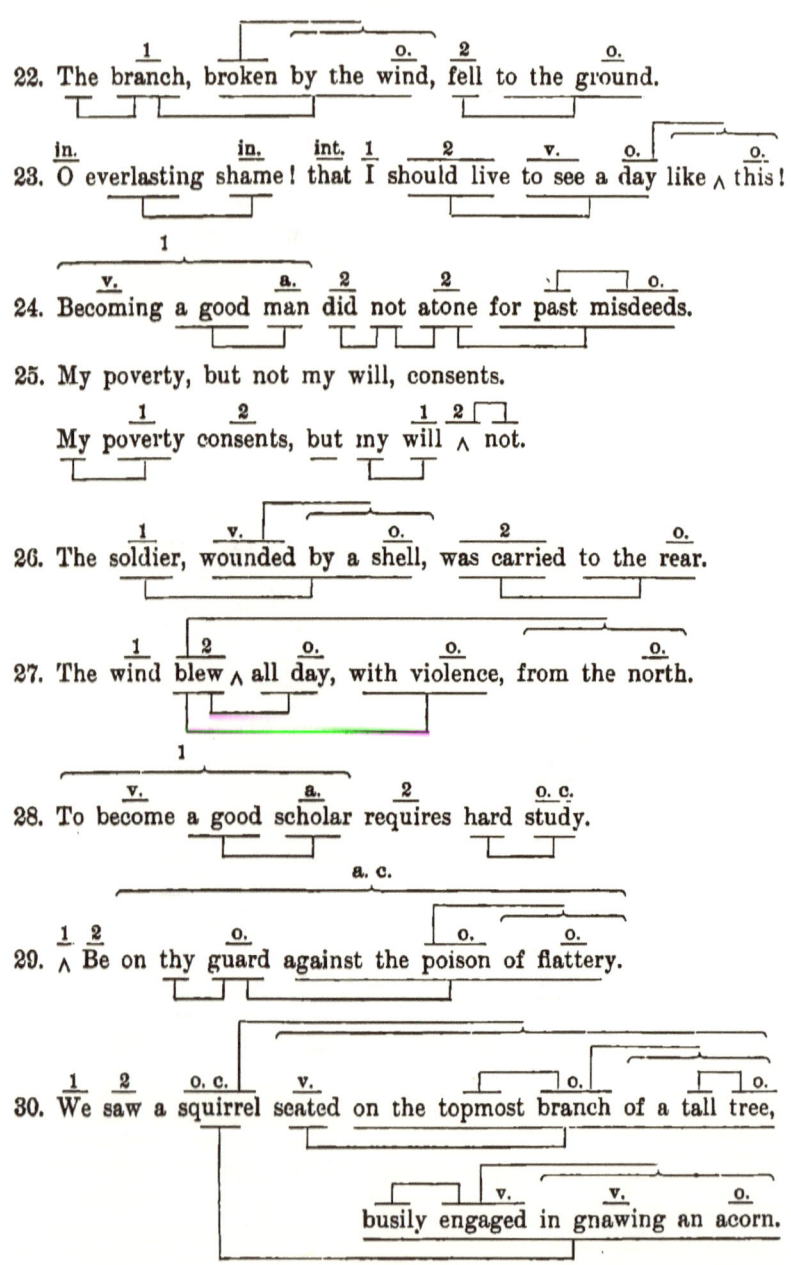

DIAGRAMMING.—COMPLEX SENTENCES.

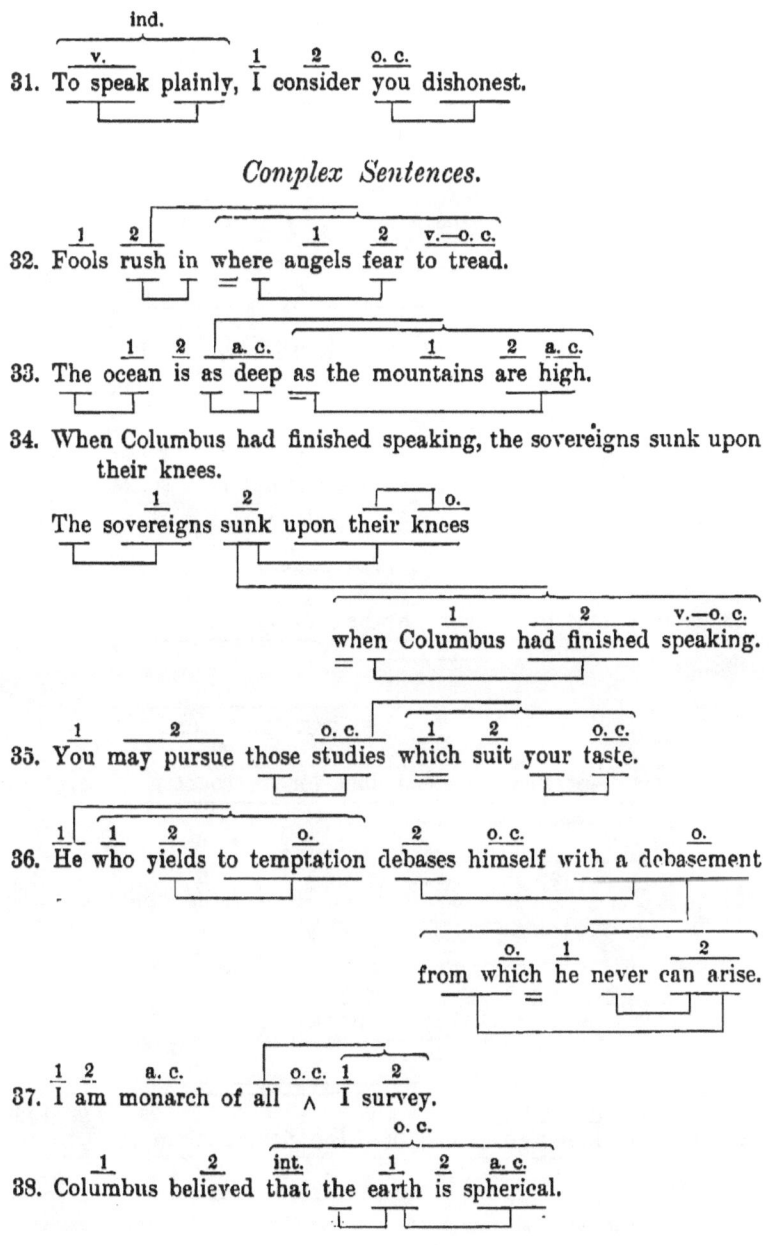

Complex Sentences.

31. To speak plainly, I consider you dishonest.
32. Fools rush in where angels fear to tread.
33. The ocean is as deep as the mountains are high.
34. When Columbus had finished speaking, the sovereigns sunk upon their knees.
35. You may pursue those studies which suit your taste.
36. He who yields to temptation debases himself with a debasement from which he never can arise.
37. I am monarch of all I survey.
38. Columbus believed that the earth is spherical.

276   APPENDIX.

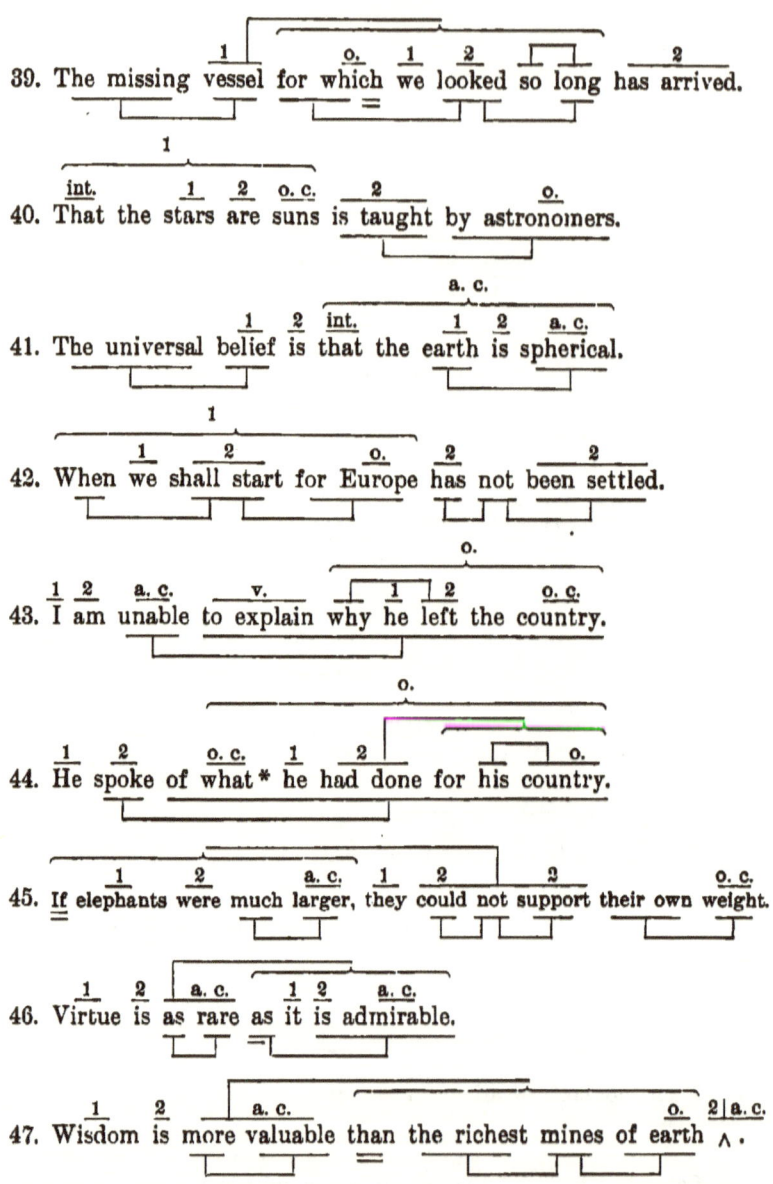

* *What he had done*, etc., as a *whole*, is the object of the preposition *of*; but *what* is the object complement of the verb *had done*.

Compound Sentences.

48. A soft answer turneth away wrath, but grievous words stir up anger.

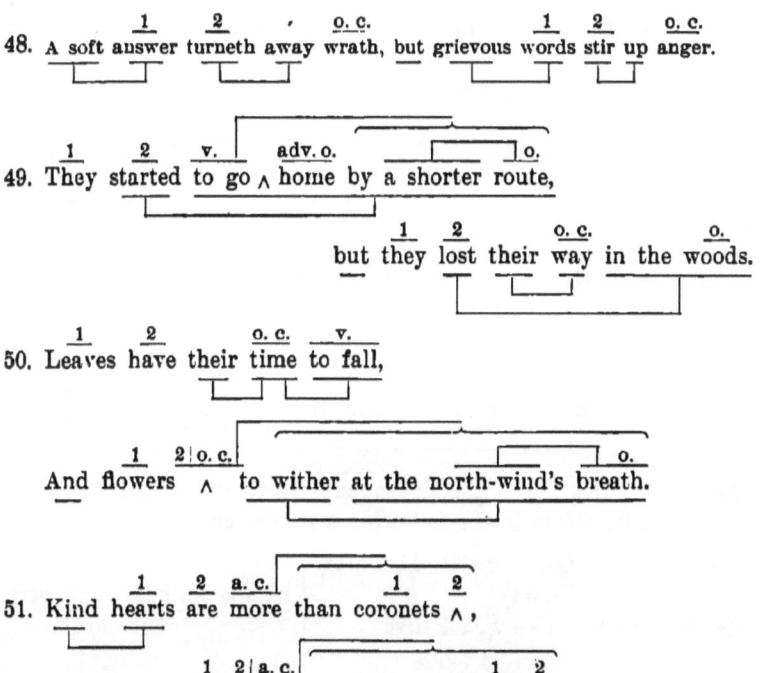

49. They started to go home by a shorter route, but they lost their way in the woods.

50. Leaves have their time to fall, And flowers to wither at the north-wind's breath.

51. Kind hearts are more than coronets, And simple faith, than Norman blood.

52. If you snap the golden threads of thought, they will float away on the air like the film of the gossamer, and I shall never be able to recover them.

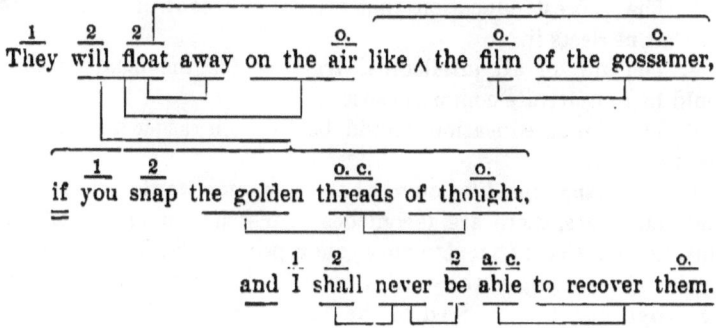

278   *APPENDIX.*

53. Seen at a little distance, as she walked across the churchyard and down the village street, she seemed to be attired in purest white, and her hair looked like a dash of gold on a lily.

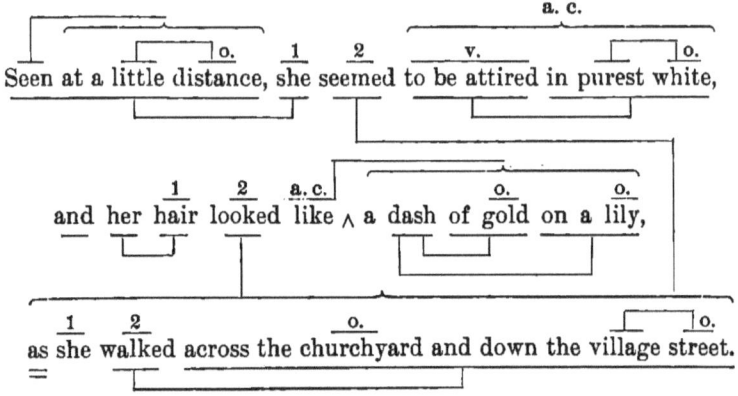

Note.—The relation of the dependent clause, in 53, to the two members may also be shown in the following arrangement:

Seen . . . . distance, she . . . . white, ⎫
            (and)   ⎬ as she walked . . . . street.
her hair looked like . . . . lily, ⎭

Sentences for Analysis.

1. An honest man's word is as good as his bond.

2. If you would not be forgotten as soon as you are dead, either write things worth reading, or do things worth writing.

3. The poorest education that teaches self-control is better than the best that neglects it.

4. The aim of all intellectual training for the mass of the people should be to cultivate common sense.

5. The aim of education should be to teach rather how to think than what to think.

6. In a language like ours, where so many words are derived from other languages, there are few modes of instruction more useful or more amusing than that of accustoming young people to seek for the etymology, or primary meaning, of the words they use. There are cases in which more knowledge may be conveyed by the history of a word than by the history of a campaign.

CCVIII.—FALSE SYNTAX.

778. Direction.—These exercises in the correction of *false syntax* may be used in the regular order of progress as fast as the text, calling for their use, is mastered; also as a review as often as necessary. Pupils should be required to refer to the text for reasons for the corrections.

In speaking and writing, care should be taken to avoid an—

(1) Improper use or omission of an article:
    1. This is an hard task [70].
    2. Nouns have two numbers; the singular and plural [454].
    3. A lion is bold* [452].

(2) Improper use of adjectives:
    1. These kind of people will never succeed [574].
    2. Have you any new children's shoes? [582].
    3. This child is real sick [620].
    4. Which of the two sisters is the tallest? [556].
    5. He always reads very slow [620].
    6. The rivers flow in two † opposite directions.

(3) Improper use of adverbs:
    1. This velvet feels smoothly [513].
    2. I feel nicely, thank you [513].
    3. We arrived home safely [513].
    4. This machine is more perfect than the other [567].

(4) Improper use of nominative forms:
    1. Who will you vote for? [357].
    2. Between you and I, he is a crank [357].
    3. He from my childhood I have known [256 (3)].
    4. Can you forgive we girls? [256 (3)].
    5. They imagined it to be she [712].
    6. The girls deceived you and I shamefully [256 (3)].

(5) Improper use of objective forms:
    1. You and me must hurry to school [256 (1)].
    2. Whom do you think was with me? [256 (1)].
    3. There was no chance of him recovering his money [657].
    4. Was it him that you saw? [501].
    5. I can run as fast as him [256 (1)].

---

* *The* lion; not any single lion, but lions as a class.
† Only *two* directions can possibly be *opposite*, therefore *two* is unnecessary.

6. Them that seek wisdom shall find it [256 (1)].
7. I am sure that it was him [501].
8. Him being disabled, we carried him to the rear [702].

(6) Improper use of possessive forms:

1. Everything is judged by it's use [237, 261].
2. They are wolves in sheeps' clothing [226].
3. John's uncle's brother's farm was sold yesterday [359].
4. I bought this book at Smith's and Brown's store [488].
5. We keep ladie's fine shoes [227].

(7) Improper use of verb forms:

1. A variety of pleasing objects meets the eye [430].
2. Each day and each hour bring new duties [331].
3. The jury is individually responsible [334].
4. Many a captain, with all the crew, have been lost at sea.*
5. Such phenomena is very wonderful [323].
6. Has the horses been fed? [323].
7. There appears to be many others interested [323].
8. He don't know his lesson [269].
9. Columbus believed that the earth was spherical [739, f. n.].
10. I seen him strike my brother [469, caution].
11. They had broke the ice before we arrived [469].
12. Plenty of oranges is brought from Florida [430].
13. Every one of them have the same answer [429].
14. That orator and statesman have great influence [329].
15. The number of voters in the district are very large [430].
16. I intended to have done it yesterday [768].
17. If he was here, he could see for himself [759 (3)].

(8) Improper use of pronouns:

1. This is the horse whom we all admire [672].
2. The lion is an animal who meets his foe boldly [672].
3. The class whom we heard recite have been dismissed [221].
4. This is the same horse which I drove yesterday [675 (6)].
5. We saw the prisoners and the arms which were captured [675 (1)].
6. The moon dispensed his silvery light [180].
7. Neither the merchant nor the lawyer made themselves rich [273].

---

* A singular subject, followed by a phrase introduced by *with*, should have a verb in the singular number.

FALSE SYNTAX.

8. Many a flower will waste their sweetness on the desert air [271].
9. Every man and every boy received their wages.*
10. That is the same' man who was here yesterday [675 (6)].
11. The boy who came late and that sits at the last desk may now recite.†

(9) Improper use of prepositions:

1. This is in accordance to your ideas [414].
2. We can not allow of such conduct [420].
3. He almost died for thirst.
4. Hurry and get in the carriage [409].
5. I was to Boston last week [408].
6. I bought this dress to Stewart's.
7. I met him out to the park.

(10) Use of inappropriate words:

1. *Every* little *girl* was dressed alike.
2. I never was as thirsty in my life [709].
3. He made no farther appeal for aid [561].
4. They will never be no wiser [593].
5. If you wish to succeed, do like I do [427].
6. O fairest flower! no sooner blown *but* blasted.
7. The teacher *learned* me how to draw good [611, 558].
8. Neither the army or the navy was represented [708].
9. We can not succeed *without* we try.
10. The death of his son greatly *effected* him.
11. He was *that* poor he could not buy a pair of shoes.
12. I *expect* he must have arrived last evening.
13. I have no other hope but this.‡
14. The opinion was more universal than I had supposed [567].
15. He does not know *if* his father is at home.#
16. I did not know but what you were angry.‖
17. I do not deny but what he is honest.‖
18. I fear lest something dreadful has happened.‖
19. Try and come early to-morrow [634, caution].

---

* When two or more singular antecedents connected by *and* are preceded by *each, every,* or *no,* they must be represented by a singular pronoun.

† When two relative clauses are connected by a conjunction, the same relative should be used in each.

‡ *Than* should follow *else, other,* and *otherwise.*

If should not be used when *whether* is meant.

‖ *But what* or *lest* should not be used for *but* or *that.*

(11) Improper *omission* or *insertion* of the adjective *other* in sentences containing comparative clauses:

    1. Milton is more sublime than any of the poets.
    2. This State exports more cotton than all the States.
    3. Hope is the most constant of all the other passions.
    4. A fondness for show is, of all other follies, the most vain.
    5. The Nile is the longest of any river in Africa.
    6. Solomon was wiser than any of the ancient kings.

Explanation.—In 1, "Milton" being included in "any of the poets," is represented as more sublime than himself. By inserting *other* between *the* and *poets* the sense is complete. In 2, the same correction should be made. In 3 and 4, *other* should be omitted to make the sense complete. In 5, say "The Nile is longer than any other river"; or, "The Nile is the longest river," etc.

(12) Improper repetition or omission of words; or the repetition of an idea in different words [tautology]:

    1. He might have succeeded and is now fully convinced of it.*
    2. The carriage was broken and they compelled to walk home. †
    3. This opinion never has and never can prevail. ‡
    4. The few who *regarded* them in their true light were *regarded* as dreamers.
    5. Hence he must necessarily, therefore, be in error.
    6. He appears to enjoy the universal esteem of *all* men.

(13) Improper arrangement:

    1. He is an old respectable man [459].
    2. It not only has form, but life [588].
    3. The sisters were nearly dressed alike [589].
    4. We can not afford such another victory [589].
    5. Adversity both taught us to think and to reason [589].
    6. A servant will obey a master's orders whom he loves [669].
    7. We saw a man digging a well with a Roman nose [373].
    8. Nature tells me, I am the image of God as well as scripture.
    9. We also get salt from the ocean which is very useful to man [669].

---

* Supplying *he* as the subject of *is*, will make the sense clear.

† An auxiliary should *not* be omitted when a second subject is of a different person or number from the first.

‡ When the principal parts of two connected verbs are of different forms, neither principal part should be omitted for the purpose of abbreviation.

CCIX.—RHETORICAL FAULTS.

779. Grammar teaches how to use language *correctly*.

780. Rhetoric teaches how to use language with *clearness, force,* and *elegance*.

781. Clearness in the use of words should be observed:
1. It is a long time since I have been devoted to your interest [obscure].
2. I have been devoted to your interest for a long time [clear].
3. I can not think of leaving you without distress [obscure].
4. I can not, without distress, think of leaving you [clear].

An improper arrangement of words, phrases, or clauses, or the omission of some necessary word, often renders the meaning more or less obscure; i. e., makes it difficult to ascertain the meaning intended, as in 1 and 3 above, and in 9 and 10, under the head of improper arrangement [778 (12)].

An obscure sentence is ambiguous when either of two meanings may be taken.

782. Obscurity is a fault that leaves us wholly in doubt as to the meaning intended.

783. Ambiguity is a fault that leaves us in doubt as to which of two possible meanings is intended; as,
1. I think he likes me better than you.
2. An ivory-handled knife was found by a child that has a broken back.
3. Robert promised his father that he would pay his debts.
4. He liked to hear her talk better than any of his associates.

CCX.—EXAMPLES IN FALSE SYNTAX.

784. Direction.—Correct the following sentences, and give reasons:

1. These apples are real good. 2. Problems of these sort are very easy to solve. 3. Nobody should praise themselves. 4. Who is like thou in heaven, light of the silent night! 5. The four sisters were greatly attached to each other. 6. There was a chance of him recovering the money. 7. Which do you prefer most, apples or oranges? 8. Run quick into the house. 9. The parent's care for her children is a divine instinct. 10. Whom do you think was with me yesterday? 11. He reads too slow. 12. How can we tell who to trust? 13. The money was divided among the two brothers. 14. There are plenty of molasses in the jug. 15. He and

APPENDIX.

they we know, but who are you? 16. In some climates the peasantry goes barefoot. 17. Twelve months' interest were due. 18. The ship with all her crew were lost. 19. Neither the army or navy was represented. 20. There was many giants in those days. 21. Do you know if the train has passed? 22. Two of the boys have swam ashore. 23. Every twig, every leaf, and every blade of grass teem with life. 24. He is older than me.

25. I lay the book on the desk, but it is now laying on the floor. 26. It was real mean of her to leave us. 27. Meteors may be looked for to-night, if pleasant. 28. Obscurity, however, is a fault quite as much as ambiguity. 29. My purpose is to bring the fact I have stated into prominence. 30. I can not deny but what he is honest. 31. I always have, and always shall, be an admirer of Whittier. 32. Where are each of the boys to stand? 33. Rid yourselves from such bad habits. 34. The farmer went to his neighbor and told him that his cattle were in his field. 35. Has the second bell rang yet? 36. The traveler by this time had took his seat beside the lady. 37. A savage is a better state of life than a slave. 38. Metal types were now introduced, which before this time had been made of wood.

39. Climbing to the top of the mountain, the Pacific Ocean was seen. 40. We had rode only a short distance, when a dark cloud arose. 41. I wish I was in California. 42. If my friend be in town, he will call this evening. 43. If I had have seen him, I should have known him. 44. If you shall call, I will be happy. 45. He knew who should betray him. 46. Had you not better lie down awhile? 47. He was completely covered over with snow. 48. Who should I meet the other day but my old friend Jones? 49. Give the balance of our dinner to the cat. 50. How many spoonsful make two cupsful? 51. We not only found the questions easy, but very diverting. 52. Jacob loved Joseph more than all his children. 53. On each side are pavements for pedestrians that are from six to eight feet wide. 54. I fear that I will never see him again.

55. The assembly was divided in its opinion. 56. He hadn't ought to ask such questions. 57. Can they not do the work equally as well? 58. He owned an old and new house. 59. I would not have dared done it. 60. That is very easy done. 61. He suffered more than me. 62. I knew it to be she. 63. Let him be who he may, I do not fear him. 64. Of all other vices, lying is the meanest. 65. Do you remember who we met yesterday? 66. The society at these places are always objectionable. 67. Who did you send the letter to? 68. Either he or I is right. 69. Was I so disposed, I could not gratify you. 70. They come soon after you had went away. 71. We had rode only a short distance when the storm burst upon us. 72. They that are diligent I will reward. 73. Here come my old friend and teacher. 74. Either you or I are to blame.

75. When will we three meet again? 76. He taught that the soul was immortal. 77. The rise and fall* of nations are an interesting study. 78. If I stretch a cord tightly between my fingers, I will make it smaller. 79. A few months before, he was willing to have hazarded all the horrors of civil war. 80. Every one must judge of their own feelings. 81. It was expected that his first act would have been to have sent for Lords Grey and Grenville. 82. Everything that painting, music, and even place, furnish, were called in to interest the audience. 83. Sorrow not as them that have no hope. 84. It is now a week since you have arrived. 85. He was not prepared to thoroughly weigh the arguments. 86. The Nile is the longest of any river in Africa.

CCXI.—FIGURES OF RHETORIC.

785. Definition.—A *figure of rhetoric* is a deviation from ordinary language for that which is more pleasing or impressive.

786. For the sake of making a stronger impression on the mind, or of producing a more pleasing effect, we often make a comparison of *one* object with another *essentially* different in its nature, but having *some* points of resemblance; as,

1. "Ingratitude! thou fiend with heart like marble."
2. "So far her voice flowed on like timorous brook."

787. Definition.—A simile is a direct comparison made in a formal way, generally by using *like*, *as*, *so*, or *resembles*; as,

1. Thy smile is as the dawn of the vernal day.
2. The troubles of a child are like an April shower.
3. As the rain and the sunshine come and go over the landscape, so do tears and smiles over the face of childhood.
4. Grateful persons resemble fertile fields, which always repay more than they receive.
5. Christianity is to the soul what light is to Nature.

788. Definition.—A metaphor is an implied simile; it is a comparison in which the resemblance is *assumed*, not stated; as,

1. He is like a lion in the fight [simile].
2. He is a lion in the fight [metaphor].
3. The sun rules the day as a king rules a nation [simile].

---

* *Rise and fall* = *history*, and the meaning is *singular*.

4. The sun is the king of day [metaphor].
5. A man should bridle his anger [metaphor].
6. As a restive horse is restrained by the bridle, so should a man restrain his anger [simile].

Direction.—In the following, change the metaphors to similes, and the similes to metaphors:

1. "Wild fancies gamboled unbridled through his brain."
2. "Friendship is no plant of hasty growth."
3. "He shall be like a tree planted by the rivers of water."
4. "Idleness is the rust of the soul."
5. "The President is the head of the nation."
6. The clouds of adversity soon pass away.
7. "Eternal smiles his emptiness betray,
    As shallow streams run dimpling all the way."
8. "On life's vast ocean diversely we sail,
    Reason the card,* but passion is the gale."

789. Caution.—Mixed metaphors should be avoided; as,

The *apple* of discord has been thrown into our midst; and, if it be not *nipped in the bud*, it will *burst* into a *conflagration* that will *deluge* the world.

790. An **allegory** is a continued metaphor.

791. A **parable** is a brief allegory.

792. Metonymy means a change of names. It is a figure in which there is used the name of a thing suggested by the real thing meant; as, "They have Moses and the prophets" [their writings]; "Gray hairs should be respected" [old age]; "He drank the fatal cup" [contents]; "The kettle boils" [water].

793. Synecdoche is a figure in which a part is called by the name of the whole, or the whole by the name of a part, or in which a definite number is used for an indefinite; as, "This roof shall protect us"; "Belinda smiled, and *all the world* was gay"; "Ten thousand fleets sweep over thee in vain."

794. Hyperbole is an exaggeration of the truth for the purpose of making a statement more impressive; as, "The waves ran mountain-high"; "Belinda smiled, and all the world was gay"; "Brougham is a thunderbolt"; "Rivers of water run down mine eyes."

---

* *Card* means *mariner's compass.*

795. Irony is language that means the contrary of what the words themselves imply, the tone or manner of the speaker generally indicating the *real* meaning; as, "And Brutus was an honorable man"; "He saved others, himself he can not save."

CCXII.—VERSIFICATION.

796. Poetry is a mode of expressing thought and feeling in a measured and musical flow of words.

797. A verse is a line of poetry containing a certain number of accented and unaccented syllables.

798. Rhyme is verse in which the endings of certain lines have similar sounds.

799. Blank verse is verse without rhyme.

800. The syllables of each line of poetry are measured off into divisions called *feet*, there being one *long* or *accented* syllable in each foot, and one or two short or unaccented syllables; as,

1. **Trochee:** Lives' of | great' men | all' re | mind' us.
2. **Iambus:** The cur' | few tolls' | the knell' | of part' | ing day'.
3. **Dactyl:** No'ble and | rare' was her | place' in so | ci'ety.
4. **Anapest:** At the close' | of the day' | when the ham' | let is still'.

Explanation.—The *kinds* of feet depend on the number of syllables in a foot, and the particular syllable accented. As is seen above, the kinds of feet called *trochee* and *iambus* have each two syllables in a foot, the former accented on the *first* syllable, and the latter on the *second*. The *dactyl* and the *anapest* have each three syllables in a foot, the former accented on the first syllable, and the latter on the third.

801. These four are the principal kinds of feet in which English poetry is written. Two other kinds, however, are sometimes used: the *spondee*, having two long or accented syllables; and the *pyrrhic*, having two short or unaccented syllables; as,

Brought' death' | into | the world' | and all' | our woe'.

Sometimes there is an omission of one or more syllables in a foot, as is indicated by this mark [○] in the following lines:

1. Rap'ping | at' my | cham'ber | door' ○.
2. Dawn' on our | dark'ness and | lend' us thine | aid' ○ ○.
3. Pa'tient, ○ | full' of im | por'tance and | grand' in the | pride' of his | in'stincts ○.

APPENDIX.

802. Scanning is dividing a line of poetry into feet, or reading it according to the accent, pausing slightly at the end of each foot.

803. Lines of poetry are also named according to the *number* of feet that compose them; as,

1. **Monometer**: Stay'ing.
2. **Dimeter**: Rich' the | treas'ure.
3. **Trimeter**: From the cen' | ter all round' | to the sea'.
4. **Tetrameter**: Fad'ed the | va'pors that | seemed' to en | com'pass him.
5. **Pentameter**: Near yon' | der copse' | where once' | the gar' | den smiled'.
6. **Hexameter**: On' a | mount'ain | stretched' be | neath' a | hoar'y | wil'low.

Direction.—The last line is composed of six trochaic feet; therefore its measure [meter] is a *trochaic hexameter*. Scan the four lines [800], and mention the kind of measure of each; also the six lines given above.

Recasting Sentences.

The following example shows some of the different ways in which a sentence may be varied without altering the sense:

1. We may derive many useful lessons from the lower animals. 2. Many useful lessons may be derived from the lower animals. 3. The lower animals afford us many useful lessons. 4. Many useful lessons are afforded us by the lower animals. 5. If we observe the habits of the lower animals, we derive many useful lessons. 6. By observing the habits of the lower animals we derive many useful lessons. 7. Many useful lessons may be derived by observing the habits of the lower animals. 8. The lower animals afford many useful lessons to close observers of their habits. 9. The lower animals afford many useful lessons to people who closely observe their habits. 10. By studying the habits of the brute creation we derive many useful lessons.

It is not possible, in varying a single sentence, to exhaust all the devices for recasting. Sentences may be varied—

(1) By changing the active to the passive form [519]. (2) By changing the declarative to the interrogative or the exclamative form [348]. (3) By the use of introductory *it* or *there* [632, 342]. (4) By changing the order of the elements of a sentence [340-1]. (5) By changing the phraseology of a sentence; i. e., by the use of synonyms; by changing an affirmative to an equivalent negative expression; by the use of several words to express the sense of one; by the abbreviation or expansion of phrases and clauses.

Sentences for Recasting.—1. Industry is the cause of prosperity. 2. The infinite surpasses all the works of human ingenuity. 3. The whale is larger than any other animal. 4. A profusion of beautiful objects everywhere surrounds us. 5. Iron is the most useful of all metals.

CCXIII.—OTHER CHARACTERS USED IN WRITING.

804. The dash is used—

(1) To set off a parenthetical expression; as,
    1. Lord Marmion turned—well was his need—
       And dashed his rowels in his steed.
    2. Tom Moore wrote politics at times—pointed, bitter, rankling politics—but he was really no politician.

(2) To denote an abrupt change in the subject; as,
    1. I have often told you that—but I will not repeat it.
    2. He said, "Bring me the"—but the man had disappeared.

(3) Before a repetition for effect or explanation; as,
    1. Never is virtue left without sympathy—a sympathy dearer and tenderer for the misfortune that has tried it, and proved its fidelity.
    2. There is one feeling, and only one, that seems to pervade the breasts of men alike—the love of life.

(4) To denote an unexpected turn in sentiment; as,
    1. The young man was in love—with his profession.
    2. He is very generous—with other people's money.
    3. He had no malice in his heart—
       No ruffles on his shirt.

(5) Before a statement of particulars, and also before a summing up of particulars; as,
    1. A solid has three dimensions—length, breadth, and thickness.
    2. Reputation, money, friends—all were sacrificed.

(6) To denote hesitation, suspense, or delay; as,
    1. This man is a—a—a—but words are too feeble to do him justice.
    2. The pulse fluttered—stopped—went on—throbbed—stopped again—moved—stopped.—Shall I go on?—No.

(7) To denote the omission of letters or figures; as,
    1. We passed through the village of D—— early in the morning.
    2. The winter of 1887-'88 was very cold.

(8) At the end of a line to mark an unfinished statement, resumed on the next line [see 804].

(9) After side-heads; as,

> *Poetic License.*—For the purpose of accommodating words to the measure of a line of poetry, they are changed in various ways [see page 259, and side-heads all through this book].

805. Marks of parenthesis are used—

(1) To inclose something incidental or explanatory, which may be omitted without injuring the sense; as,

> 1. Know then this truth (enough for man to know),
> Virtue alone is happiness here below.
> 2. It behooves me to say that these three (who, by the way, are all dead) possessed great ability.

806. Brackets are used—

(1) To inclose words used for the purpose of giving an explanation, correcting a mistake, or supplying an omission; as,

> 1. Yours [the British] is a nation of unbounded resources.
> 2. Do you know if [whether] he is at home?
> 3. He is not so tall as his brother [is tall].

807. The index [☞] is used to point out a passage to which special attention is directed.

808. Marks of reference are used to direct attention to notes in the margin, or at the bottom of the page; as,

(1) The asterisk [*]; the dagger [†]; the double dagger [‡]; the section [§]; the parallel [∥].

INDEX.

[The numbers refer to paragraphs.]

A or *an*, 66, 69, 70.
Abbreviation, 132–136.
Adjectives, 49–52; modifying elements, 53, 54, 58, 266; definition, 55, 60, 61, 544–588; arrangement, 457–459; used as complements, 495; not to be used as adverbs, 513; numeral, 546 (2); inflection, 552–571; double comparison, 572; plural adjectives, 574; phrase-adjectives, 583; ending in *ly*, 608; position, 266, 575–579; participial, 643; parsing, 285; used as nouns, 550, 610.
Adjective pronouns, 547, 549.
Adverbs, 77–86; definition, 87; same form as adjectives, 89, 611; position, 138, 339, 591; interrogative, 350; not to be used as adjectives, 513; comparison, 590; office, 592; double negatives, 593; *rather*, 596: independent, 599; responsives, 600; conjunctive, 606; classes, 606; formation, 607; parsing, 285; modal, 592.
Adverbial phrase, 363, 623 exp.
Adverbial clause, 665, 709, page 211.
Adverbial objective, 377, 615.
A few, 583.
Ago, 597.
A little, 583.

Alone, 581.
Allegory, 790.
Ambiguity, 783.
Analysis, definition, 62. Oral models, 63, 80, 92, 101, 113, 153, 154, 242, 365, 394, 478, 503, 531, 624, 629, 644; complex sentences, 662, 663, 713. Written models, 120, 367; complex sentences, 663, 679.
And also, 333.
And not, 333.
And yet, 707.
As well as, 333.
At once, 398.
Another, 586.
Antecedent, 145.
Anticipative subject, 632 f. n.
Apostrophe, 226–228, 231.
Apposition, 473–482; case, 479, 480, 487; position of an appositive noun, 486; appositive phrase, 476; parsing, 481.
Articles, uses, 73, 74, 448–456.
As, joining words in apposition, 484; relative pronoun, 676; conjunctive adverb, 661.
Asterisk, 807.
Attribute complement, 493–502; similarity to appositive use, 494; parsing, 504.
Auxiliary verbs, 299–301, 469–471, 736.

Bad construction improved, 654, 720.
Be (verb), 505–508, 511, 761; conjugation, 757.
Beside and besides, 405.
Between or among, 119 note, 415.
Brackets, 806.
But, conjunction, 418, 612; adjective or adverb, 612; preposition, 418, 612.
But if, 707.
But that, 707.
But what should not be used for but that, page 281 f. n.
Capital letters, 19, 23, 130, 131, 542, page 11 f. n.
Case, definition, 252. Nominative, 229, 248, 256; independent by address, 527; by pleonasm, 703; absolute, 702. Possessive, formation, 226–228, 249, 254, 256, 487–489. Objective, 250, 255, 256, 357, 481, 622, 639.
Caret, 141.
Clauses. Adverbial, 659; condensed, 665, 702; clauses of comparison, 718; conditional clauses, 718. Adjective (relative) clauses, 668, 669; position, 693; restrictive, 680–684; office, 697; condensed, 700. Substantive, 711.
Clearness, 781.
Comma, rules, 102, 155 exp., 369, 372, 432, 440–446, 477, 485, 532, 653, 661, 683.
Comparison, adjectives, 552; adverbs, 590.
Complements, object, 106; attribute, 493–495.
Complex sentences, 659–714; classification, 714.

Compounds, words, 156; sentences, 97, 100; classification, 715; contracted, 147–152.
Composition lessons, 32, 75, 94, 137, 139, 155, 199–201, 224, 246, 296, 316, 336, 352, 396, 490, 685, 701, 720.
Composition writing, arrangement, 31; directions, 64, 65; topical outlines, 65, 75, 104, 224.
Conditional clauses, 758–760.
Conjunctions, 96, 99; primary use, 152; elements they connect, 437; co-ordinate, 704–706; subordinate, 707; correlatives, 708.
Conjunctive adverbs, 660, 661; parsing, 664.
Conjunctive pronouns, 666.
Contractions, words, 231, 267–269; sentences, 147–152, 434–438; clauses, 700, 702.
Conjugation, 739–757.
Copula, page 168 f. n., 511.
Dagger, 807.
Dative object, 378 f. n.
Declension, definition, 259; personal pronouns, 261; relative pronouns, 673.
Dash, 804.
Defective verbs, 766.
Dependent clauses, 659, 667, 709–712.
Diagramming, simple sentence, 121, 154, 367; complex sentence, 663, 679; simple, complex, and compound, 777.
Different from, 412.
Each other, 587 f. n.
Element, definition, 57.
Elder, 560.
Ellipsis, 376.

INDEX. 293

Elliptical phrases, prepositional, 376–378; infinitive phrases, 630, 631.
Elliptical clauses, 718.
Elision, 763.
Else, 581; some one else's book, 489 rem.
Enough, 581, 604.
English grammar, definition, 34, 779.
Etymology, 36, 162.
Examples in false syntax, 784.
Explanatory *or*, 484 note.
Expletive, page 201 f. n.
False syntax, 778.
Factitive object, 481 note.
Farther, further, 561.
Figures of rhetoric, 785.
Finite verb, page 196 exp.
From after *different*, 412.
Gender, 162–182; definition, 169; forms, 171–173.
Get, 425.
Grammatical subject, 59 f. n.
Had rather, had better, 397.
Hyperbole, 794.
Hyphen, 31, 140.
Ideas, 1–4; related ideas, 93, 100.
Indicative mode, 733–744, 758.
Idioms, 397; idiomatic phrases, 398, 399, 603.
If instead of *whether*, page 281 f. n.
Imperative mode, 755.
Indirect object, 378.
Indefinite *it*, 290.
Independent element, 526–543.
Infinitives and infinitive phrases, 621–635; used as adjectives or adverbs, page 196 exp., 623, 624; used substantively, 628; tense, page 253; elliptical infinitives, 630–633; have indirect subjects, page 196 exp., 712 exp.; used as predicate-verb, in a dependent clause, 712; uses, 767–769; parsing, 625, 629.
Interjections, 534–543; parsing, 543, in model for analysis.
Intermediate expressions, 431.
Interrogative adjectives and adverbs, 349, 350.
Interrogative pronouns, 694.
Intransitive verbs, 108, 109.
Inverted order, 340–342, 496, 661 note.
Is gone, are come, 523.
Irregular verbs, 461, 465; list, 764.
Irony, 795.
Introductory *it*, 632; introductory *there*, 598.
Letter-writing, page 52.
Like and *unlike*; as adjectives or adverbs, 380; as prepositions, 427; not to be used as conjunctions, 427.
Lie and *lay*, how to use, 491.
Logical subject, 59 f. n.
Many a, 583.
Means, singular or plural, 217, sentences 3 and 4.
Members, 98.
Merely, 589.
Metaphors, 788; mixed, 789.
Metonymy, 792.
Modal adverbs, 592.
Mode, 730, 731.
Modified subject, 59.
More than, 603.
Misused words, 424–427.
Names, 5, 6.
Name-form of nouns, 229, 251.
Near, nigh, 381.
Nearly, 589.
Negative adverbs, 91, 593.
No, none, 585.

Not only, 589.
Nominative case, 229, 248, 256, 527, 702, 703.
Nouns, 7-12; proper and common, 122-131; abstract, 215; inflection, 162-231; collective, 218-223; relation forms, 225-241; used independently, 526-531; used absolutely, 702; parsing, 284.
Number, 189-217; proper nouns, 211, 212; letters and figures, 203.
Objects (things), 1-9.
Object complement, 106; def., 111; kindred meaning, 116; indirect object, 378; factitive object, 481 note; object of prepositions, 356, 357; object of an infinitive, 623; object of a participle, 639, 640; object phrase, 628, 646; object clause, 697, 711.
Obscurity, 782.
Of late, 603.
Of old, 603.
Older, elder, 559, 560.
One, other, 587.
Only, 581, 588.
Opposite, 381.
Or connects nouns in apposition, 484.
Order, natural, 337, 339; rhetorical, 340-342, 496.
Orthography, 35.
Parable, 791.
Paragraph, 31.
Parenthesis, 805.
Parsing, def., 244; written models, 245, 258; remarks, 281; oral models for nouns, personal pronouns, adjectives, adverbs, and conjunctions, 282-286; verbs, 324; prepositions, 375; noun in apposition, 481; attribute complement, 504; passive verb, 520; active verb, 525; interjections, 541, 543, in model for analysis; infinitive verb, 625, 629; participles, 645; conjunctive adverb, 664; relative pronoun, 692, 695, 699; verbs, 749; analytical parsing, 343-347.
Part of speech, 40; def., 41.
Participles, 461-463, 636-658, page 253; adjective use, 641; substantive use, 646; def., 649, 652; modified by a possessive, 657; kinds, 651, 755; have indirect subjects, 637 exp.; parsing, 645.
Passive voice, 518-524.
Person, 185.
Personification, 178-182.
Phrase, def., 355; subject, object, attribute, 628.
Phrase, prepositional, 360; office, 363; position, 364; arrangement, 368, 373, 374; object omitted, 382; compound, 383; complex, 391-393.
Phrase, infinitive, 623.
Phrase, participial, 640.
Phrase, idiomatic, 398, 399, 603.
Phrase-adjective, 583.
Phrase-adverb, 602.
Phrase-preposition, 403, 404.
Pleonasm, 530, 703.
Poetry, 796.
Poetic license, 763.
Potential mode, 745-749.
Predicate, def., 44; simple, 47; modified, or entire, 77, 78; principal part, 112.
Predicate-verb, 78.
Prepositions, 353-395; def., 361; office, 362; list, 362; omitted, 376, 379; used as adverbs, 382; proper use, 405-418; unnecessary use,

INDEX. 295

420; improper omission, 421; used as adjectives, 422; parsing, 375.
Pronouns, 143; antecedent, 145; kinds, 232, 292, 547, 668–693; singular and plural number, 146; agreement with antecedent, 175, 270–278, 691.
Pronouns, personal, 232; def., 233; relation forms, 237–241; double possessives, 287–289; compound, 291; parsing, 283.
Pronouns, interrogative, 694.
Pronouns, relative, 292–295; 666–693; parsing, 692, 695.
Proper nouns, 22, 122–131.
Punctuation, period, 23, 28, 133; interrogation point, 26; exclamation point, 31, 533, 536; quotation marks, 31, 279; semicolon, 721–725; colon, 726: comma, 102, 155 exp., 369, 372, 432, 440–446, 477, 485, 532, 653, 661, 683.
Quotations, 31, page 11 f. n.; direct and indirect, 279, 280.
Rather, 596.
Recasting sentences, page 288.
Redundant verbs, 765.
Relations of words in a sentence, 243.
Relation-forms of words, 229, 237–241, 247–266.
Relative pronouns, 292–295, 668–693; compound, 671; declension, 673; the relative *what*, 677 f. n.; *that* preferable to *who* or *which*, 675; *as* a relative, 676; restrictive clause, 680–684; unlike personal pronouns, 686, 687; gender unimportant, 688; position, 693; ellipsis, 698; parsing, 692, 695.
Relative adverbs, 710 f. n.
Responsive adverbs, 600, 601.

Responsive pronouns, 696.
Review by sentences, 351, 385–390.
Rhetoric, 780.
Rhetorical figures, 178–182, 785–795.
Rhetorical faults, 779–783.
Rhetorical order, 340–342, 496, 661 note.
Rules for capitals, 774.
Rules for semicolon, 721–725.
Rules for colon, 726.
Rules for construction, case, 256; agreement of pronoun with antecedent, 271–273, 691; agreement of verb with its subject, 323, 327–333; object of a preposition, 357; noun in apposition, 480; attribute complement, 501, 775.
Rhyme, 798.
Senses, the five, 2, 3.
Series of words, 439–441.
Sentences, 13; def., 15, 20. 93; declarative, 21; interrogative, 25, 117, 348; imperative, 25, 118; exclamatory, 30; simple, 95; principal parts, 112; compound, 97; contracted compounds, 147–152; classification, 715; complex, 659–698; classification, 714.
Shall and *will*, uses, 741 f. n., 770–772.
Should and *would*, 773.
Same, 676.
Simile, 787.
Sit, set, how to use, 491.
So, 617, adverb or adjective.
Subject, def., 43; simple, 47; modified, 59; grammatical, 59 f. n.; logical, 59 f. n.
Subject-phrase, 628, 646.
Subject-clause, 697, 711.
Subjects for composition, 776.
Such, 676.

INDEX.

Substantives, 627.
Substantive phrases, 628, 646.
Substantive clauses, 697.
Subjunctive mode, 750-754, 759, 760.
Syntax, 38.
Synecdoche, 793.
Synopsis, 762.
Synthesis, 75 f. n., 103, 119, 155, 246, 296, 316, 352, 366, 396, 490, 685, 701.
Tautology, page 282 (12).
Than after *different*, 412; should follow *else*, *other*, and *otherwise*, page 281 f. n.
That, uses, 549, 574, 710; plural, 574.
The, 66, 67; an adverb, 452.
There, introductory, 598.
Tenses, 297-310, 735, 739-744.
Transitive verbs, 106, 107, 110, 114-116.
Transposed order, 340-342, 496, 661, note.
Unthought-of, *unheard-of*, etc., 422.
Unlike, 380, 427.
Variety of expression, contracted sentences, 147-152, 434-438, 700, 702; arrangement of phrases, 368, 373; rhetorical order, 340-342, 496, 661; changing a direct to an indirect quotation, 279, 280; changing declarative to interrogative sentences, 348; changing complex to simple sentences, 702; compound to complex sentences, 717; active voice to the passive voice, 519; clauses to phrases, 702; recasting sentences, page 288. See also 119, 155, 685.

Varying parts of speech, 609-619.
Verbs, 16-18; def., 45; transitive, 106, 107, 110, 114-116, 515; intransitive, 108, 109, 514, 521, 523, 524; transitive or intransitive, 114, 115; complete and incomplete, 107 f. n., 505; number-forms, 199-201, 311; s-form, 312-317, 739, 740, note, 751; agreement with subject, 199-201, 318-335, 429, 430; tense, 297-310, 735, 739-744; verb-root, 309; regular and irregular, 461-466; principal parts, 301, 466; auxiliary, 299-301, 469-471, 736; uses of auxiliaries, 467-472; progressive form, 468, 761; passive forms, 515, 516, 524, 761; list of irregular verbs, 764. Modes, 730; def., 731; indicative, 733, 734, 758; potential, def., 745; subjunctive, 750-754, 759, 760; imperative, 755; conjugation, 739-744, 745-749, 754-757; voice, 517.
Verbs *appear*, *feel*, *look*, *smell*, *taste*, *become*, 505, 509, 510.
Verbals, 626, page 203 f. n., 756.
Verse, 797.
Versification, 796-803.
Voice, def., 517; active voice, 517; passive voice, 517.
Will, 741 f. n., 770-772.
Would and *should*, 773.
Worth, 588.
What, 677 f. n.
Whether, page 281 f. n.
Yet, 618.

THE END.

www.ingramcontent.com/pod-product-compliance
Lightning Source LLC
Chambersburg PA
CBHW022107230426
43672CB00008B/1311